AUTOBIOGRAPHY OF A
SPY

AUTOBIOGRAPHY OF A
SPY

BY MARY BANCROFT

William Morrow and Company, Inc. | New York | 1983

Library of Congress Cataloging in Publication Data

Bancroft, Mary.
Autobiography of a spy.

Includes index.
1. Bancroft, Mary. 2. World War, 1939-1945—Secret
service—United States. 3. Espionage, American—
Switzerland. 4. Hitler, Adolf, 1889-1945—Assassina-
tion attempt, 1944 (July 20). 5. Spies—United
States—Biography. 6. Spies—Switzerland—Biography.
I. Title.
D810.S8B353 1983   940.54'86'73   83-5384
ISBN 0-688-02019-4

Printed in the United States of America

First Edition

1 2 3 4 5 6 7 8 9 10

BOOK DESIGN BY LINEY LI

For Mary Jane

AUTOBIOGRAPHY OF A
SPY

On a sunny, blustery day in April, 1919, five months after the Allied victory in World War I, I stood beside my father on the steps leading up to the equestrian statue of General Sherman in front of the Plaza Hotel in New York, watching with envious eyes as Colonel William J. "Wild Bill" Donovan led his famous regiment—"the Fighting 69th"—up Fifth Avenue.

Although it was customary for the colonel of a regiment to ride at the head of his troops, that morning the newspapers had reported that Colonel Donovan had told the press he intended to march. What was good enough for his men was good enough for him.

As I watched Wild Bill and the Fighting 69th sweep past with flags flying and bands playing, I wondered disconsolately if anything exciting would ever happen to me. Other girls my age—I was fifteen at the time—might dream of getting married and living happily ever after. Not me. I longed for a life of adventure. I wanted to go everywhere, see everything. I had been terribly disappointed when I learned that, because I was a girl, I couldn't fulfill my most cherished ambition of becoming a cop. I probably couldn't even be a glamorous spy like Mata Hari, whom the French had shot. There was nothing glamorous about me. My mood of teenage despair grew blacker by the minute.

If anyone had told me then that twenty-five years later I would be working with the Office of Strategic Services, the intelligence organization that Wild Bill Donovan would head during World War II, I might not have been so despondent or so envious of Wild Bill. Naturally, it never occurred to me that I would eventually meet many fascinating and important people, live for a year in Cuba, and for twenty years in Switzerland, where I would work and study with the famous psychologist Carl Gustav Jung. During World War II, I would work for—and fall in love with—Allen Dulles, at that time head of the Office of Strategic Services (OSS) mission in Switzerland and later head of the Central Intelligence Agency. I certainly never imagined that Allen would use me as a contact with the group of German civilians and military officers who, on July 20, 1944, staged an abortive attempt on Hitler's life. In 1919, when I watched Wild Bill Donovan lead the Fighting 69th up Fifth Avenue, nobody knew who Adolf Hitler was and I had never heard of Allen Dulles.

I was a wildly imaginative and insatiably curious child. There was nothing on the face of this earth that didn't interest me or that I didn't long to investigate. I wanted to discover the Truth about everything. According to Emerson, "God offers every mind its choice between truth and repose." Granted my curiosity, the choice was simple. I could do nothing with repose.

When I was nine, I wrote in my journal, "I am *almost* an adult." When I was twelve, I noted, "I am now an adult, but nobody seems to realize it."

Usually I felt quite able to handle my problems myself, but periodically I would feel a need for the help of a higher authority. I would then steal into the telephone room under the front stairs. Carefully closing the door so no one would hear me, I would pick up the telephone receiver, hold down the hook from which it was suspended on the old-fashioned instrument, and telephone God. I would point out to Him that I was doing the very best I could. I knew that He was responsible for sending me down on this earth. I felt a great responsibility for His property, namely *me*. Occasionally, however, life seemed beyond the limits of human endurance, as when, for instance, Grandma had refused to believe that I, Pancho Villa, the Mexican bandit, had been forced to hide in an empty garbage can. Otherwise the neighborhood children, in the guises of the Unites States Cavalry, would have captured and killed me. God understood—but not Grandma.

I loved Grandma and knew that she adored me. I was her "Precious Doll" and she spoiled me unmercifully. I had lived with her and my grandfather Bancroft at 12 Ware Street, in Cambridge, Massachusetts, ever since my Irish-Catholic mother had died of an embolism when I was only a few hours old. At that point, Grandma, accompanied by the Irish coachman, Nolan, who was carrying a huge laundry basket, had appeared in my parents' apartment. I was placed in the basket and carted off to my grandparents' home, where I was to live for the next fifteen years. Carrying me off like that had been, according to Grandma, to keep the Catholics, in this instance my mother's Cogan relatives, from "getting" me. Her greatest fear was that the pope would move to Washington and "put an end to our liberties." But her dislike of Catholics was only slightly stronger than her distaste for the Irish. She repeatedly cautioned me never to tell anyone I was Irish, something that Nolan claimed would not be too easy: "Not for you, Miss Mary, with the map of Ireland on your face!"

Grandma had bright blue eyes, very pink cheeks, a sweet expression, and her snow-white hair was twisted in a knot on top of her head and arranged in a pompadour with a "rat" inside it. She bought her hats, so like those of Queen Mary of England, at a milliner's on Copley Square in Boston. And after the horses were replaced by a Cadillac limousine, she often tried on her hats in the car so as to be sure they wouldn't hit the roof if the car happened to go over a bump.

Although everyone else in the family seemed to know who their ancestors were, Grandma would only say, "I was born in Nova Scotia. My name was Mary Shaw." My father told me that he had repeatedly tried to find out more about her family, but all he had been able to determine was that she had a half-brother, in whose home she had grown up and who owned a fish market in Salem. Only when I published my first novel in 1952 did I learn more about her family and perhaps why she felt as she did about both the Catholics and the Irish. In my novel I had fictionalized her and my grandfather under the names of General and Mrs. Dana. I had given General Dana approximately my grandfather's real background and said he had met his wife when she was a waitress in a hotel in Nahant, Massachusetts, where the Harvard crew, of which he was captain, had staged their annual celebration.

I was signing copies of my novel in a bookshop in Cambridge when an elderly lady handed me a copy of my book that she had previously purchased and asked me to autograph it. Leaning across the table, she whispered, "I was *so* interested in reading your book to find that you *did* know about your grandmother! My family always wondered if any of you Bancrofts knew the truth!" She then proceeded to tell me that my grandmother, as a young and very pretty Irish-Catholic girl, had been a chambermaid in her family's home when my grandfather started courting her. At that time in Boston, it was still possible to see want ads reading NO IRISH NEED APPLY. For a man with my grandfather's background to have married an Irish-Catholic girl in those days could be compared to the son of a southern plantation owner marrying a black girl in the days before the Civil War. Apparently Grandma had dreaded having clouds of sham-rocks and legions of priests and nuns casting shadows over the fine new life she had made for herself.

Her attempts to keep the Irish—and the Catholics—from getting me, however, were doomed to failure. My nurse, the three maids in Grand-ma's home, and Nolan were all Irish and staunch Catholics. When I was only a few weeks old, my nurse, with the help of Nolan, spirited me away to the Catholic church where my Cogan aunts were waiting and I was duly baptized in the Catholic faith, although I have been a wandering lamb ever since. All through my childhood, I watched Congregationalists and Catholics struggling for dominion over the spirit of a little child not interested in becoming a Christian anyhow.

I loved going secretly to early mass with the maids and Nolan and being fussed over after the services by kindly souls with thick Irish brogues. I liked the smell of incense, the flickering candles and the tiny, tinkling bells. The Congregational Church where I was taken later in the morning by my grandfather, General William A. Bancroft, in a cutaway and top hat, seemed a bleak and dismal place by comparison. I never thought my grandfather enjoyed it very much either, for he invariably dozed off during the sermon. Grandma never accompanied us to church on Sunday but devoted the morning to writing her weekly letter to my Aunt Catherine Haviland who lived in Limoges, France, where my Un-cle William Haviland owned a china factory.

My grandfather was a tall, handsome man with an erect and military bearing, hazel eyes, high coloring, and a moustache that resembled that of Kaiser Wilhelm II of Germany. He was vain about his appearance and spent considerable time in front of the full-length mirror in his bedroom.

He had graduated from Harvard in the class of '78, had been first marshal of his class and a member of the A.D. Club. He had captained the first Harvard crew to row against Yale at New London, and in the third-floor hallway were his oars and pictures of him and his crew mates, all with sideburns, looking much older than Harvard students of my day.

In 1893 he was elected mayor of Cambridge and was subsequently reelected three times. He then became president of the Boston Elevated

Railway and a trustee or director of many financial and educational institutions, as well as an overseer of Harvard from 1893 to 1903. He was a brigadier general in the United States Volunteers in the Spanish-American War, retiring with the rank of major general. To my disappointment, he never fought in Cuba with Teddy Roosevelt and his Rough Riders.

On one occasion there was talk of my grandfather running for governor of Massachusetts, but nothing came of it and I never learned the reason why. There was something about him that touched me even as a small child, something that made me feel he had dreams of glory that he sensed would never be fulfilled. He was a great admirer of Napoleon, whom he referred to as "Bonaparte." In the library there was a steel engraving of Napoleon looking very sad. Entitled "The Last Phase," it hung between plaster busts, on tall mahogany pedestals, of the two Caesars, Julius and Augustus, whom my grandfather also admired. There were many books in the library, but the only books I ever saw him read were the novels of Sir Walter Scott. He would read them, one after the other, until he had finished the entire set, handsomely bound in bright blue and gold. Then he would start at the beginning and read right through them all again. For several hours after dinner he would read a Scott novel, seated in his large, leather armchair in front of a full-length portrait of himself in the dress regalia of the state militia.

My grandfather was interested in genealogy and enjoyed researching the Bancroft family tree. Originally, he told me, the family had come from Derbyshire, England. I was, my grandfather said, "a tenth-generation American," which made me feel extraordinarily old. There was one ancestor in the family tree of whom I was rather proud: Mistress Ann Hutchinson. It seemed that in her day she had been regarded as a witch— and I enjoyed the idea of being descended from a witch. But there was another ancestor who embarrassed me: John Alden. When he had been sent by his friend Miles Standish as an emissary to ask the hand of "the maiden Priscilla" in marriage, Priscilla had asked, when he blurted out his mission, "Why don't you speak for yourself, John?" I would have greatly preferred Miles Standish, killer of Indians, as an ancestor. I thought it humiliating to be related to a man who couldn't speak for himself.

My mother, Mary Agnes Cogan, was the youngest of five children of Joseph and Rosanna Owens Cogan and the only one to marry.

My grandmother Cogan was born in County Kildare, Ireland, but brought to the United States by her parents when she was only two. She was a small, gentle woman, who dressed very simply and was the only member of the Cogan family that Grandma Bancroft claimed to be able to "tolerate."

My grandfather Cogan was also born in County Kildare. He was a tall, spare man with a square-cut gray beard, very active in Catholic affairs, a member of the Common Council of Cambridge for several years, and a member of the Cambridge Board of Alderman from 1884 until 1888, shortly before my grandfather Bancroft became mayor of Cambridge.

My mother's elder brother, Joseph, was a doctor in private practice in Boston and my favorite among my Cogan relatives. He spent his summers on Monhegan Island off the coast of Maine. After I went to live in Europe, he'd send me a postcard each summer: "Nothing between you and me but the broad Atlantic!" A graduate of Harvard and the Harvard Medical School and aware of my grandmother Bancroft's distaste for the Irish, he always spoke with a heavy Irish brogue in her presence and delighted in her obvious annoyance. He lived to be ninety-six.

Aunt Clara was my godmother and particularly disturbed at my lack of Catholic religious instruction. She lived to be ninety and spent her last days seated in front of her television set, phoning me late at night to announce she was in love with Perry Como.

Aunt Esther, next in line, was the most fashionable and opinionated of my Cogan aunts. A tall, handsome woman dressed in the latest styles, she always wore flowered toques, preferring roses or violets. When I moved to New York in 1926, she wrote me a letter warning how, having been "gently reared" and "both innocent and trusting," I must be very careful with whom I became "intimate" in New York. "That metropolis," she wrote, "is full of people just off the ship, with backgrounds *very* different from yours!"

Aunt Emma, who did the housekeeping for the family, reminded me of Mrs. Tittlemouse in Beatrix Potter's tale. She was a plain, gentle creature, with fine, wispy hair knotted in a tight bun on top of her head. She was devoted to my uncle Will, the youngest member of the family, who had been an invalid since his freshman year at Harvard, when he had been struck in the head by a snowball and permanently blinded. It depressed me to see him, pale and wan, sitting patiently in an armchair in the front room of the Cogan home in North Cambridge, his sightless, clouded eyes, unable to see the brightly colored stuffed birds—a robin, a blue bird, a blue jay, and a Baltimore oriole under a glass bell on the mantelpiece—that so enchanted me. But with the invention of the radio, Uncle Will's whole life changed and I no longer found it so painful to visit him. He enjoyed the comedians most and when he'd laughingly repeat their jokes to me, I realized he had the same sense of humor I had, and that made so many things such fun for us both.

The Cogan house was one half of two attached wooden structures of three stories each, painted a dreary shade of gray with dark green blinds. It sat practically on the brick sidewalk, with only the tiniest strip of scraggly grass between it and the bricks. The rooms were small, furnished sparsely with heavy, elaborately carved furniture of very dark wood, and all the chairs were upholstered in dark red velour. Until long after most people in Cambridge had installed electricity to light their homes, the Cogans continued to use gas. Although the house seemed small to me, I considered it adequate for "those Cogans," as Grandma called them. But I sensed a significant contrast between it and the large house on Ware Street with its five acres of lawn, where I lived with my paternal grandparents. Actually, I felt protective about the Cogan house when Grandma criticized it. It was there that my father and mother had been married. I was very romantic about my mother and heartbroken that I had never known her.

In the parlor on Ware Street there was a portrait of her in a yellow brocade evening gown with a fichu of white lace around her neck, her golden hair piled high on her head. I would sit in that room by the hour, gazing at that portrait, wondering what she had been like, and imagining how different my life might have been if she had not died.

She and my father had been childhood sweethearts. Grandma had opposed the match, but when my father told her that they were going to get married, no matter how she might feel about it, she gave up the battle. That my grandfather Bancroft didn't share her views about either Catholics or the Irish was undoubtedly a factor in her surrender.

All I have of my mother's are a theme, "The Progress of Arts and Sciences in France During the Seventeenth and Eighteenth Centuries," on which she got an A at Radcliffe when she was nineteen, some snapshots, and a few letters. In a letter she wrote to her brother, Joseph, from Groton, where my grandfather and grandmother Bancroft had a summer home, she gives a picture of her own rather delicate health as well as of how his parents felt about my father, Hugh Bancroft.

Dear Joe,
*   It is dull this* A.M., *so I'm going to take the opportunity to write a few letters, and I think I owe you the first. That tonic you sent me has done me much good—at least I have some color now in my lips and face.*

*My knees, too, are much better. Hugh bought me a pair of Dr. Brad-
ford's shoes to wear about the house. Their feeling is really delightful,
although they are much too ugly to wear when I am dressed up.*

*The Bancrofts are very early risers. We all get up at 6 A.M. and
breakfast at 7. That, of course, leaves us a very long morning, but I help
in the housework and the exercise does me good. . . .*

*Every P.M. we take a long drive with the general's new span. The
general firmly believes that this country or the countries abroad contain
no such spot as Gibbet Hill and it truly is a beautiful place.*

*This is Hugh's twenty-third birthday and he is to have a birthday
cake tonight for dinner. The Bancrofts think there is no one like Hugh.
Mrs. B. says he is the smartest person she ever heard of. As soon as he
opens his mouth at table to speak, which isn't often, his father makes
everyone else hush up, afraid he won't catch every word. He has just
given Hugh a good job to do for the Boston Elevated Railway which
will bring in money and little time need be given to it. He is very
thoughtful in this way and he is just great to me.*

Why don't you write to me if it isn't too much bother?

Love,
Mary

The trouble with her knees was apparently some form of tuberculosis
of the bone that was not taken too seriously. It was a shock to everyone
when she died a few hours after my birth, although she lived long enough
to know she had a nine-pound daughter and even held me briefly in her
arms.

My father was a tall, distinguished-looking man with hazel eyes behind
rimless spectacles, a ready smile, and a hearty laugh. I thought there was
nothing he didn't know, nothing he couldn't do. I always felt completely
safe and secure in his presence, although it hurt me that he never showed
the slightest interest in the report cards of which I was so proud. Nor
could I understand what he meant when he said that what people learned
at school or college was of no use "in the terrible things that happen to
them in later life." I imagined that perhaps what he meant was that what
he'd learned at school and college had not helped him when my mother
died.

Grandma claimed that he could read the newspapers before he could
walk, which I didn't believe. But he entered Harvard at the age of fourteen, graduating *summa cum laude* after three years. Then after taking his

master's, he went on to Harvard Law School, so that by the time he was twenty-one he had three degrees from Harvard. He also rowed on a Harvard crew and enjoyed both tennis and horseback riding. After law school, he opened a law office in Cambridge and shortly became, according to Grandma, "the youngest district attorney in Massachusetts."

At the age of thirty, he was appointed director of the Port of Boston and was responsible for building the Commonwealth Pier, large enough to accommodate the ships of the Hamburg American Line. I can still remember officials of that company, as well as officers of the company's ships, being entertained by my father and how impressed I was that the world was populated not only by Americans, English, and French, but also by Germans. Of course, I was aware of the Chinese, as was my friend Charlotte Clapp, who lived down the street. We spent several years digging a hole in the backyard with kitchen spoons in an attempt to reach China.

Throughout my childhood, Nolan was my beloved friend and confidante; I trusted him completely and he never betrayed that trust. I wish that every child might have a friend like Nolan. I realized, of course, that he was an adult—one of Them. But he saw things from my point of view, understood that flowers, trees, shrubs, even grass, were alive, just like people, and that animals had thoughts and feelings, only they expressed them differently than we did. He thought the white bull with one brown and one blue eye on the farm at Groton was so ferocious because he'd been mistreated as a little calf, long before my grandfather had bought him and turned him over to Henry Fitzgerald—"a kindly soul"—who ran the farm at Groton. But this was no reason, Nolan cautioned me, to try to change the white bull's character by sneaking into his stall to give him hay. Nolan believed that bright colored birds flew around in my head. When I told this to Grandma, she said, "Don't lie, Precious Doll!"

Nolan had come to Boston as a young lad from Cork, where he was born, to work as a stable boy for the then governor of Massachusetts. His second position was with my grandparents, first as coachman and handyman, then after the horses were sold, as chauffeur. But his heart was never in being a chauffeur. He had loved the horses: Dick, the spirited stallion with a wicked gleam in his eye, that my grandfather rode each day at dawn through the streets of Cambridge, and Douglas and Dundee, the chestnut pair. I have a snapshot of Nolan, seated on the box of an open carriage, reins in hand, whip cocked at a rakish angle, taken in front of my grandparents' summer home. I am posed on the steps of the carriage in a frilly white dress and a large floppy white hat. On the back of the snapshot in Nolan's careful script is the date and the comment: "This is Miss Mary's own pose. She requested to be photographed thus." I was five at the time.

Nolan's salary never exceeded seventy-five dollars a month, but by shrewdly investing his money in real estate—corner lots in what he termed "expanding neighborhoods," rolling the phrase off his tongue with great solemnity in his lilting Irish brogue—he managed to leave a sizable estate when he died in 1937. EX-CHAUFFEUR LEAVES ESTATE OF $60,000—CHARITIES BENEFIT BY THOMAS NOLAN'S WILL, the headline in the Boston *Herald* read.

Nolan's very carefully considered disposal of his estate reflected not only his great love for his church and his affection for children, but his interest in the Holy Ghost Hospital for Incurables, a huge yellow-brick building not too far from Ware Street. To be incurable seemed to me a terrible fate, and I'd nag Nolan to tell me stories about the people there. This he only too willingly did, embellishing these stories with the kind of detail that thrilled a child with my particular brand of dramatic imagination.

Nolan was devoted to my grandfather, whom he referred to as "the General," but he and Grandma were "enemies." He always called her "she." To her, Nolan was "that impossible creature."

Fortunately, Grandma never set foot in the backyard or stable and only very seldom on either of the broad lawns with their forsythia and lilac bushes, their magnolia tree and blue spruces. Whenever Grandma opened a window and called, "Where are you, Precious Doll?" I'd call, "Here I am!" and rush around in front of the window. "What are you doing, Precious Doll?" "Playing with Charlotte," I'd reply—even if Charlotte hadn't appeared that day and I was following Nolan around as he did his chores or sitting at his feet in the harness room, listening with rapt attention while he talked with Father Flaherty, the neighborhood priest, or with one of the cops from the local precinct.

At the time of the Boston police strike, when my father and grandfather were discussing how sure they were that the police would *not* strike but would "go along with Jim Storrow's compromise," I piped up to announce, "Oh, no! The police *are* going to strike!" Grandma, flushing scarlet, turned reproachfully to my grandfather: "You see, William? That child has been in the stable with that impossible creature again!"

And why not? In the stable I learned what was actually going to happen. What the family thought was going to happen, somehow never did.

Even as a very small child, I hungered for reality. My own imagination provided all the fantasy I needed and often far too much.

||

have no idea just how old I was when I first developed an absorbing interest in the "news," something else that I shared with Nolan. In those days, five or six newspapers were published in Boston. My grandparents subscribed to them all.

Each morning before breakfast I would dash downstairs and gather up the papers that a newsboy had earlier tossed up on the front steps. Nolan, raking the driveway, would call, "Well, Miss Mary, what is the news this morning? Is there a great diss-ast-er in mid-ocean? Is there a ship oopside down?"

Nolan shared my fascination with disasters—earthquakes, hurricanes, typhoons, blizzards, volcanic eruptions—anything that proved the insignificance of man when measured against the elements. I think the reason I felt this way was because such things made me feel less menaced by "Them," those people who with their edicts were always spoiling all the glittering possibilities that life offered. Nolan, on the other hand, related such things to the awesome power of God. This didn't bother me. I was convinced that God was on my side. There was often news of various catastrophes, but there had never been any news of a disaster at sea, something I had hoped to find in the papers ever since I had read *Robinson Crusoe, The Swiss Family Robinson,* and a fascinating book about shipwrecks.

Then one spring morning when I was eight years old, and I went down to get the papers as usual, Nolan, instead of raking the driveway, was standing by the front steps with the newspapers in his arms, scanning the headlines with an expression of astonishment on his face. Looking up, he said, "Well, Miss Mary, today there *is* a great dis-ass-ter in mid-ocean! There *is* a ship oopside down!" The date was April 15, 1912, and that ship was the *Titanic*.

For the next twenty-four hours no one talked about anything else. Grandma even forgot to brush my curls. Until the excitement died down after about a week, Nolan and I saved all the papers that had anything about the disaster in them. So many rich people having "disappeared without trace" impressed Nolan and consequently impressed me. Actually, the identifying mark of a true disaster, Nolan thought, might be that the rich suffered as well as the poor.

I didn't like thunderstorms, or rather I didn't like the thunder. Thunder, however, was the only thing I remember being afraid of, except possibly my grandfather's stallion Dick, who would look at me in a way that made me feel it would be prudent to keep my distance. Otherwise, to be told something was dangerous sent me rushing off to do it, whether to climb up and walk along the ridgepole of the stable, to scramble up to the top of the tallest tree or, when I visited my father and stepmother at Cohasset, Massachusetts, in the summer, to go swimming out over my head.

Still another disaster at sea nearly caused a permanent break in my relationship with my friend Charlotte Clapp. One day Charlotte and I were in the backyard, digging our hole to get to China, when I heard Grandma calling, "Where are you, Precious Doll?" Rushing around in front of her window, I was startled to see Grandma's eyes red from weeping and one of her fine linen handkerchiefs wadded up in one hand. I couldn't imagine what had made Grandma, usually so serene, cry. "A terrible thing has happened, Precious Doll," she said. "The *Lusitania* has been sunk!" "By an iceberg?" I asked, remembering the *Titanic*. "No," said Grandma, her voice quavering and tears starting to roll down her cheeks, "by those terrible Germans!" With this she banged down the window. I dashed back to give Charlotte the news, filled with a sense of great importance. "What's the *Lusitania*?" asked Charlotte, staring blankly up at me. I could have strangled her. Was this any way to greet the bearer of such dramatic tidings?

Tossing my curls back over my shoulders and pulling myself up to my full height, I said icily, "If you don't know what the *Lusitania* is, Charlotte Clapp, I think you had better go home this minute—and perhaps you had better never come back!"

"Oh, all right," said Charlotte, jumping up, "if you think you're so smart!" And she ran up the driveway and headed down the street to her own house.

But Nolan's reaction more than made up for Charlotte's. Pushing his cap to the back of his head, he said in solemn tones, "Well, Miss Mary, this means that the United States will now get into the war!"

I was absolutely thrilled by the prospect of the United States entering the European war. Ever since its outbreak, Nolan and I had followed its course with passionate interest. I had bought the sheet music of some of those stirring songs with lines about home fires, long trails and the distance to Tipperary. I would sit in the parlor banging them out of the Steinway grand, singing off key, until Grandma called down from the upstairs sitting room, "That's enough, Precious Doll!" Then I'd dash out to find Nolan and we would sing them together, me still off key, he in his lovely, true tenor.

I'd lie awake in my bed at night, while the robins chirped mournfully in the elm tree outside my windows, softly reciting to myself Captain John G. McCrae's poem:

> *In Flanders fields the poppies grow*
> *Between the crosses, row on row,*
> > *That mark our place; and in the sky*
> > *The larks, still bravely singing, fly*
> *Scarce heard amid the guns below.*
>
> *We are the Dead. Short days ago*
> *We lived, felt dawn, saw sunset glow,*
> > *Loved and were loved, and now we lie*
> > *In Flanders fields.*

Nolan's favorite was Alan Seeger's poem:

> *I have a rendezous with Death*
> *At some disputed barricade*
> > ** * **
> *When spring trips north again this year,*
> *And I to my pledged word am true,*
> *I shall not fail that rendezvous.*

My fascination with disasters and my interest in the war in Europe were not actually as bloodthirsty as they may seem, because of Nolan's attitude toward death. My own attitude toward it grew out of my conversations with Nolan about my "beautiful mother who was an angel in heaven," as well as my longing to know where she was buried. Whenever I asked Grandma, she'd frown and say, "Don't be morbid, Precious Doll!"

Then one fine spring day Nolan took me to her grave in a cemetery in North Cambridge and picked me a tiny bunch of yellow pansies growing by her headstone, which I pressed in my favorite book, *The Little Lame Prince*, and kept until they turned to dust. Somehow Nolan managed to make death seem gentle and kind, a sad experience, of course, for those who were left behind, but not for those who had gone ahead. The dead were able to wander through the heavenly pastures, where the sun always shone, butterflies fluttered over the myriad flowers, and turtles sunned themselves on the banks of streams over whose surface darted dragonflies with iridescent wings.

Once I was dreadfully upset when I found a dead robin under the privet hedge and ran sobbing to Nolan, who came loping back with me to pick up the robin and carry it tenderly back to the stable, where he found a little tin box to put it in on a cushion of fresh wool waste. Nolan thought a cat had killed the robin, but not our cat, Marty, the huge tiger cat with round green eyes who slept in the kitchen window most of the time and refused to play with a Ping-Pong ball the way Charlotte's gray cat did. Nolan thought "a roving tomcat" had done the dire deed and he promised to keep his eye out for the villain, maybe take a shot at him with his BB gun. The robin's death, he said, had actually been "natural"—killing birds was "the nature of cats." I shouldn't hold it against them. And I never did.

We buried the robin in a corner of the backyard where later there were other graves for other birds, an occasional mouse, and even a grave for a rabbit, one of a pair I was given one Easter. Nolan made a tiny picket fence around the graveyard, painted the pickets white, and planted a small rosebush at one corner. He handled the tiny corpses I'd bring him with the greatest tenderness and afterward invariably took time out from his chores to sit in the harness room with me and speculate on the arrival of the latest victim of death in the heavenly pastures. The pictures he painted for me were so happy that death became for me nothing more than the quiet opening of a door, "A r-r-r-e-lease," Nolan said in his inimitable brogue, "from this vale of tear-r-rs."

I hated the idea of any living thing suffering. I tiptoed around anthills and begged the cook to kill the flies, stuck and struggling on the sheets of flypaper she laid out in the kitchen pantry. I never thought of the people caught in disasters or fighting in wars as suffering. Dying, yes, but never suffering. Only when I realized that in war soldiers were wounded, lost arms, legs, eyes, did war become repulsive to me. Even then it took quite a while for the horrors of war actually to be brought home to me.

When war broke out in Europe in the summer of my eleventh year, I thought of it only in terms of bands playing, flags flying, poppies growing in Flanders's fields, and larks singing in the sky. If the *Lusitania* being sunk now meant, as Nolan said it did, that the United States was going to get into the war, I felt that at last I, too, would be a part of those marching bands and flying flags. But actually two long years were to elapse before my fantasy became a reality. In the meantime, names like the Somme, the Marne, and particularly Verdun, where the name of Marshal Pétain first entered my consciousness—a name that was to have a far different significance for me many years later—became as familiar to me as the names of places around Cambridge and Boston.

The eastern front held little interest for me. My notion of the Russians had been formed by Rudyard Kipling's "The Truce of the Bear," from which I concluded that it was advisable to proceed with extreme caution when dealing with the Russians.

Grandma was greatly disturbed by the Russian Revolution. She was sure it was going to spread and endanger my Aunt Catherine Haviland and the hospital for American wounded that she had opened at her château near Limoges in France. Grandma worried so much that I wrote Aunt Catherine, begging her to be careful of what she said in her letters to Grandma:

> *She worries frightfully about you people over there. I find her alone in her room, crying over your letters. She's afraid you will all be murdered by the Bolsheviki. I try to cheer her up by saying I'm sure conditions over there are no worse than here with all these strikes in the mills at Lawrence and Lowell. But she won't believe me. She just goes on saying she is sure you will all be murdered by the Bolsheviki. . . .*

Of course, the Bolsheviki had murdered the Czar and his family, although the Czar, who looked so much like his cousin, King George V of England, appeared quite harmless to me. I had seen a picture of the Czarina's sitting room, very much like Grandma's, with its white wicker furniture and its tables covered with family photographs. I envisaged the life of the Czar and the Czarina, as well as that of King George V and Queen Mary—in my eyes permanent fixtures on the throne of England—as very much like that at Ware Street. I assumed that, when European royalty put on their crowns and velvet robes and performed their royal duties, it was not very different from when my grandfather, in his major general's dress uniform of the state militia, and Grandma, wearing her pale blue brocade with a train, drove off to some mysterious destination and I was able to spend the evening in the kitchen. There the Irish maids entertained the cops from the local precinct and the conversation—as well as the horseplay they frequently indulged in—was so much more fun than anything above stairs.

This downstairs world gave me a sense that there was not just one point of view, one set of values. It gave me the ability to differentiate instinctively among people, their perceptions, and their problems. I saw people who worked for my family going about their daily tasks and realized that they were judged on the excellence of what they did. It was this that first taught me the importance of work and the value of excellence. I came to understand that there was nothing in the least demeaning about any kind of work, domestic or otherwise. Actually, my family, with the single exception of Grandma's attitude toward Nolan, regarded those who worked for them with genuine affection, even as members of the family.

The Germans in their spiked helmets, their goose step, and their ferocious-looking Kaiser, with his upturned, waxed moustache, were, of course the Enemy. The Austrians were the Enemy, too, but in my eyes far less dangerous than the Germans. "The Blue Danube" and other lovely waltzes that we danced to at dancing school came from Vienna. The aged Emperor Francis Joseph was "bowed with sorrow." His beautiful wife, Elizabeth, had been stabbed to death by an anarchist in, of all unlikely places, Switzerland. His only son, Archduke Rudolf, unable to marry his commoner sweetheart, had first shot her, then himself, at his hunting lodge in a place with the romantic name of Mayerling. In my omnivorous reading I had gleaned that when the Turks of the Ottoman Empire had been stopped in their conquest of Europe by the Austrians at Vienna, they had left lilacs as their legacy to that city. Over Austria hung an aura of beauty and melancholy, and in my imagination the fragrance of lilacs enveloped everything Austrian.

Actually, the Austrians had started the war in a place referred to as "the powder keg of Europe." I envisaged it as a huge ammunition depot, without human inhabitants, a concept that had to be drastically revised when Queen Marie of Rumania, together with her son, Prince Nicholas, and her daughter, Princess Ileana, came to stay with my stepmother's stepfather, Clarence W. Barron—or "CW" as I called him—publisher of *The Wall Street Journal.* The Queen, a granddaughter of Queen Victoria, had been educated in England and spoke flawless English. She was a strikingly handsome woman of regal bearing, arrayed in silks and satins, with ropes of pearls the size of small birds' eggs around her neck. Friendly and gracious, she put everyone, including me, instantly at ease. To the American public, she was the prototype of a Queen, known for her work for the Red Cross during World War I when her country fought on the Allied side. CW was greatly taken with her, and nothing annoyed him more than rumors that she was only using him to get a loan for her country.

CW had married, rather late in life, a widow with two daughters whom he had adopted, the elder of whom became my stepmother. He was exactly fifty years older than I was, but I adored him, and he was a tremendous influence in my life.

A short man, about five feet five inches tall, weighing well over three hundred pounds, CW had rosy cheeks, bright blue eyes twinkling behind rimless spectacles, and a beautiful white beard that he combed with a small gold comb at the table after meals, much to my stepmother's annoyance. Until I was six, I thought he was Santa Claus.

When at home from his many travels, he entertained lavishly both at his house on Beacon Street in Boston and his summer place at Cohasset. In the downstairs front room on Beacon Street, a white bear rug with head attached lay on a highly polished floor. I loved to stick my fingers in the bear's open mouth with its bright red tongue, thrilled by the thought that the bear might come alive and bite my fingers off.

There was a large conservatory off the dining room where several brilliantly colored macaws squawked from their perches among CW's magnificent orchid collection. Huge fantailed goldfish swam in and out among tiny stone castles in a pool over which an illuminated fountain played on the nights when CW entertained. The whole house smelled of fresh flowers, and the meals there were delicious.

This setting was very different from the world into which CW had been born. His family had been of extremely modest means. His father worked as a teamster all his life to support a wife and many children, of whom CW was next to the youngest and the only one to achieve such worldly success.

CW was *the* pioneer in financial journalism as we know it today, the first to tie the industrialization of the country into its history, the first to realize that the "news" lay not only in the building of railroads and the establishment of corporations but also in the character and mode of operation of the men involved. He knew and interviewed them all. Even those who were up to no good realized it was not in their best interests to refuse him an interview. Not only was he a crack reporter and the proprietor of an influential newspaper, but he was also the owner of an important news ticker service over which he exercised strict control. No company was mentioned on the Dow Jones tickers that CW had not investigated, either personally or through the gifted reporters in his employ.

In his vest pocket he always carried a pack of three- by four-inch white cards on which he'd quickly jot down shorthand notes during an interview. He would later use these as reference points for enlarged reports about the people he'd seen, what they'd said, as well as what they were planning to do and how this fitted into the larger picture. He worked at such a pace that he had two, sometimes even three, male secretaries dancing attendance, living at the house when he was home, or accompanying him on his travels.

He would stay in bed, dictating until noon, for he seldom retired before two, three, or even four A.M. I learned more on a wide range of subjects when I dropped in on those morning dictating sessions than I ever learned at school. I became familiar with names like Morgan, Rockefeller, Schwab, Carnegie, Frick, Harriman, Ford, Du Pont; with what these men were thinking; what they were planning; and how they intended to go about it. I learned what was happening in the stock market, in railroads, oil, mining, shipping, public utilities, the automotive industry, and on the commodity markets. I learned how the stock market itself operated, about mergers, options, "puts" and "calls," about "buying on margin" and "selling short."

CW always kept a volume of the Bible on his bedside table and read in it first thing on arising in the morning and before retiring at night. He gave me what he considered the most useful edition of the Bible, "The Oxford Self-Pronouncing Bible—S. S. Teacher's Edition," printed on extremely thin paper, with many excellent maps and an elaborate Cyclopedic Concordance. He often quoted the Bible to make a point in the letters he wrote me from his travels and on his return would question me as to what I thought of the relevance of the quotes. His letters meant so much to me that I pasted them into a special scrapbook. And I am still amazed at the way in which he was able to write to a girl fifty years younger than he was in a way that meant so very much to her at the time.

His letters were full of anecdotes about the people he met. And scattered throughout were bits of advice that I have never forgotten such as: "Always put the unpleasant truth in the interrogative form" and "Remember that facts are not the truth, but only indicate where the truth may lie."

When my first husband, Sherwin Badger, was working for the United Fruit Company and we were spending a year in Banes, Oriente, Cuba, I wrote CW how unhappy I was with the life in the company-owned sugar mill town, how disgusted by the intrigues and disloyalty that I saw around me. In answer to my letter, he wrote,

> *It doesn't make any difference where you take hold of the world, whether in Cuba or South Boston, if you only get down to the bottom and master the situation there. The railroad presidents are the men who came up from the coupling pins. They do not graduate from Harvard or Yale as a rule, but from the college of hard knocks. . . . We should be grateful to our Heavenly Father if we get the rough experience of life in early youth and learn the lesson it provides. . . . You will run up against a lot of adventurers, I believe, in Cuba, a lot of bad politics, bad manners, disloyalty, and dishonesty. But never hesitate to meet people from all walks of life—even gamblers and crooks—always study them and learn to differentiate clearly between the good and bad you find everywhere, not only among people, but within individuals themselves.*

I was only twenty-one and CW's comments struck just the right note, making it possible for me to look at my surroundings with different eyes. I realized that no matter what happened, I had CW's backing. He was always there to help me incorporate the most bizarre experiences, the most unconventional thoughts and feelings into an enlarged and more detached view of the world. There was no one else in my life in those days with his particular type of vision, or anyone I felt had such a genuine affection for me as I actually was. I could confide in him exactly how I felt, exactly what I thought, and he would not pooh-pooh it as nonsense. Nothing seemed strange to him. He was interested in everyone and everything in some particular way, and he took endless pains to explain to me just what that way was. He was my one real and trusted friend from the time I was fifteen until I was thirty, and the second real friend I ever had, the first, of course, being Nolan.

CW urged me to keep a line-a-day diary and a journal in which to write about anything that interested me. And he persuaded me to learn to type and to set up my own files of subjects for articles and stories. Because I felt he cared for me and was interested in my having a life that satisfied me, I eagerly followed everything he suggested.

He'd send me packages of books on every imaginable subject with no rhyme or reason in their selection. And he'd enclose a note asking me to write him what I thought of the books after I'd read them. He took all my ideas seriously and spent time, either arguing with me or questioning me as to why I felt as I did.

I have never known anyone more alive than CW. Even today when I think about him, as I do so often, I cannot help smiling to myself and feeling the same warmth I always felt in his presence. He made the world seem a glittering, exciting, and very worthwhile place to be and that it was a privilege merely to be alive.

He thought I should try my hand at journalism, not only because I could "express myself," as he put it, but because he thought I had what he called "a nose for news." Later, after I had worked with Professor Jung, I realized this nose for news was, in Jungian terms, nothing but a highly developed and extroverted intuition. Needless to say, CW himself had an extraordinary nose for news. Once, when crossing Texas on a train, he suddenly insisted that the train be stopped at an unscheduled way station because he was convinced that the Supreme Court was about to hand down an extremely important decision. There was absolutely no reason for this hunch. He had simply picked it out of the air. However, the result was that the reporter from *The Wall Street Journal* was the only newspaperman present when the Supreme Court handed down its decision on the Teapot Dome case, a decision that had not been expected for several months.

I was present myself on one occasion when CW's "nose" was at work. We were playing bridge at his home in Cohasset. CW was an excellent bridge player, but on this particular evening he revoked several times and, finally flinging down his cards, said he couldn't continue. Important news was about to break. Every ten minutes or so he sent one of his secretaries to phone the office to see what was coming in over the wires. For over an hour the secretary would report that there was nothing. Finally he returned to say there was still nothing—except that President Warren G. Harding, on a visit to California, had had crabs for dinner and was suffering from an upset stomach. "That's it!" CW exclaimed. "Get me the Vice-President!"

Calvin Coolidge, the Vice-President and a good friend of CW's, was visiting his father at his home in Vermont. CW finally got in touch with him, told him about Harding, and added that Coolidge should stay where he was and be sworn in as President of the United States by his father—a notary public—preferably by candlelight as that might be more picturesque. My stepmother was greatly annoyed with CW for "burying poor Mr. Harding before he is even dead." But CW was adamant. He was positive Harding was going to die—and, of course, he did. Calvin Coolidge was sworn in as President of the United States by his father—and by candlelight at that.

At one point during his presidency, President and Mrs. Coolidge came to lunch with CW in Cohasset. They arrived on the presidential yacht, the *Mayflower,* which required deeper water than that provided by Cohasset Harbor. So the *Mayflower* had anchored offshore and the presidential party had arrived by launch at the dock on CW's property. Mrs. Coolidge was all charm and animation, but the President was his usual dour self. The lunch consisted of boiled lobsters that CW knew were a particular favorite of the President's. The other guests began to argue about the rise and fall of the tides in Cohasset Harbor, while Secret Service men lurked among the shrubbery outside the windows. Some people thought the tide rose six feet, others said seven. At that point, the President put down the lobster claw he was cracking and announced in a surprisingly loud voice, "Nine feet!" Needless to say, he was right.

One of the stories current during Coolidge's term was that once, when he had opened his mouth, a moth had flown out. I heard him tell my father that he had decided he could either talk or be President. He couldn't possibly do both. On several occasions, however, I heard him not only talk but tell very amusing stories in his dry, New England way.

CW had a photograph of Henry Ford given to him by Ford himself. It was an unusual picture with a kind of gold finish that made it gleam as if it were actually illuminated. CW, noticing the President looking at it rather crossly, began to explain its history, when Mrs. Coolidge interrupted, saying, "Calvin doesn't like Henry Ford! He gave him a maple sugar bucket for the Wayside Inn and Ford used it as a wastebasket!" Coolidge nodded and, without changing expression, said, "That's right!"

My father liked to tell of the time when, spending a few days in Washington, he was asked to stay at the White House. Shortly after his arrival, he encountered the President coming down a White House corridor. The President's greeting was, "Located?" and when my father said, "Yes, thank you . . . ," the President nodded and proceeded on his way.

In the last years of his life CW was subjected to increasingly severe attacks of bronchitis. Consequently, because of the severity of Boston winters, he spent the winter months on his houseboat, the *Edna B.*, among the Florida Keys. On several occasions I went down to spend some time with him and play "bumble-puppy." "Bumble-puppy" was his name for a kind of idiotic bridge he would play when he had as a guest someone from whom he was trying to extract a story for *The Wall Street Journal.* When playing "bumble-puppy," CW would play bridge as if he were a complete idiot, carrying me as his partner, and playing for extremely high stakes. He would whistle and hum, trump his partner's ace, seem astonished when he lost a trick, and all the time amid the whistling and humming, shoot sudden questions at his victim. I was amazed at how well this strategy worked. I watched him get information out of W. C. Durant of General Motors on one occasion and out of the head of the Whelan Cigar Store chain on another, information that I am sure neither man realized he was revealing until he read later what CW wrote about him in *The Wall Street Journal.*

The winter I was fourteen, my grandfather had a slight stroke from which he recovered completely. But in the spring of the following year, he had another and much more serious one that left him almost completely paralyzed. Most of the time Grandma's eyes were red from weeping and the house on Ware Street became more like a hospital than a home. It broke my heart to see my handsome, vigorous grandfather lying helpless and shriveled in bed, trying to reach out to take my hand with tears streaming down his cheeks when I went in to see him. As the sun set each day, he began to whimper, then gradually the whimpering grew louder, until the sound of huge, shattering sobs filled the entire house. He had to have nurses around the clock and my room was needed for them. So it was decided that I should go to live with my father, my stepmother, and their three little children in their home on Beacon Street in Boston, several doors up from where CW lived.

At the same time I transferred from the Cambridge School for Girls to the Winsor School in Brookline. I was not worried about being able to keep up with my lessons in my new school. Getting good marks had never been a problem for me. But I was concerned about being "popular," which seemed to be the most desirable goal in life. Everyone wanted to be popular. Newspapers and magazines carried articles about the importance of popularity. Books were written about how to achieve it. Products were advertised as cures for such impediments to popularity as greasy hair and acne. Girls were urged to use Listerine as a daily mouthwash so as not to risk being "always a bridesmaid, never a bride."

At Winsor I quickly divided my classmates into four categories: the Elect, the Belles, the Poor Boobs, and the Majority. The Elect had shiny hair, faultless complexions, got good marks in their studies, were splendid athletes, lived in Boston or Chestnut Hill, and had parents who had known each other since childhood. The Belles were extremely pretty girls, interested only in boys of whom they knew masses at Middlesex, Milton, St. Paul's, and, of course, Groton. I had no intention of being a Poor Boob. This left only the Majority. But being accepted by the Majority was not as easy as it might have seemed for two specific reasons: first, everyone in the class wore the same type of two-piece dress of some shade of pastel jersey, with a round, white linen collar and a knife-pleated skirt, whereas I had only plain white shirtwaists and a couple of plaid skirts that Grandma had bought me at Jordan Marsh, a store at which, I quickly learned, my classmates turned up their noses. When I told my stepmother this, she quickly remedied the defect by getting me several dresses like the other girls.

But my other handicap was subtler and at first I feared would be impossible to remedy: I had grown up in Cambridge. Although I now lived in Boston, who had ever heard of anyone growing up in Cambridge? Of course, Cambridge was better than Newton, where some of the Poor Boobs actually lived, but unquestionably Cambridge carried a certain stigma. This depressed me inordinately during my first weeks at Winsor until I began to realize that in the eyes of the Elect, Cambridge didn't possess any negative connotations. In fact, being so sure of themselves and consequently much more independent in their judgments, the Elect seemed to think a Cambridge background rather exotic. So I decided to concentrate on becoming popular with the Elect. The rest was easy. Once the other girls noticed that I had been accepted by the Elect, they trooped along like so many sheep. By the end of my first year at Winsor I could relax, safe in the realization that I had become at last that most desirable of creatures, "a popular girl."

Three years later I graduated from Winsor and in June was sent abroad with three other girls from my class. We were accompanied by two chaperones who took groups of girls abroad each summer to give them a bird's-eye view of European culture to enhance their charm when they made their debuts the following winter. I now think that the chaperones' steamy devotion to each other was open to a far different interpretation than was given it at the time.

Just before we sailed, my father asked me if I would like to have a coming-out ball at the Hotel Somerset. If so, he must get in touch with the hotel to reserve a date. I thought not, although I did not tell him why. In spite of my popularity with my classmates, I had realized there was something permanently "off" about me ever since I had overheard the mother of one of the Elect, at whose house I was spending the night, telling a friend, "I never mind the Bancroft girl spending the night here. The servants love her and never make a fuss about the extra work. She's the daughter of Hugh Bancroft's *first* wife, you know. . . ." In other words, the Irish again. If I had a coming-out ball at the Hotel Somerset, my Cogan aunts would be sure to appear and kiss me in front of the whole world.

So I told my father I would much rather have a *thé dansant* at the house to which only my contemporaries would be invited. Galvin, the florist, constructed a wall of smilax against which my stepmother and I received, with huge baskets of flowers on the floor on either side of us. Music was provided by a small orchestra that played for the dancing songs about a poor butterfly, Avalon beside the bay, and about a baby in tulip time—maybe.

The rest of the winter passed in a whirl of festivities—luncheons, teas, dances, balls, and house parties. At the dances and balls there was always a huge stag line of Harvard students so not even the Poor Boobs were wallflowers.

After Christmas several of the Belles announced their engagements. By spring a few of the Elect had followed suit. Obviously, for me with my eye still on popularity, the situation was becoming critical. I must now either get engaged, go to college, or risk the humiliation of being "on the shelf"—the pits as far as popularity was concerned.

I studied a list of boys that I'd kept ever since I'd first gone to dancing school. I didn't feel particularly romantic about any of them. They were just there, in reserve, like money in a piggy bank, to be used when a need arose for guests at a dinner or house party, not necessarily for anything as serious as marriage. Occasionally, I shifted the names around, promoting some boys, demoting others, depending on whether a book I had read or a movie I had seen had given me a new idea about the kind of man I might like to marry—Heathcliff, for instance, or Gary Cooper.

One boy, Sherwin Badger, whom I had known longer than any of the others, had always ranked near the top of the list. His father, Dr. Badger, was our family physician, and the Badgers also had a summer place at Cohasset. Sherwin and I had played tennis, golf, and gone sailing to-

gether each summer. The Badgers' winter home was near us on Marl-
borough Street. Sherwin, then a junior at Harvard, coxswain of the
varsity crew and figure skating champion of the United States, was frequently at our house. In my last year at Winsor he had been in love with
one of the Belles in my class. I had furthered this romance in every way I
could, although I was not sure that the Belle was as enchanted with him as
he was with her, particularly since her mother was set on her making a
brillant marriage. Sherwin might be a good marriage, but certainly not a
brillant one.

Sherwin's crush on the Belle continued during the first months of our
coming-out year. Then, suddenly, after Christmas, she announced her
engagement to her mother's choice, a man from New York.

Sherwin was shattered. He moped around, looking like a sick calf. I did
my best to console him, pointing out that "there are as many good fish in
the sea as have ever been fished out"—a standard mode of comforting the
lovelorn in those days. One evening, driving me home from a dance, he
announced abruptly, "Perhaps you and I ought to get married!" I was
startled. However, I had no intention of being accused of "catching him
on the rebound," a particularly frowned-upon maneuver in our crowd.
Besides I wasn't sure he meant it. So I didn't say anything or react in any
way, but decided to abandon the idea of marriage and go to college
instead.

Grandma had always been opposed to college, claiming that all girls
learned there was "how to walk, talk, and think like men." My father,
with his attitude about the uselessness of what he himself had learned at
college, was naturally not too keen on my going either. "Whatever do
you want to do that for?" he demanded. "I certainly hope you aren't
planning to earn your own living and take a job away from some man
who needs it to support his family, are you?" But to me college seemed
the best, if not the only, solution.

I had already passed my college boards and been accepted at Smith, so
that autumn I set out for Northampton. On the way I was followed into
the ladies' room of the Hotel Kimball in Springfield by several Smith
upperclassmen and pledged to a secret society known as AOH. There
were two of those secret societies at Smith in those days: AOH, which
stood, appropriately enough in my case, for Ancient Order of Hiber-
nians; and Orangemen. Both societies took in twenty freshmen each
year, and it was a great honor, a confirmation of "popularity," to be
chosen for either of them. I found that ceremony in the ladies' room both

embarrassing and ridiculous, but I was properly grateful for the solution to the popularity problem it offered for the next four years.

I had hoped to find at Smith answers to the multitude of questions seething inside my head, evoked by the omnivorous reading I had done ever since I could remember. I had particularly looked forward to studying philosophy and was bitterly disappointed when I discovered that I couldn't even begin to study philosophy until at least my junior year and even then the courses offered didn't look too promising. The classes I was able to take as a freshman were so dull and boring that I had difficulty even staying awake. The professors were also singularly uninspiring, not even as interesting personalities, as were some of my teachers at Winsor.

Late in October, "Nightie Night" was held for the freshmen pledges to AOH. The freshmen, ordered to appear in long white nightgowns, were herded into the center of the room, while the upperclassmen formed a circle around them. An upperclassman would call out the name of a freshman and order her to be funny. But no matter what any freshman did—I stood on my head—it was greeted by a chorus of "Do you call *that* funny?" Before the meeting broke up, we were informed that for two weeks after the Christmas vacation each of us would have to be a "slave" to one of the upperclassmen and do anything we were ordered to do. This seemed a horrendous prospect and I began to toy with the idea of abandoning my college career. But how without losing face and landing back "on the shelf"?

While I was pondering this, Sherwin phoned to say that he was driving up for the weekend, so I decided to bring up the possibility of our getting married after all. But I was spared this humiliation. Sherwin brought it up himself. We spent the weekend walking, talking, and eating by candlelight in various Tea Shoppes, trying to figure out the best way to approach our parents. We anticipated little difficulty. Sherwin would be graduating from Harvard in June and already had a job lined up with the United Fruit Company. Our parents liked each other and I was sure my father would be relieved that I was abandoning a college career. We agreed that the best time to tell them of our plans would be during the Christmas holidays.

Everybody was delighted—so delighted, in fact, that for me life took on an unreal quality like that described by George Santayana when he wrote, "The world is a perpetual caricature of itself; at every moment it is the mockery and contradiction of what it is pretending to be. But as it nevertheless intends all the time to be something different and highly dignified, at the next moment it corrects and checks and tries to cover up the absurd thing it was; so that a conventional world, a world of masks is superimposed on the reality, and passes in every sphere of human interest for the reality itself."

Up until that point in my life, I had known what goals I had been trying to reach. I had never had the slightest doubt about who I was or where I stood in the picture. But after I became engaged, I began drifting away from that clear concept of myself into other people's assumptions about me: that I was in love, that I was blissfully happy, that I was looking forward to getting married, that I was enchanted to be assembling a trousseau and thrilled by taking a course at Fanny Farmer's cooking school. The edges of who I actually was began to blur. The pressure of the assumptions about me was so great that the temptation was not just to engage in role playing but actually to become whatever role was being attributed to me.

Our wedding ceremony was held at the Church of the Advent and the reception took place at my father's home on Beacon Street. Nolan, in a brand-new suit, a new green necktie, and highly polished black buttoned boots, came down the receiving line while Grandma, red-faced with annoyance, glared at him. Aunt Clara and Aunt Esther Cogan, in large flowered toques, kissed me and gushed over me as I'd dreaded they would if I had had a debutante ball. And Sherwin's mother, a tiny, pink-faced woman with beautiful white hair, couldn't stop weeping from what I hoped, but doubted, was joy. We left amid a shower of rice and rose petals in the family's chauffeur-driven Pierce Arrow for the New England inn where we were to spend our honeymoon.

That night, our bedroom was suffocatingly hot. During the months of our engagement, we had done some rather heavy necking, but had never gone what was somewhat inelegantly known as "the whole hog." I had assumed that Sherwin was much more experienced than I was in such matters, he having insinuated as much after he'd returned from a European trip during the summer of his sophomore year at Harvard. But I quickly discovered he was just as ignorant as I was. We'd agreed that we didn't want to have a baby right off, and I'd been told that the best way to avoid that was to take a Lysol douche. But I put in so much Lysol that I burned myself badly, and any attempts at lovemaking were out for the rest of our honeymoon.

It rained every day. I sat in our bedroom, writing thank you notes for the 232 presents we had received, while Sherwin went for long walks in the rain by himself. Then at meals we talked in a curious kind of baby talk that we had never used before, but apparently had invented in a vain attempt to hide from each other how miserable we felt.

I grew even more discouraged when we returned from our honeymoon and settled down in a house in Cambridge that we had rented and my stepmother had fitted with furniture that reflected her taste far more than mine.

After we had been home for two weeks, I woke up one morning with a very bad case of the mumps. Sherwin, claiming that he might become "sterile for life" if he caught them, quickly threw a few essentials into an overnight bag and fled back to his parents' home, while a practical nurse was sent for to take care of me.

No sooner had I recovered from the mumps than I became pregnant with an ectopic pregnancy and had to have an operation that left me feeling weak and even more seriously depressed. Why had I ever gotten married? Even Smith would have been better than this.

In the meantime, Sherwin's job at the head office of the United Fruit Company was turning out to be far less interesting than he had anticipated. One evening he suggested he might ask for a transfer to one of the company's sugar mill towns in Oriente province at the eastern end of Cuba. What did I think of that idea? I thought it enchanting. The prospect of a year in the tropics suddenly revived my drooping spirits, and I urged him to try for the transfer as soon as possible. My idea of the tropics had been formed by the writings of Somerset Maugham, and I could hardly wait for us to become involved in what I envisaged as a life of fascinating intrigue in a warm and luxuriant setting.

IV

After about six weeks Sherwin's transfer came through. We put our things in storage, sublet our house, and sailed on a ship of the Munson Line for Antilla, a port on the northeastern end of Cuba, not too far from the company's sugar mill town of Banes, where we were to be stationed.

On the trip down the sea was choppy and the sky overcast. The ship's doctor, at whose table we sat, warned us that we'd have to be careful in the tropics. "Practically everyone you meet has a dash of the tarbrush!" he said, giving a short, cynical laugh.

All during the voyage, the meals had been poor, but on the last night the Captain's Dinner was delicious. The dining salon was decorated with festoons of red, white, and blue crepe paper. By each place there was a menu engraved in gold, paper hats, whistles, and other noisemakers. The captain, a short, stocky, fair-haired man with shrewd gray eyes and blond eyelashes, led the hilarity.

Afterward, in the smoking room, the captain, slightly drunk, tore up two packs of cards with his bare hands. Then, tossing the torn cards aside, he announced that he was going to teach us not to play cards with strangers. Summoning the steward, he ordered him to bring two new decks that he explained to us had been marked so that only the dealer would be able to win.

As I glanced from the captain's shrewd, red face to the incredulous, slightly terrified expression of a large, blond woman—a Christian Science healer on her way to visit a married daughter in Santiago—I remembered a sign I had once seen in the lounge of the French liner on which I had gone to Europe with my classmates and our two chaperones:

MONS. LES PASSAGERS SON MIS EN GARDE CONTRE LES JOUEURS PROFES-SIONELS QUI VOYAGENT PARFOIS SUR LES GRAND PAQUEBOTS. *("Passengers are warned that occasionally professional gamblers travel on large ocean liners.")*

I couldn't help reflecting how different the scene before me was from the vision of diamonds and gaming tables that elegant-sounding sign in French had evoked in my imagination!

Few of the passengers went to bed that night. Sherwin and I slept very little because of the running up and down in the corridors and the sound of champagne corks popping to the accompaniment of the toots of penny whistles, mingling with bursts of shrill, hysterical laughter. I told myself that even Somerset Maugham had probably run into such dreary, childish celebrations. But I had a nagging feeling that the romantic year in the tropics that I had envisaged was nevertheless beginning somewhat inauspiciously.

The next morning as we steamed into Antilla, the sun shone brilliantly in a cloudless sky. No breeze was stirring and the air was oppressively hot and humid. We had been told that we would be met at Antilla on our arrival. This seemed to be all that Sherwin could think about. It irritated me that he placed so much significance on being met. We knew where we were going, didn't we? Surely we'd be able to find our way there somehow, even if we weren't met officially by a company representative. But Sherwin was always nervous when he imagined anything concerning his status was at stake, unable to recognize that this very fact often laid him open to exactly the kind of snub he most dreaded. Headwaiters would take one look at him and show us to the worst table in a restaurant, where Sherwin would fidget and complain throughout the meal. If I tried to explain to him what he had done wrong, we'd end up quarreling.

Antilla was small and, even as port towns go, quite incredibly dirty. Open sewers ran along its main street and the odor floating out to us as the ship was docking was nauseating. Yet clusters of huge pink and yellow roses hung over the ramshackle wooden customs shed, and along the water's edge stood tiny donkeys, weighted down with large saddle baskets of overripe bananas which their riders, with occasional outbursts of song, were attempting to sell to our fellow passengers leaning over the ship's rail. Why couldn't Sherwin see that at least the scene was *picturesque?*

Suddenly he pointed to a man standing on the pier near where the gangplank was coming to rest. "There's David Armstrong!" he exclaimed. "He's the manager at Banes. I recognize him from his photographs."

Sherwin hurried to the top of the gangplank up which the man was now striding, showing remarkable vigor for a man obviously in his middle years. Stockily built, with a small, bristly black moustache and shrewd dark eyes behind horn-rimmed spectacles, David Armstrong was wearing a leghorn straw hat with a brightly colored band and a black alpaca suit. He shook hands first with Sherwin, then somewhat perfunctorily with me, his glance lingering much longer than necessary, I thought, on my legs.

I sensed a definite hostility in his manner as he chatted with Sherwin and continued to cast sly glances at my legs. Only much later did I learn how uneasy he had been about our arrival. Born in Jamaica, with that "dash of the tarbrush" that the ship's doctor had warned us was so common in the tropics, David Armstrong had devoted his entire life to the company. Now that he was getting on in years, there were rumors of impending changes in the company's administration. When he'd learned that Sherwin's father was a friend of the company's new president, he feared that Sherwin might have been sent to Banes to check up on him. During the entire time we were in Banes he seldom addressed a word to me, and then on only the most banal of subjects. However, sometimes at a party after everyone had drunk far too much planter's punch, I would catch him staring appraisingly at my legs. When he realized I had caught him at this, he'd raise his glass, wink, and give a short, nervous laugh.

We made the trip from Antilla to Banes in a small handcar with a Cuban driver on a narrow-gauge railway that ran through fields of sugar cane, which stretched as far as the eye could see in every direction like rows of tall, untasseled corn with a silvery sheen in the sunlight.

The engine in the handcar made so much noise that conversation was impossible. I was grateful for this as it permitted me to let my imagination run riot as we whizzed through tiny villages, past rickety huts, where dark-eyed women with clusters of naked children by their sides stood in the doorways, gazing sullenly at us as we passed. They looked to me like creatures from another planet, and I was appalled by the poverty in which they lived.

The trip in from Antilla took about an hour, but once there I was impressed by the size and modernity of the Banes station. As the handcar came to a halt, the driver jumped out and began carrying our suitcases over to an ancient Studebaker touring car before which stood a tall, very dark black man in a white linen suit and a large panama hat. "This is our chauffeur, Luis," said David Armstrong. Luis bowed with great dignity but with no change of expression.

As we lurched around corners and dashed up short, sun-baked streets, I glimpsed bright yellow bungalows, hidden among luxuriant growths of tropical shrubs. Native women with ramrod straight backs were striding along the cement sidewalks, huge baskets of fruit balanced precariously on their heads. We narrowly missed hitting several grizzled old men jogging along on tiny donkeys with live chickens hanging upside down from their saddle cloths.

Suddenly the Studebaker stopped in front of a high hedge of pink and white oleanders.

"There's Susie!" exclaimed David Armstrong, pointing to a woman in a blue chiffon dress, hurrying down a gravel path toward us from a large, two-storied house that loomed in the background.

A short, heavyset woman with slender, shapely legs and tiny feet encased in high-heeled beige pumps, Susie Armstrong had fine, straight blond hair streaked with gray and gathered in a small chignon at the nape of her neck above a roll of muscle and fat. Her eyes were a pale, almost milky blue, with blond eyelashes, creating the impression that she had just missed being an albino. Her complexion was a curious shade of pinkish lavender, and in the deep lines on either side of her thin-lipped mouth with its yellowish irregular teeth lingered a light residue of whitish powder. Yet despite her rather unattractive appearance, she exuded a magnetic vitality that was almost hypnotic in its effect.

Without her it is doubtful that David Armstrong would have ever reached the position in the world he had. She worshiped him, and he had been as helpless to resist the force of her ambitions for him as if he had been an insect impaled on a pin. She, too, was convinced that Sherwin and I were company spies.

Each morning after we finally moved from the Armstrong house, first to the company club, then eventually into our own bungalow, she would telephone me promptly at nine o'clock and outline what she had planned for me that day. She ran the entire social life in the Division, as the company part of Banes was called, with an iron hand. She decided who was to ask whom to dinner when, who was to play bridge with whom at the afternoon bridge games, and who was to be whose partner against whom at the biweekly tennis afternoons for the ladies. She drank to excess, yet never appeared drunk, swore like the proverbial trooper, and had a prurient interest in everyone's sex life.

By the time we reached Banes, she was rapidly becoming an object of pity even for those who disliked and resented her most. For some time she had been having fainting spells, diagnosed as the petit mal form of epilepsy. Shortly before our arrival, these attacks had deteriorated into a more serious type of epileptic seizure known as grand mal. In those days there was no known way of controlling such seizures, and Susie was now having these spells at increasingly short intervals.

At bridge games and dinners, as well as on the tennis court, everyone watched her nervously for the first dreaded signs of an attack, when she would begin to chew her tongue, her head would start rolling from side to side, and she would start to tear off her clothes while uttering a string of obscenities. If David Armstrong were present, he would struggle with her to try to prevent her disrobing, holding her jaw so that she wouldn't bite her tongue. Otherwise this task fell to the strongest among the women. Once the seizure was over and she had emerged from the twilight condition of its aftermath, she apparently had no recollection that anything untoward had occurred and she would start to berate those present for "sitting there like fools, instead of getting on with the game." To me what was most painful about Susie's seizures was the way David Armstrong—if he were present—would look at her as she was coming out of them, as if he would have gladly killed her.

Her health was a constant subject of conversation, of even more interest than the weather or the potential sugar content of the crop. No one was callous enough to remain impervious to the spectacle of this still-strong and unbelievably iron-willed woman disintegrating before their eyes. She spoke faultless Spanish—the only woman in the Division to do so—and had many friends among the Cubans throughout the island. She talked blithely about how she and David planned eventually to retire to Jamaica.

But there were those who thought David had other plans. Some claimed he would put her in an institution and "get himself a rich widow." Others felt he would "just disappear with Kitty," the Armstrongs' housekeeper, a beautiful, soft-voiced mulatto girl with long, slender arms, who glided silently about the Armstrongs' house, eavesdropping on all conversations. Kitty was the mother of two little girls, both of whom bore a startling resemblance to David Armstrong and of whom he was extraordinarily fond. Susie joked openly about the chil-

dren's resemblance to David, claiming that it was only natural for a man
to want children and, of course, she, to her great sorrow, had never been
able to give him any.

When I tried to tell Sherwin how Susie's constant interference in our
lives made me feel, he was unable to grasp what I meant. He was still
absorbed in mastering his work at the office and enchanted at being able
to play polo after work on a pony that David Armstrong had provided. If
he was enjoying life in Banes, why wasn't I? We were married, weren't
we? We were married all right, but to me marriage meant sharing and
there was apparently nothing about life in Banes for us to share.

The first person I made friends with, at the biweekly tennis games for
the women, was Mrs. Moore, wife of the manager of the Royal Bank of
Canada, the only bank in the Division. The Moores, not being employed
by the company, felt no need to follow Susie's rules of protocol. One day
Mrs. Moore asked me if Sherwin and I would like to drive out to the
beach on Sunday for a swim. I longed for another view of the countryside
that had so fascinated me on our way in from Antilla. But Sherwin was
reluctant to accept the Moores' invitation because David Armstrong had
asked him to play in a polo game on Sunday. When I told Mrs. Moore
this, she said, "Well, you come anyway!" So I did.

But I had to pay heavily for it. Susie lectured me endlessly about this
unconscionable breach of protocol, went on at great length about her low
opinion of Mrs. Moore, and how, in her view, no banker could be
trusted. But this time I turned a deaf ear to her reproaches and frequently
accompanied the Moores to the beach on Sundays and during the week
sometimes went riding with them in the late afternoons when Sherwin
was practicing polo.

I found the Cuban countryside breathtakingly beautiful, particularly a
stretch of road on the way to the beach that ran through a thick swamp.
There, huge trees locked their branches overhead and delicate streamers
of gray-green moss floated down around their massive trunks. Large,
blue-green land crabs would dart off the road at our approach, then turn
and stare at us with an evil gleam in their protruding eyes as they sought
refuge beneath the lush foliage of the mallow plants by the roadside.
Further on we'd pass open sheds used as living quarters by the Haitians
imported annually to harvest the sugar crop.

In the mornings when we lived at the club, I would try to read, but I
was unable to concentrate because our room was stiflingly hot and there
was such commotion issuing from the club kitchen. There was much

shouting by the woman known as "Sweetheart," who ran the club together with Percy, a slender, bad-tempered Jamaican who swished about
serving as her assistant, and much running up and down stairs, while in
the background a phonograph wailed what we called the company hymn,
"Yes, We Have No Bananas," and, "It Ain't Gonna Rain No Mo'."

Finally our own house was ready. It was the smallest type of bungalow
provided for company employees in accordance with Sherwin's rank in
the company hierarchy. Painted bright yellow inside and out, with a red
roof, it had a living room and dining room on one side and two bedrooms
joined by a bath on the other. Beyond the dining room was the kitchen,
originally a native house, with a servant's room attached. Everyone in the
Division had servants, the number depending on their position in the
company. Susie had hired a Jamaican girl for me, Clarice, who had a little
daughter named Delith Joyce Francis. "Naturally," Susie told me, "Clarice is *not* married!"

At the club we had had lamps to read by. In our own house there were
only single light bulbs dangling down from the center of the ceiling, and
no floor sockets for lamps, which we were told were against regulations.
We tried installing stronger bulbs in the dangling lamps, but blew out the
fuses, so in the evenings it was impossible to read. When there wasn't a
dinner party arranged by Susie and in which we were included, there
was nothing to do but sit on the small screened porch until it was time to
turn in. If we had had anything to talk about, those evenings might not
have seemed so endless. If I began speculating about the people we were
meeting, Sherwin merely grunted, and I wasn't in the least interested in
his bookkeeping problems at the office. I tried to show an interest in the
tips he was getting about improving his polo game, but I was far more
interested in the overseers who came to play in the Sunday games than I
was in the game itself. Sunburned, dashing-looking men, the overseers
seemed fascinating to me. But to Sherwin they were "just overseers." So
again we were at an impasse. The feeling I had had on our honeymoon
that, by the single act of getting married Sherwin and I had become
strangers to each other, began to overwhelm me again, and I became
increasingly restless and frustrated.

Gradually, through the Moores and the Newtons, another couple who
showed more defiance of Susie's regulations than anyone else in the Division—for the simple reason that they were financially independent—I began to meet a few Cuban couples and some of the overseers and their
wives. Sherwin usually begged off from accompanying me on these expe-

ditions with his favorite excuse of polo practice or because he had something important to do for David Armstrong at the office.

It was then that I began pouring out my heart in long letters to CW
and receiving from him those wonderful, understanding letters that
meant so much to me. I wrote about the people I was meeting, both in the
company and through the Moores and Newtons, described my view of
the company's business, reported all the talk about the sugar content of
the crop and what was being said about Cuban politics, including the
general belief that eventually Fulgencio Batista y Zaldívar would take
over as President of Cuba from Gerardo Machado y Morales and things
would "improve," whatever that meant. The only connection between
the Cuba I knew and Fidel Castro was that sometimes the Moores and I
rode out to those mountains in which Castro holed up with his first small
band of followers before he swept over the island with his revolution and
threw out of office that same Batista who in our day was supposed to
"save" Cuba from the corruption of Machado's government.

As our year in Banes was drawing to a close, my father wrote that, as
he had some business in Havana, he and my stepmother were planning to
come down to visit us in Banes and accompany us back to the States. It
would be ridiculous, he wrote, for us to leave Cuba without seeing
Havana.

During my family's visit, Susie didn't have any fits, thereby convincing
my stepmother that my descriptions of them were exaggerated. My father charmed everyone. Sherwin was the star of the Sunday polo game
and my stepmother praised him to the skies. She had always been nicer to
him than to me.

The morning we left for Havana everyone came to the station to see us
off. My last view of Banes was of a group of waving, smiling people, with
Susie in the forefront and, off to one side, David Armstrong in his wrinkled, dark alpaca suit, his old leghorn straw hat pushed to the back of his
head, a defeated and desperately unhappy man. It was midmorning. The
sun beat down mercilessly. High in the sky several buzzards circled
ominously. I only learned much later that just that morning David
Armstrong had received word he was being replaced as manager of the
Division by a younger man.

was enchanted by Havana, its harbor, its beautiful beaches, and the casino, where I won eight hundred dollars at bingo. At some point my father asked Sherwin if he wouldn't like to work for the Boston News Bureau. Sherwin was delighted and so was I. After the experiences of the previous year, working for the United Fruit had lost all its charm.

As soon as we reached Boston, Sherwin joined the staff of the Boston News Bureau. We got our furniture out of storage and set up housekeeping in an apartment in a two-family house in Brookline. I still felt trapped in the role of a young married woman. And what was a young married woman supposed to do? Have a baby, of course. I got pregnant almost at once—and hated every minute of it. I couldn't understand why women found this a "fulfilling" experience.

As the time for the baby's birth approached, I began to panic, afraid I would die in childbirth as my mother had done. I certainly didn't want to die before I had even begun to live. But again I had no one with whom to share my feelings. During the last month or so I suffered from a kind of hay fever accompanied by mild asthmalike attacks that obliged me to sit up all night in a chair in the living room, only dozing off occasionally. By the time the labor pains started, I was not only thoroughly terrified but utterly exhausted.

Finally, after a long and difficult labor lasting nearly three days, the baby arrived. He was a beautiful, seven-pound boy, and for the first time since I had left Ware Street, I felt genuinely happy and contented. Perhaps life as a young married woman might be worth living after all.

When I returned home, I took the nurse I had had in the hospital with me. But after ten days she left and I started taking care of the baby myself. One day, when I was giving him his bath, I noticed a miniscule scratch under his left eye. I assumed he had scratched himself flailing about with his little hands, so I carefully trimmed his tiny nails—and thought no more about it.

The next morning the left side of his face was flaming red and badly swollen. I took his temperature and my heart nearly stopped when the thermometer registered over 106 degrees. I knew babies ran very high fevers, but not that high. I rushed to the phone and called the doctor, who arrived shortly. He took one look at the baby and said he wanted to call in another doctor for consultation.

While we were waiting, the doctor suggested that I call Sherwin and ask him to come home; and also that I try to get in touch with the nurse, for the baby would need to have special care for a few days at least. Fortunately, I was able to reach the nurse, who promised to come at one—then I called Sherwin. He became quite hysterical, asking all kinds of questions I couldn't answer. The nurse arrived first, then Sherwin looking ashen.

No sooner had he taken off his hat and coat than the second doctor arrived. Something about the speed with which all this was happening, as if everyone sensed some intangible danger, only added to my anxiety. I had been terrified that, when I had washed the baby's face, I had some-how been responsible for the infection getting into the scratch under his left eye. My doctor assured me this was not so, but I couldn't overcome the feeling that maybe I might unwittingly have killed my baby.

The two doctors spent only a short time in the baby's room, then rejoined us. My doctor, looking extremely grave, said that the baby had a severe case of erysipelas, a fever-inducing disease that results in severe inflammation of the skin and subcutaneous tissues. When I asked if that was serious, the doctors glanced at each other. Then the second doctor said, very gently, that erysipelas was extremely serious in old people and babies under a year old, adding much less gently, "Frankly, I've seen over a dozen small babies with erysipelas—and I have never known one to recover." For me, the baby died at that instant. Sherwin, however, imme-diately began thinking of endless reasons why *our* baby would be an exception.

The baby was terribly ill, with the same high fever and the infection spreading over his entire head for a week. The apartment was filled with an etherlike odor from the compresses the nurses applied to his head to reduce the swelling. His nearly continuous, pitiful whimpering was almost more than I could bear. Sherwin's determined cheerfulness was too much for me, and fortunately after the second day I was able to persuade him to return to the office. My father telephoned several times a day, sounding miserable. My stepmother's calls reflected an optimism equal to, if not surpassing, even Sherwin's.

At the end of the week the baby's temperature was down and the swelling seemed to be diminishing. I hadn't been out of the house since he had been taken ill and one evening Sherwin persuaded me to drive to Boston to have dinner with him at his parents' home.

Just as we were beginning the main course, I felt as if two icy hands were gripping me by the shoulders. Jumping up, I said we must return home at once. I was convinced something dreadful had happened to the baby. The others tried to persuade me that my alarm was simply the result of the nervous strains of the previous week. But I was adamant.

The nurse met us at the door, looking extremely worried. "I tried to reach you," she said. "But you had already left. The baby has had a convulsion. The doctor has already been here. The baby's all right now. He's sleeping peacefully."

I dashed into the baby's room to see for myself. He did seem all right, but I was not entirely reassured. I could still feel those icy hands on my shoulders. Sherwin suggested we have a nightcap, but not even a good, strong drink diminished my feeling of terror. Once in bed, however, I was so exhausted that I feel asleep immediately.

As the first light of dawn was coming through our bedroom window, the nurse rushed in crying, "Come! Come quickly!" I leaped out of bed and, followed by Sherwin, hurried into the baby's room. But we were too late. He was already dead. I laid my hand on his little swollen head, something I wish I had never done, for the sensation was to haunt me for years.

I have no recollection of the next ten days. I was told that on the afternoon of the baby's death I came down with chills, followed by a high fever, and was delirious for ten days. The doctors were unable to determine what was wrong with me. They thought it might have been some kind of brain fever.

Shortly before I regained consciousness, I dreamed that I was floating down a swiftly flowing river toward a very high waterfall. I realized that I was going to be swept over the waterfall, at which point I would be dead. At that exact moment, I heard a woman's voice saying, "I think she's gone!" Suddenly I was filled with a tremendous rage at such presumptuousness. And the river began suddenly flowing in the opposite direction, carrying me away from the waterfall. I realized I was not going to die after all. I opened my eyes. Two nurses were standing by the side of the bed and my father, huddled in an overcoat—for it was January and the windows were open—was seated in an armchair in the corner of the room.

In the meantime, of course, the baby had been buried. Everything that might have reminded me of him had been removed from his room, which had been transformed into a kind of study. I realized this had been done out of consideration for me, but it made me feel as if the baby had never actually existed, which added to my depression and sense of loss.

Everyone was very nice to me and I received many letters of sympathy. But no matter how kind and sympathetic people were, they would invariably tell me that what I ought to do was have another baby, just as quickly as possible. I knew they meant well, but my reaction was an overwhelming desire to strangle them.

I knew that we would have to get out of Boston as soon as possible or there would be no chance at all of saving our marriage. When I spoke to Sherwin about it, he agreed. Actually, he said there had been some talk of his being transferred to New York to work for *The Wall Street Journal*. Maybe this was the moment to do it. Why didn't I speak to CW about it?

So I did. CW thought it a splendid idea. It would certainly be good for Sherwin's career. And it would be good for me too, he thought, to have completely new surroundings.

A few weeks later we moved to New York. Sherwin started working for *The Wall Street Journal* and we took a small apartment on lower Fifth Avenue. I did the housework and helped Sherwin with articles for the paper, occasionally doing a theater review myself and later a column summarizing world news for *Barron's*, of which Sherwin was eventually to become the editor.

The bull market had not yet hit its peak—it was still only 1927—and everyone in the country seemed to be making money in Wall Street. Employees of the *Journal* were not allowed to speculate in the market and if caught doing so were promptly fired. But nothing was said about employees' wives. So I decided I would try my hand at playing the market.

Although I knew my family could be considered wealthy by any standard and consequently I would probably never lack for life's necessities, nevertheless I felt very insecure about money. Everything connected with it seemed beyond my control. I felt that if just once I could make some money through my own efforts, this debilitating insecurity would vanish. From the time I had started school, my father had given me a generous allowance, increasing it over the years and doubling it when I had married. There was absolutely no reason why this state of affairs shouldn't continue indefinitely.

But I suspected that being basically dependent on my father for money had a lot to do with my feeling of insecurity, and for a rather curious reason: My father had never mentioned my mother to me, but if anyone commented, when we were together, about how much I looked like her, afterward he would give me money, small sums when I was younger, larger sums as I got older. This had the effect of getting money all entangled with love in my mind and making me feel that if I lost one, I would automatically lose the other—and not just as far as my father was concerned, but in general. When I was twenty-one, my father had given me a portfolio of blue-chip stocks, advising me to put them away in a safe-deposit box and forget about them, which I had done. I now decided to take some of these stocks and use them to speculate in the stock market by opening a margin account.

I selected a brokerage house where I was sure neither my father nor CW had any contacts, so whether I was successful or not, nobody but Sherwin would know what I had been doing. CW had always said that there were two ways to speculate: "diversify" or "put all your eggs in one basket—and watch the basket!" I decided to begin by diversifying. After some weeks of spectacular success with this method, I decided to shift gears and put all my "eggs" in one basket. The eggs I chose were the common stock of a utility company that Sherwin had written several articles about and that we were both bullish on—one of the few times we ever agreed on anything connected with the market. Almost immediately this stock began to soar with dizzying rapidity, so fast in fact that it made me nervous. Against Sherwin's frantic pleas, I sold out and returned to diversification, which was much less nerve-racking and actually, in my opinion, much more fun.

By now I had increased my original investment so substantially that my panic about money was beginning to recede. I took the stocks I had used to open my margin account, put them back in my portfolio, and continued to speculate furiously with the money I had made from my "eggs." Gradually I became so self-confident, so sure of my judgment, that when I began to suspect that the financial picture was not as rosy as it seemed, I began taking more and more money out of my brokerage account, buying small lots of blue-chip stocks with it, and returning them to the safe-deposit vault, too.

When the market finally broke wide open on October 29, 1929—my twenty-sixth birthday—my losses were not disastrous because of my having cut back steadily on my speculations and bought common stocks with whatever profits I had made. The whole experience had been very much worthwhile. I was now sure I could make money if the need ever arose, even if there would probably never be anything quite like the bull market of the 1920's again. And it was not just having proved to myself that I could make money on my own that gave me self-confidence. It was that I now felt I could trust my hunches, the intuition that I had never quite dared trust before, no matter how often it had proved to be right.

Ever since Sherwin and I had settled into our small apartment, we had been getting along better than at any time since our marriage. I was interested in his work and enjoyed helping him on articles. He was fascinated by my success in playing the market. Sometimes we would have early supper and head uptown to Texas Guinan's, where Texas, perched on a stepladder, greeted her customers with her familiar, "Hello, sucker!" or to the club where Clayton, Jackson, and Durante were putting on their act. Nightclubs in those days were tawdry, ill-lighted places where illegal liquor was sold at outrageous prices. But even Sherwin enjoyed watching the floor shows and the customers. However, on the evening when the famous gangster "Legs" Diamond, in a natty, pin-striped suit and a flipped-down gray felt hat that he didn't deign to remove, accompanied by two blade-thin gentlemen, similarly attired, strolled in and sat down at a table next to ours, Sherwin muttered, "Let's get out of here!" We left precipitately, even before the floor show in which on other evenings we had both enjoyed watching an adorable, dimpled little girl called Ruby Keeler dance up a storm.

Several evenings a week and again on weekends, Sherwin and I went skating at the New York Skating Club atop the old Madison Square Garden. Sherwin was to represent the United States in the men's singles at the 1928 Winter Olympics to be held in St. Moritz and subsequently at the World Championships in London. Together with his partner, Beatrix Loughran, national women's champion, he was entered in the pair skating at both events. It was essential that he keep in practice. I didn't particularly enjoy skating, but for anyone who had spent as much time in sports as I had, some exercise was necessary. So I was quite willing to settle for skating, since it was so important for Sherwin.

What really made life enjoyable that first year in New York was that CW kept an apartment at the Ritz and was often in town. His death in the autumn of 1928 was a terrible blow to me. My only consolation for his loss was that he had been spared all knowledge of the stock market crash of 1929. I'm afraid that it would have broken the heart of one whose faith in the economy of this country was literally boundless.

Early in January 1928 Sherwin and I sailed for Europe with other members of the United States figure- and speed-skating teams on one of the huge ships of the White Star Line. After a few days in Paris, we went on to St. Moritz. This was my first visit to a place that was to become very dear to my heart, with its lofty mountains and beautiful valley studded with lakes. We stayed at the Palace Hotel, still one of the world's great hotels, where we saw what was virtually the end of truly elegant European society. Each evening we waited in the long hall for famous beauties, such as Lady Ribblesdale, to come down to dinner around ten o'clock, resplendent in exquisite gowns and magnificent jewels.

During the aperitif hour, the Duke of Alba, many times a grandee of Spain, sat in an exquisitely tapestried armchair beneath one of the Old Masters paintings that graced the walls of the large salon, a prototype of the authentic aristocrat. On a couch not far away lounged Michael Arlen, author of the international best-seller *The Green Hat,* whose heroine, Iris March, drove a yellow Hispano-Suiza and "was beautiful and loose like the emerald ring on her finger."

I spent most of my mornings watching Sherwin and the other figure skaters train on the Kulm rink. Sherwin liked to get there very early while the ice was still fresh. But no matter how early we arrived, we always found a young Norwegian girl in a short robin's-egg-blue panne velvet skirt, a beige cloche jammed down over her golden curls, practicing her school figures. I was sure she would win the championship. Her school figures, even the most difficult, were virtually flawless. But Sherwin said we would have to see if her free skating was as impressive.

On the day of the women's free-skating competition. this slender, golden-haired girl raced out onto the ice on the points of her skates, swooped around the rink at breakneck speed, and executed a difficult and spectacular jump, literally soaring up, up into the air like a bird, followed

by a perfect landing. The program that followed was greeted with outbursts of applause and cries of "Bravo!" from the spectators. Her performance easily won her the gold medal. Sonja Henie, that slender,
golden-haired girl, had changed the art of figure skating forever.

There was another young champion at the Winter Olympics that
year—an American, Billy Fiske, who created a sensation by steering the
American four-man bobsled team to victory down a dangerous and icy
run. He also broke the record for a single sled on the even more dangerous Cresta Run. In 1948, when the Winter Olympics were again held
at St. Moritz, the same sled was mounted on a wall at the Kulm Hotel
beneath a plaque hung in his honor.

During World War II, when I watched American bombers, the sun
glistening on their wings, flying in formation high up in the bright blue
sky over the snow-covered peaks of the Engadine to bomb the cities of
southern Germany and Austria, I often thought of Billy Fiske and the
day I had watched him break all the records on the Cresta. Naturally, I
had never dreamed that that young, freckle-faced boy would be the first
American to lose his life in a war that no one foresaw at that time.

Sherwin did not win a medal at the Olympics in either the men's
singles or in pair skating, but he and Beatrix Loughran placed third in the
World Championships in London which somehow made the whole trip
seem worthwhile.

As soon as we were back in New York, I discovered that I was pregnant again. I didn't have any of the cravings for exotic foods that so many
women seem to have, but I had a longing that amounted to an obsession: I
wanted to be a Typical Suburban Housewife, to have a kitchen with
everything marked with a *Good Housekeeping* seal, and to have all the
problems of the women in the stories in the women's magazines.

As our apartment was obviously too small to accommodate a baby, we
decided to buy a house in the suburbs. Each weekend we looked at houses
in Westchester, first in Bedford Hills and Mount Kisco. But the houses in
those places were too large, too elegant, too isolated. They were for
people older than we were, who had been through more, who longed for
solitude, nature, and long country walks. I just wanted to live in the
suburbs, to participate in community affairs, and, when our children were
older, to belong to the PTA. Each weekend for a month we toured
Westchester, finally settling on a choice between two houses—both in
Scarsdale, both newly built and as yet unlived in—one a white, imitation

colonial and the other a stucco-and-brick fake Tudor. We eventually decided on the latter.

Our new fake-Tudor mansion was set fairly close to its neighbors, in a hollow where it got only morning sun. We were to discover that the soil around it was so rancid that everything we planted—grass, shrubs, and flowers—promptly died. Neither the heating nor the plumbing worked. The roof leaked. And the men summoned to make repairs were either incompetent or surly, more often both. But as we drove away that first Sunday and I looked back at our new home, I was convinced that I was about to embark with the greatest satisfaction on my role as a Typical Suburban Housewife. Little did I realize that within less than a year, the mere word *Scarsdale* and all it implied would be anathema to me.

Our baby, a son, was born in Bronxville on July 26 and named Sherwin, Jr. This time I was not afraid of dying as I had been the first time and the birth was shorter and much less difficult.

Sherwin was beside himself with joy that we'd had another boy. But instead of spending the first evening with me in the hospital, he telephoned his parents with the good news, then took the car and went for a drive up along the Hudson by himself, exulting in being a father again. The baby, unlike my first baby, was not pretty. He yelled a lot and was ravenously hungry. But all this comforted me, for I felt it meant he was intended for this world. Still, from the moment he was placed in my arms, I fought against loving him too much, so if he, too, should die, I wouldn't be hurt the way I had been when we had lost our first baby.

The disappointments and disillusionments of the following months were nightmarish. Sherwin hated commuting and in the evenings was exhausted. There was no more helping him with articles, and I missed having that crutch in our relationship. None of the neighbors came to call, and I didn't know how to go about finding out what community activities there were, if any. By the end of the year it was obvious to us both that our marriage was rapidly disintegrating as it had begun to do toward the end of our stay in Banes. So we put the Scarsdale house on the market, sold it—at a profit—surprisingly quickly, and moved back to the city into a large, comfortable apartment with a magnificent view of the East River. From then on I was so busy that in retrospect it seems to me that I was leading half a dozen different lives rather than merely one.

The first thing I did was to hire competent household help—a German couple named William and Mary. Mary helped me with the baby, taking him to the park in the afternoons and doing most of the housework, while William did the cooking and occasionally acted as chauffeur.

Two of our Boston friends, Ruth and Lyman Paine, had moved to New York and gave wonderful parties in their West Side apartment. We met a lot of their friends, mostly in the arts. Ruth was a painter. Lyman, an architect, was interested in what he termed "the ultimate reality," which I interpreted as my old friend, Truth. Lyman and I had endless discussions about this ultimate reality while sipping highballs of bathtub gin and ginger ale that would have taken the varnish off a table if they had happened to spill. Usually one of the guests played the piano while others argued or danced. Some couples occasionally disappeared for protracted periods of time.

Those were the days of Judge Ben Lindsey of Colorado proclaiming his theories of companionate or trial marriage and of Bertrand Russell trumpeting the joys of free love. There was plenty of experimenting with different partners and a general feeling that to suppress one's desires could well be responsible for the alarming increase in cancer.

Certainly none of us wanted to risk getting cancer. Many years later when the so-called sexual revolution hit this country and there was such lamenting over the habits and customs of the young, I couldn't understand why everyone was so excited. With the sole exception of the use of hard drugs, particularly heroin, I couldn't see that the young were behaving any differently from my own generation.

The only real difference was expressed very well, I thought, by Margaret Mead when she said that girls in college were not doing anything different from what they had always done, except that now they were doing it in front of the dean of women. Our generation was much more discreet. We went out of our way to cover our tracks, and I still think our way was best. Scheming not to get caught not only added to the excitement but, in my opinion, increased one's ingenuity in ways that were very useful later in life.

Shortly after we moved back to the city, there was an exhibition of the work of Cézanne, van Gogh, Gauguin and Seurat under the auspices of the Museum of Modern Art, located at that time in an office building at the corner of Fifth Avenue and Fifty-seventh Street. The effect of that exhibition on me was a kind of inner explosion. I felt that those four artists "saw" things as I did, only unlike myself they were able to transfer their visions onto canvas. I decided I wanted to learn to paint, so I enrolled at the Art Students League, only to realize that I'd never be able to paint as I wished until I first learned to draw. This required too much hard work and far more time than I, in my impatience, was willing to give to it. As quickly as I took it up, I abandoned that project and settled down to write a novel about our experiences in Cuba.

In the meantime, among the people we had met at the Paines' parties were Marya Mannes, a talented writer, and her brother, Leopold, a pianist and composer then working with Leopold Godowsky on a process of color photography that eventually became known as Kodachrome. Leopold's wife, Edie, was also a painter. Through them we met Marya and Leopold's parents.

Clara Mannes, a formidable lady and a fine pianist, was the sister of Walter Damrosch, for many years conductor of the New York Philharmonic. David Mannes, an excellent violinist, was at the time conducting free concerts at the Metropolitan Museum of Art. Together they ran the Mannes Music School. They were both devoted to Marya and Leopold, making no secret of the fact that they considered them geniuses. I was deeply impressed by the family's relationships with each other and by the cultured atmosphere in the Mannes home.

The stock market, after wobbling around for several weeks, had begun to head downward with alarming rapidity. Everyone, whether ordinarily familiar with the market or not, realized that something serious was happening. This created that undercurrent of excitement that all catastrophes seem to drag in their wake. On the day the stock market broke open, I felt very much as I had on the day the *Titanic* sank. We were fortunate, however, that the crash did not affect our personal lives in any tangible way.

About that time a friend asked me why I didn't have another child. Although I was immediately on the defensive, I still asked myself, why indeed? I knew I cared almost too much about Sherwin, Jr.; panicked if he so much as sneezed. Perhaps if I had another child, I would not be so nervous about him. It couldn't really be good for him to have such an anxious mother. So I got pregnant again and on May 15, 1930, our daughter, Mary Jane, was born.

Toward the end of the summer of 1930 I went up to spend a few days with Ruth Paine at her family's summer home on Naushon Island off the coast of Massachusetts. One afternoon we sailed over to see Leopold and Edie Mannes at their home on Martha's Vineyard. For the first time since we had met over a year before, I got the distinct impression that

Leopold was attracted to me. But I thought he and Edie had such a perfect marriage that I told myself I was just imagining it.

Shortly after we were all back in New York again, however, I realized that Leopold's interest in me had not been my imagination. It was a fact, and for me an overwhelming one. We could not have been more different in a great many quite obvious ways. Our greatest lack of compatibility, however, came not on the intellectual but on the emotional level, although at first neither of us had any inkling of this. The overpowering physical attraction we felt for each other was too strong.

The effect on me of this *coup de foudre,* as the French call it, was to fuse all my thoughts, feelings, ideas, hopes, into one single powerful emotion focused entirely on Leopold. On his side the emotion itself was as powerful, but it had a subtle objectivity and detachment that my feeling for him lacked, a certain impersonality that I came to realize only gradually. For me everything was completely subjective and personal. I loved *him,* and the love I felt for him could not, in my eyes, have possibly been induced by anyone else. But he seemed to feel that something had *happened* to us—the same thing that had happened to other lovers throughout history. In short, what for me was something personal and unique was for him but a part of the general human experience.

At first this didn't bother me, but then it began to make me feel as if we were not having a marvelous, private experience but instead were suffering from a common, universally acknowledged disease. Not that he ever denied that he was caught up in the same irresistible whirlpool of emotions as I was, but whereas I was amazed at how ruthless I suddenly became about everything else and took this as a sign that our love would last forever, he took what I can only describe as a more scientific approach. He did agree that we should both get divorced as soon as possible so we could marry each other, but he didn't seem to feel the same optimistic conviction as I did about how long our love would last. It wasn't that he felt getting married wouldn't work, but there was a vague "we'll have to wait and see if it lasts" about his attitude that gradually began to disturb and unsettle me.

Leopold's father came to see me, all suavity and charm, talking vaguely about life and its meaning, but carefully avoiding any specific comments about the actual situation. I was both touched and amused by how he handled it, until I learned through Marya that he had actually been sent as an emissary by his wife, who certainly would not have been too pleased if she had realized how well he succeeded in finessing the situation. Mrs.

Mannes was not upset by the idea of Leopold getting a divorce, but she was violently opposed to his marrying me.

When I wrote my father that I was planning to divorce Sherwin, he made a hurried trip to New York to try to dissuade me. In a conversation extremely painful to us both, he told me what he couldn't bear was the thought that by divorcing Sherwin I would be doing to my children what he had never ceased to reproach himself for having done to me. He felt he had neglected me by leaving me for so many years with my grandmother and seeing me only on Sundays and for some weeks in the summer. He had said that he felt that, in my marrying again and possibly having other children, I would be passing on to my own two children what he felt was the unforgivable neglect he had shown toward me. He concluded by saying, "If you were only doing this because you were in love with someone else, then perhaps I could understand it."

He looked so utterly miserable and dejected that I burst out with, "But I *am* in love with someone else!"

I had not intended to tell him about Leopold, figuring that would make him more, rather than less, unhappy. Actually my instinct was correct, for when he found out I was in love with Leopold, he exclaimed, "What? A *musician*? And a *Jew*?" It was impossible to tell which he considered the greater liability. There was no question which bothered my Cogan relatives most. Aunt Esther wrote pages about "that other person and his *background*." People who had repeatedly told me that they thought that Sherwin and I were not right for each other suddenly revealed a hitherto well-concealed streak of anti-Semitism that horrified me with its viciousness.

None of this affected in the least my decision to marry Leopold, but the prejudice that was being clamped down on him made me feel extremely defensive about everyone who was Jewish. The fact that I didn't tell him about any of this created a very subtle barrier between us, for until this vicious prejudice had raised its head, I had shared absolutely everything with him. Also, I had begun to sense that he was troubled by what I knew was his mother's opposition to our marriage.

Eventually, Mrs. Mannes asked me to have tea with her alone. She told me quite frankly that although she had no objection to Leopold divorcing Edie, or even to what she termed his "close relationship with you," she was unalterably opposed to Leopold marrying me. He had far too much on his mind, with his music and his work in color photography, for him even to consider taking on a new wife with two small children. Besides, she considered us basically unsuited to each other. "Actually," she said, "I consider you too much for Leopold!" I was both hurt and astonished. I had always felt that Leopold had far more energy and vitality than I had, but obviously his mother saw things differently, and she and Leopold were extremely close.

That afternoon marked for me the beginning of the end as far as Leopold and I were concerned. I sensed that he would never be able to defy his mother's opposition. She had by far the stronger character of the two and he was devoted to her. I never really lost touch with Leopold until his death at a comparatively early age. By then he had completed the invention of Kodachrome and paid off his backers. His last years were consumed largely by the problems of the family's music school and by the obligations of his second marriage to a woman of whom his mother thoroughly approved.

VI

Although my relationship with Leopold had not worked out as I had hoped, my marriage to Sherwin was definitely over. I got a divorce in Reno and in the summer of 1933 sent the children to visit him and went abroad with Ruth Paine. We planned to spend the entire time at St. Jean-de-Luz in France, near the Spanish frontier, for neither of us could envisage a summer that didn't encompass being by the sea.

Early in July we sailed on one of the ships of the French Line bound for Bordeaux. The first night out we were invited to dinner at the captain's table. I sat beside Jean Rufenacht, who was on his way home from Japan after having audited the books of a Swiss silk company with offices in Tokyo. When I asked Jean his nationality, he said, "I'm Swiss," to which I had replied, not too politely I fear, "How dull!" He gave me a quick, speculative glance, and added, "Actually I was born a Turk. My family only acquired Swiss citizenship later!"

This, of course, was much more intriguing. I thought of the Turks as a wild and savage folk who killed unfaithful wives with the most imaginative forms of torture. I asked Jean if this were true. He nodded. "Oh, yes, the Turks understand very well how women should be treated!" I was fascinated.

For the rest of the voyage, he regaled me with stories of life in the Middle East. He was fourteen years older than I and physically not at all the type of man that I usually found attractive. He was heavyset and bald, but he had an intriguing twinkle in his eye and spoke half a dozen languages fluently. With my distaste for provincialism in all its forms, I liked what I regarded as his worldliness, his facility with languages, and his extensive knowledge of gourmet food and wines.

Ruth and I debarked at Bordeaux. Jean, continuing on to Calais, promised he would come to St. Jean-de-Luz to see me. I didn't put much faith in this promise. He would have to travel across France to get from Zurich to St. Jean-de-Luz. I knew all about the traditional fragility of shipboard romances, or thought I did. So I just laughed and dismissed the idea.

Consequently, I was both surprised and pleased when he appeared, unannounced, in St. Jean-de-Luz two weeks later. We spent a delightful week, sunning ourselves on the beach and dining at the little restaurants that Jean always managed to discover no matter where we went. As he was leaving, he suggested that I postpone my return home for a few days and visit him in Zurich. I told him I would let him know.

After his departure, I consulted Ruth. "Oh, go ahead!" she urged. "You know you are dying to find out if your Turk will kill you!"

Actually, she was right. Believing as I did that Jean was a Turk, I fancied myself in some mysterious kind of danger. A delicious thought. Most people apparently pull back at the mere thought of danger. That has never been my reaction.

So I set off for Zurich, where I learned that Jean was not a Turk at all, but a French-Swiss who had simply told me he was Turkish because I had told him I thought the Swiss were dull. To pretend he was Turkish had been an easy masquerade for him to carry off. He had gone to Turkey as a very young man to work for the secretary general of the Anatolian-Bagdad Railway, eventually working up to that position himself. He had spent nearly twenty years in Turkey. On his return to Switzerland after Mustafa Kemal had come to power and Swiss interests in the railroad had been liquidated, he had become associated with an affiliate of one of the large Swiss banks and traveled frequently to the Balkans and the Far East on business.

On the last day of my visit, Jean asked me to marry him. I was tempted to say yes, but I had been brought up to believe that you should never marry a man until you had seen him in your own home environment. When I told him this, he was greatly amused. He agreed though, saying he would be returning to the Far East shortly and would travel via the United States to meet my family.

As his ship left Cherbourg, he received a wireless message that his father had died unexpectedly and minutes later another from me saying that my father had committed suicide. Both deaths had occurred at approximately the same moment. This eerie coincidence gave us a feeling that fate had somehow taken a hand in our relationship.

During my father's life he had had several nervous breakdowns, as they were called, when he wouldn't speak to anyone for weeks on end and had to have someone constantly with him so he wouldn't, I was told, "harm himself." His breakdowns were a terrible experience for me, during which I felt the whole world was about to collapse. But then he would snap out of them and the sun would break through the clouds again.

He never mentioned his breakdowns to me until several months before his death. One afternoon before I left for Europe I was watching him chop wood at Cohasset when he suddenly put aside his hatchet and sat down dejectedly on the tree stump he used as a chopping block. "You know, Mary," he said, "I'm afraid I'm going to have another breakdown." I had never seen such an expression of misery on anyone's face. I leaned over and kissed him, murmuring something about how I was sure that everything would work out all right somehow.

"I certainly hope so, darling," he said sadly.

He had never called me "darling" before. I felt a quiver of happiness. Perhaps, I thought, he might be going to talk to me about my mother. Instead he began to describe what his depressions were like, how at such times he felt that he was balancing precariously on the edge of an abyss, overwhelmed by a desire to throw himself into it and "finish with everything once and for all." Then he asked, "Can you understand that?"

"Of course!" I said, hoping he wouldn't notice that I was trembling.

"Can you really?" he asked.

"Naturally," I said. "Everyone feels that way sometimes."

"Do you?" he pressed.

"Of course," I said. "But let's not think about such things!"

He smiled wanly. "Weren't you planning to play tennis?"

I felt immeasurably relieved. "Oh, that's right!" I said. "I guess I'd better hurry!" Leaning over, I kissed him again.

"Have a good game!" he said.

And as I hurried off to my tennis date, he picked up his hatchet and started chopping wood.

While I was at St. Jean-de-Luz with Ruth, I had heard that he had had a breakdown, then that he was much better—in fact seemed quite himself again. Later we learned that at the exact moment when he had seemed to be coming out of his depression, he had taken a book on poison gases out of the Boston Public Library. He subsequently purchased the necessary

ingredients for the gas he intended to make, at different places throughout
the city on the pretext that he wanted to get rid of an infestation of rats
on his property at Cohasset. After he had assembled the necessary mate-
rials, he locked himself in a toolshed on his property at Cohasset and
concocted a poison gas that killed him instantly.

I have no idea what caused his suicide, but I have always felt it had
something to do with how his intelligence was exploited at a very early
age by his parents, and how after my mother's death he retreated into
himself. At first he had lived with his parents—actually until I was four
years old; then he had married again. I knew that the fact that I didn't get
along with my stepmother made him unhappy.

I always felt that there was a deep division in him between the person
he was before my mother's death and the person he became after he
married my stepmother. That division grew steadily, creating that abyss
that he had told me about and into which he finally toppled. He was also
very attached to his mother, whom he telephoned every night at exactly
eight o'clock, no matter where he was. My grandmother Bancroft didn't
like my stepmother any better than I did, and the tensions growing out of
this relationship added, I think, to my father's emotional difficulties.

My father's suicide really did not surprise me, and not just because of
what he had told me about how he felt in his depressions before I had left
for Europe. I had always had a vague intuition that something like that
might happen. I had learned, just how I no longer remember, that once
when I was having some kind of a problem he had said he worried
sometimes about me committing suicide. This had astonished me then,
because I knew that was the last thing I would do. Why had the thought
occurred to him? Could it be that it was something he felt himself capable of ?

I was too full of life and living, however—actually too young, I suppose—to worry too long or too deeply about such things. But the mere
fact that I *had* thought of them at all took some of the surprise and shock
away from it when it finally happened. In some curious kind of way, it
was a relief.

I had been concerned about just how I was going to tell my father
about Jean. I had not forgotten his reaction when I had told him I was in
love with Leopold and planned to marry him. The fact that Jean was a
foreigner and that I would be going abroad to live was also, I felt, a
complicating factor. I had never shared with my father my own sense of
adventure, how I really wanted to go everywhere and see everything,

that feeling that had filled me with envy of Wild Bill Donovan when at the age of fifteen I had watched him lead the Fighting 69th up Fifth Avenue. My father had made many trips to Europe and he had little use for Europeans as a whole. I was not sure he would even like Jean as an individual. I knew Jean would like him. Jean admired successful and prominent men. My father certainly belonged in that category.

All these worries that had been upsetting me were now suddenly removed. I naturally felt sad over my father's death, even sadder about all the suffering he must have endured before resorting to such a drastic measure as taking his own life, but I did feel a strange kind of relief, as if the slate had been suddenly swept clean and I would now be able to start life on my own. I now had only my stepmother left to deal with, and I felt sure I could deal with her. I had been told that she dreaded seeing me after my father's suicide, claiming I would doubtless blame her for it. I had no such intention, particularly after I had been told of her dread. Consequently, I didn't mention it. I think that this fact alone resulted in my being able to get along with her much better, in fact very well, until her own death many years later.

When Jean arrived in New York, he was darling to me and quite overwhelmed by the fact that we had both lost our fathers at approximately the same moment. He, as well as I, saw in this mutual loss some kind of karmic significance. After a few days we left for Boston to stay with my stepmother. She had none of my father's prejudice against foreigners. In fact, she rather liked them, as had her own mother, whose views so colored her own. I didn't doubt in the least Jean's ability to charm her. He had quite a way with the ladies. Furthermore, he knew my stepmother was wealthy. Like all Europeans, he believed in the importance of being in good standing with such people. In fact, even before my father's death, when we had been talking about my own financial problems, he had pointed out to me the advantages of getting on well with her.

My stepmother took an immediate fancy to Jean. She even got some of her most valuable pieces of jewelry out of the vault to wear for his benefit. Jean was halfway between me and my stepmother in age, so they could both remember life before World War I. They spent many evenings lamenting the various vanished attributes of a more orderly society. When, after about two weeks of a most agreeable visit, Jean was making his adieus before his departure for Japan, she glanced sternly at me and said, "You are a very lucky girl, Mary! Jean is going to be a very good rudder for *your* ship!" I took this as meaning that she thoroughly approved of our marriage.

For by now I had decided that I would marry Jean, although I was not in the least in love with him. When I had first told him about myself, my early years at Cambridge, my difficulties with my stepmother, my marriage to Sherwin, our life in Cuba, the loss of our first child, and my affair with Leopold, he had listened with an interest and sympathy no one had ever shown me before. Several times his eyes had filled with tears, and when I had finished, he patted my hand. "You poor thing!" he had said. No one had ever called me a poor thing before or ever shown he felt in the least sorry for me. All I'd ever heard was that I could do anything in the world if I only put my mind to it.

It was wonderfully comforting to have someone pity me, and I reveled in it. I knew that pride was one of my greatest vices, that all my life I had tried to conceal my feelings when they were hurt. I had been deeply impressed by the line from Browning, "Smiling, the boy fell dead." And one of my favorite stories was about the little Spartan boy who took his pet fox to school hidden under his jacket and let the fox eat out his heart without flinching rather than risk having the teacher take his fox away. I figured—quite foolishly as it turned out—that I could learn to love Jean. Besides, if he wanted to marry me as much as he apparently did, I would give him the chance that Leopold had been unwilling to give me.

VII

After Jean's departure, I settled down on Henderson Place off Eighty-sixth Street in New York with the children and my writing. One of the first things I did was send for Leopold so I could tell him about Jean. It was an extraordinary encounter. Leopold acted as if nothing had happened, as if our breakup and my subsequent behavior was a thing of the past and without significance. He still insisted that he was in love with me and wanted to marry me as soon as possible. I could scarcely believe my ears. I repeated that I was planning to marry Jean on his return from Japan. Leopold, who had been pacing nervously about the room, suddenly stopped in front of me. "Oh, very well," he said. "Marry your Jean! At least you'll learn to speak German!" And that was that. But it left me in a state of emotional turmoil. I realized I was still very much in love with Leopold, but felt I'd gone too far with Jean to be able to get out of it.

I finally recovered from the emotions of my encounter with Leopold, worked each day at my writing and enjoyed myself thoroughly in the evenings. I was determined to spend the time until Jean's return having as much fun as I possibly could so that I'd be ready to settle down as a model Swiss housewife after our marriage. I certainly managed to have an amazing amount of fun, particularly with Muriel Draper and the people I met at her Thursday afternoons where just about every well-known name in the arts and celebrities from other walks of life were apt to show up.

Muriel, who had very little money, lived in a tiny, dilapidated house in the East Fifties, so ramshackle that there was not even a lock on the front door. Through a hole in the living room floor it was possible to see down into the kitchen, where a tall, willowy black man by the name of Earl, with the scalloped-out crown of an old felt hat atop his head, muttered and sang as he boiled the water for tea. Muriel, wearing a hat and flourishing a long cigarette holder, would serve the tea, seated on a huge gold throne at one end of the whitewashed living room.

Muriel was an extraordinary-looking woman, with chalk-white skin, small, pale green eyes, and lips on which she wore a particularly startling shade of bright red lipstick. Her conversation was extremely witty, and I was always writing down in a notebook things she'd said that I wanted to remember, such as, "A horse is not a *criticism* of an automobile!" or observing that, "Leonard Amster looks like an authentic El Greco whereas his brother Jimmy more closely resembles a spurious Veláz-quez."

I still have a folder of letters she wrote me during the time I knew her that seem as vivid and relevant as when I had first received them. They are largely about my attempts to write. The care with which she read my novel about my days in Cuba as well as some short stories I had been struggling with meant a tremendous amount to me. It was not only her comments about the writing itself that were so helpful but her insights about what I had been trying to do. Lincoln Kirstein had told me before I met her that Muriel was a "catalyst," and that was precisely what she was. She had the gift of perceiving what one's intent was, as well as the ability to state it lucidly yet in the most tactful and constructive way imaginable. She was certainly among the handful of people who have helped me most in my life and I still feel it was a privilege to have known her.

While he was in Japan, Jean wrote to me regularly. At first his letters were full of adoration of me and details of his life and work. But gradually the tone began to change. He would ask me why I had written I had done such and such on an evening when he knew quite well I hadn't. Sometimes he was right. Sometimes I had lied about what I was doing; at other times I shaded the truth somewhat so that it wouldn't seem that I'd been having as much fun as I actually had, going to the theater, to parties, dancing the night away in different nightclubs, and dating a whole series of attractive men. Finally, in answer to a letter of mine asking when we would be married, he replied that we would be married whenever I wished, provided that since his departure nothing had been done against what he termed his "honor." I found this a ridiculously old-fashioned phrase and wrote him a rather sarcastic letter asking him to define just what his "honor" was. Nevertheless, I felt distinctly uncomfortable, and we started quarreling in our letters about the fact that when he'd been in New York he had told me that Arnold and Meela, the couple who had replaced William and Mary, who had returned to Germany, were not the kind of people I should have working for me. At the time I had accused him of being suspicious, "like all Europeans." To be sure, Arnold did have a chip on his shoulder and felt that the whole world was against him. But I attributed this to a wretched childhood in the slums of Hamburg and to the headaches he had because of a silver plate in his head, the result of a wound in World War I. It still annoyed me that Jean had taken one look at him and Meela and had judged them so harshly.

Eventually, this long-distance quarrel reached a point where I felt I had to make some kind of a gesture. Jean had repeatedly suggested in his letters that, if I would only join him in Japan, he felt sure that the misunderstandings that were springing up between us would be quickly resolved in a face-to-face encounter. But I didn't want to go to Japan in case I decided not to marry him after all. I felt that such an apparent wild-goose chase might weigh heavily against me with my stepmother, on whom I was partially dependent for support. However, I did think I could explain meeting him in Hawaii on his return voyage on the pretext of needing a little vacation. He was delighted with the idea.

We spent two days in Hawaii enjoying the beauties of the island. But he constantly evaded my attempts to have a serious conversation about when we were going to get married. On the evening we sailed for the States, as we were having drinks in his cabin, I brought up the subject again. He opened a briefcase, took out a package of letters, slapped it down on the table, and said angrily, "We will get married as soon as you have explained *these!*"

"These" were letters that Arnold had written to him in Japan, outlining everything I had done since Jean had left the States and listing everyone who had come to the house. The letters were in German, and beside quite a few of the names listed were written in parentheses *Jude.* Each letter was signed *Heil Hitler!*, followed by Arnold's signature. I knew Arnold was an admirer of Hitler, about whom we had just begun to read in the papers. On several occasions he had told me that when Adolf Hitler came to power in Germany, as he was certain he eventually would, that would be the day for people like himself, by which I took it he meant the poor and the oppressed.

After I'd glanced at the letters, I felt sick. I didn't know what to say or do. I was horrified by the letters themselves, as well as by the fact that Jean had not told me when he had received the first one. As I sat there in a state of near paralysis, Jean handed me over a sheaf of papers that, judging by the letterhead, were the report of a detective agency on my standing in the community. The report said that I apparently came "from a wealthy family," was known in the neighborhood as "a respectable person" who paid her bills promptly. But when the author of the report had telephoned to speak to me personally, I had sworn at him in a way that had surprised him, coming from a person of my apparently elevated social standing! I actually found this report quite funny, clearly remembering the incident. An oily-voiced individual had phoned me and started asking me questions about my credit standing but refusing to tell me why he wanted to know. My laughter broke the tension. Jean laughed, too. But I still refused to make any comment on Arnold's letters, and Jean suggested we go down and have dinner.

From then on, until we got back to New York, I continued my silence about the letters and behaved as if everything was all right between us. The reason I didn't say anything was that I didn't know what to say. I was quite out of my depth in a world where a butler wrote scurrilous letters about his employer and a man put a detective on the trail of the woman he intended to marry. I think I felt that if I didn't say anything, the whole matter would go away. But, of course, it didn't. On our second evening home I told Jean that I thought it would be better if we didn't get married. Jean hauled off and hit me such a blow with his fist that it knocked me out. I knew that such things happened. But to me?

When I came to, Jean was very contrite and apologetic. Could I possibly forgive him? Realizing that if he really knew all the things I had been up to during his absence, his hitting me might well be justified. I said I'd forgive him. Besides, my pride was involved. How could I explain my getting mixed up with anyone so volatile, especially since I thought myself such a good judge of people? In reality, his hitting me was the beginning of my being afraid of what he might do the next time if sufficiently aroused.

There was also something else about him that had begun to disturb me. At times he would seem like quite another person. Ordinarily, he could—and did—drink quite a bit without any change of personality. But then periodically there would come other moods that lasted for several days, during which he made me extremely nervous. Actually, he was what the Swiss call a *quartal Saufer*—a person who every three months or so drinks to excess. During the time I had known him, he had made an enormous effort to control himself during these periods. But later, after we were married, he let himself go and these episodes were a terrible experience for me.

For several days beforehand he would be extremely irritable, yelling at me that everything was my fault and attacking everything American. Then he would start to drink—drink himself into a stupor and lie for two or three days on his bed with the tears streaming down his cheeks. After these bouts were over, he would be quite himself again. But he would never admit what had happened. If I tried to ask him about it, he would clench his fist and make a menacing gesture as if he were about to hit me. That promptly shut me up. It was only after we had been married for quite a while that I came to understand what the real problem was. One thing that made it particularly difficult for me was that there was something about his moods as he was heading into one of his drinking spells that reminded me of my father's moods before his depressions that ultimately resulted in his suicide.

After the scene in which Jean knocked me out and I subsequently said I forgave him, I steered clear of any talk of my activities during his absence in Japan. I didn't want any discussion as to whether or not his "honor" had been violated. For it most certainly had been, and this naturally had involved others; if he learned who they were, how did I know what this wild man might do?

There still remained the question of Arnold and how that situation should be handled. I felt that in some way Jean, being so much smarter than Arnold, had been responsible for Arnold writing those letters; that Arnold had been only a pawn. Jean pleaded with me to let him prove to me that Arnold was not what I thought he was, that he had been justified when he had said Arnold was not the kind of person I should have in my home. By then I had become rather curious about what Jean had based his judgment on, so I finally agreed to let Jean run what he called a "test."

The test he suggested was that I go to his hotel room and conceal myself in a closet. He would then have Arnold up to the room and let me listen to their conversation. If after that I didn't agree that he was right about Arnold, good. He'd go his way and I could go mine. Under such circumstances, we obviously had nothing in common. I found his test sneaky and underhanded and told Jean so in no uncertain terms. His only reaction was a snort of disgust and some unflattering remarks about American naiveté. I still resented his equating what I regarded as my compassionate understanding of Arnold's problems with naiveté. I believed, I stated loftily, in practicing the Golden Rule and found his lack of sympathy with the poor and oppressed positively offensive. Furthermore, in any situation involving himself and Arnold, he, an educated man of the world, had Arnold at a great disadvantage. I personally believed in noblesse oblige. All I got was another snort of disgust and more derogatory comments about American ingenuousness.

After several days of increasingly acrimonious discussions, I finally went to Jean's hotel room and hid in the closet. At the appointed hour there was a knock on the door of the room and in strolled Arnold.

The next ten minutes were among the most painful I have ever spent, even more painful than when Jean had slapped that package of Arnold's letters down on his cabin table the night we left Hawaii. There was nothing about Arnold's voice or demeanor that bore the slightest resemblance to the man I had known for the previous three years. The conversation opened by Arnold saying how much he had enjoyed his meetings with "a fine European gentleman" like Jean, who was willing to help him acquire the little restaurant in Germany that he had always wanted. This was news to me. I had no idea that Jean had ever seen Arnold anywhere except in my home. They were talking German, so I missed some of the conversation, but I caught enough to gather that they had met on several previous occasions, at least one of which when they had been joined by a man who had worked as a butler for a member of my family. Arnold asked if perhaps Jean would like a look at the "plans." Jean said he would be delighted. These "plans," it seemed, were diagrams of my relative's home, indicating where she kept her jewels and other valuables, as well as plans of several other houses in the neighborhood that Arnold and his friend intended to rob. What had so far prevented them from doing so, Arnold pointed out, was that neither he nor his friend felt competent to organize such a robbery themselves. They were uneducated people without experience in organizing anything. They needed help from a man of the world, and Arnold felt that Jean was exactly the person to provide it.

The sweat poured off me as I heard Jean, in the most friendly tones, expressing great interest. Yes, he thought he could help them, but first he must study the plans. Would Arnold leave them with him overnight, or better yet for several days? He would like not only to study them himself, but by chance a friend of his, an expert in such matters, just happened to be in New York and he would like to consult him, too. Arnold fell right into the trap.

Through a crack in the door I could see him pointing out details of the plans to Jean. Then Jean, with a great show of ceremony, gathered up the plans and slipped them into his briefcase. Arnold admired the briefcase. When Jean said he had purchased it in Paris, Arnold expressed great distaste for the French and asked Jean his opinion of Hitler. Jean, lying through his teeth, said he had the greatest respect and admiration for Hitler. I shall never forget Arnold's comment. *"Ach ja!"* he said. "When Adolf Hitler comes to power, *that* will be the hour for men like me!"

There was a bit more chatter, but Jean didn't waste too much time in getting rid of Arnold. As the door closed behind him, I expected Jean to open the door of the closet and ask for my reactions. Instead he crossed the room, sat down in a chair by the window, and picked up *The New York Times.*

I wanted to die right then and there. My pride lay in shreds at my feet. Today, I always think of that moment as the time when I learned the meaning of Good and Evil—for until then I had always thought that everyone was basically good if he or she were treated properly. I stayed in the closet for what seemed to me an eternity, but Jean said it was only a minute or two.

"Well?" he asked when I finally emerged.

"What are you going to do?" I demanded. "Are you going to the police?"

"Of course not," said Jean. "Arnold hasn't done anything. Besides, I have the plans."

"In any case, I shall fire Arnold and Meela this evening," I said. "Pay them two weeks' wages and ask them to leave at once!"

"You'll do nothing of the kind," said Jean firmly. "You will behave as if nothing has happened, just as you have been doing, until it's time for us to sail. You just leave Arnold to me."

I was so shaken that I couldn't have done anything else. But I spent a most unpleasant few weeks before we sailed. I never asked Jean how he dealt with Arnold nor brought up the subject again, although I did notice that Meela's eyes were red from weeping most of the time. And there was something servile and cringing about Arnold's manner that made my flesh crawl.

Jean and I finally sailed for Europe on the *Paris* of the French Line, Jean preferring the French Line because of the excellence of its food and wine. I had arranged again for both my children to spend the summer with their father and his wife. And I had told my family that Jean and I would be married as soon as we got to Switzerland, giving as an excuse for not getting married before we left the fact that Jean had none of the necessary papers with him that were required for a Swiss. This was in a sense true, but I was not yet sure we would get married, Jean hadn't brought up the subject again after saying that's what we would do. I certainly wasn't going to mention it, because I really didn't know if I wanted to marry him and couldn't think of how to get out of it without risking getting knocked out again.

VIII

My first glimpse of Europe had been when I was five and Grandma had taken me to spend the summer with my Aunt Catherine Haviland at her château outside Limoges. My memories of that first summer in France were naturally somewhat limited, but I could remember that it had infuriated me that everyone, including my cousins, spoke French. The adults attributed my temper tantrums to the fact that I, having been the sole object of attention at home, hated sharing the limelight with other children. But I laid the blame squarely on the French.

On our way home we had stopped for a few days in England. At the London Zoo a large bird had tried to pick the bows off my pink kid slippers, of which I was inordinately proud. In my eyes, this bird was English. Consequently, I had decided I didn't like the English any better than I liked the French.

Then, of course, eleven years later, together with three classmates from the Winsor School, I had been chaperoned through five countries in six weeks. As a result of that cram course in culture, I had developed a permanent aversion to sightseeing in all its forms and had no great enthusiasm for Europe.

In subsequent years, on other trips, my attitude toward Europe changed, but I still felt like an outsider looking in. Actually, only after I eventually married Jean and went to live in Switzerland did I begin slowly, often quite painfully, to work my way *in,* to acquire what has been called "the European optic." Not that I always liked or felt comfortable with what I "saw," but at least I felt I saw it. I took my first step toward acquiring that European optic during that summer in Europe with Jean before we were married in September.

We landed at Cherbourg and spent two days in Paris, where I met Jean's brother, Andre, a large, quiet, gentle homosexual. Andre worked in an antique business with his partner, a small, dainty Frenchman with whom Andre had shared an apartment for many years in a state of wedded bliss. Jean had not told me about Andre's sexual proclivities. I realized after I met Andre that Jean had been somewhat nervous about my reactions, for he was very fond of this younger brother. But I liked Andre, whose manner was friendly but somewhat formal and who had large, plump hands on which the nails of the little fingers had been allowed to grow to an inordinate length.

After two days of lunching and dining with Andre and his friend, we went straight through to Zurich. I took a room in a hotel off Bahnhofstrasse while Jean returned to the Pension Schlichter, where he had kept two rooms since his return from Constantinople after World War I. My room had a large, comfortable balcony on which I set up my typewriter and spent my mornings writing. Jean and I lunched together, and after he returned to his office, I went back to my balcony to do some more writing or reading. I found this way of life ideal. For the first time in my life I was able to live completely in my imagination without any outside disturbances or responsibilities of any kind. This provided what was for me a novel sense of inner peace. In the evenings Jean and I dined in various Zurich restaurants, all of which were excellent. On the weekends we made excursions to different mountain resorts. It was all very pleasant, and Jean had none of those mysterious spells that so alarmed me.

Toward the middle of August, Jean announced that he had arranged his business affairs so that he would be able to accompany me to the States to pick up Mary Jane. We had heard from my lawyer that Sherwin felt that it would be better if Sherwin, Jr., continued to stay with him so he could go to school in the States. Of course, that had upset me at first, but Sherwin was our son's legal guardian and I could see the logic of a boy being educated where he would eventually be making his living. Even Jean had felt that was reasonable, so I thought it unwise for me to make a fuss about it. However, Jean said that I must insist that Mary Jane be returned to me, and because he sensed Sherwin might make some difficulties about this, he wanted to be with me when I went to get her. In order for him to have what he called "a position to have some say in the matter," we should now be married as soon as possible, especially since we would be sailing for the States in the first part of September.

At this point we ran into bureaucratic difficulties with the Swiss. I had my birth certificate and my passport with me, but I did not have a copy of my Reno divorce papers, and my passport was in the name of Mary B. Badger. In Switzerland, when a woman gets a divorce, she takes back her maiden name. Why hadn't I taken back mine *if* I were divorced? Because American customs were different. Well, how could they be sure I was really divorced? Where were my divorce papers? I only learned later that in Switzerland bigamy is regarded as a crime second only to murder, so I couldn't understand why the Swiss were so adamant. I continued to argue with them until they finally suggested that I write to Reno for a copy of my divorce, duly notarized.

I was afraid that all this would take much longer than the time we had before we planned to sail home. Besides, I had no great faith that the Reno authorities would act expeditiously, if at all. So I went to the American consulate to explain my problems. Fortunately, the American consul general was a gentleman from Mississippi whose heart was deeply touched by the difficulties of what he termed "the finest Yankee lady I've ever met." He suggested that I ask the Swiss if they would accept a letter from him guaranteeing the validity of my divorce, plus a new passport made out in my maiden name with another letter from him explaining that, because of the pressure of time, I had not been able to get a new passport before I sailed. This was quite acceptable to the Swiss, who promptly agreed to issue a marriage license.

We were married at the Zurich city hall, with an American vice-counsul and his wife as witnesses, and afterward were given a pamphlet on the duties and responsibilities of marriage, which I found touching but which irritated Jean. It might have been only my second marriage, but it was Jean's *third*. His first wife had been a Spanish girl, who had died in childbirth and the baby had died too. His second wife had been half-French, half-Armenian. He had divorced her because she had "betrayed" him, he said, although I learned later that she had divorced him because of his drinking. And now he was marrying an Irish-American—quite "a League of Nations," according to him, and he didn't need any pamphlet outlining the duties and responsibilities of marriage.

We sailed for the States the second week in September, only to discover on our arrival that Jean had been right in his suspicions that Sherwin would pose difficulties about returning Mary Jane to me. Actually, he flatly refused to do so. By then he was completely under the influence of his second wife, who certainly wasn't crazy about me. The situation was not helped by the fact that Sherwin had constantly sung my praises to her and was so fond of Sherwin, Jr., and Mary Jane.

There were painful negotiations, acrimonious disputes, legal threats, and general unpleasantnesses over the next few weeks. My lawyer wrote detailed memos of every encounter, and it quickly became clear that it was not so much Sherwin as his wife who was the real problem. Sherwin would agree to some arrangement involving summer visits of both children, while agreeing to permit me to exercise my legal rights to Mary Jane and to take her abroad with me. Then he'd go home, talk to his wife, and show up with a whole new set of propositions.

The situation dragged along until Jean had finished his business and risked trouble with his home office if he stayed in the States any longer. So he sailed back to Europe, leaving me in New York to continue negotiating.

Finally, Mary Jane was returned to me; two weeks later she and I sailed to Europe on the steamship *Rex* of the Italian Line. Jean met us at Genoa and we went straight through to Zurich, where Mary Jane and I stayed at first with Jean at the Pension Schlichter, which occupied an entire floor in the same building that housed the *Neue Zürcher Zeitung,* Zurich's leading newspaper. Trams clanged by outside windows framed by heavy, mustard-colored draperies. Steel engravings of stags at eve and hunters, gazing out triumphantly over dead chamois at their feet, decorated the dark green walls of the high-ceilinged rooms. A large rubber plant and a massive fern, in elaborate jardinieres, stood in the long hallway with a linoleum-covered floor. The whole atmosphere was lugubrious.

But there was nothing lugubrious about Fräulein Schlichter, a tiny pouter pigeon of a woman, with snow-white hair, flawless skin, rosy cheeks, and shrewd blue eyes, whose glory days had been spent as a maid for Sarah Bernhardt. Fräulein was a bundle of energy—cleaning, waxing, polishing everything in sight, scanning the ads in the local press in search of bargains, and raging morning, noon, and night against the perfidies of Adolf Hitler. On the wall of her sitting room hung a framed cartoon, published in the Swiss weekly *Nebelspalter* during the week that Hitler had become Chancellor of the Reich. It showed a tiny Hitler, perched on the edge of a huge, golden throne, and bore the caption, *Kleiner Mann, was nun?* ("Little man, what now?")—the title of a German runaway best-seller about a young couple trying to survive during the devastating inflation of the twenties.

One Friday evening I could see Jean was heading into one of his mysterious spells. It so happened that Andre was coming in from Paris to visit us. On Saturday afternoon Jean and Andre went off together, and when they returned, Jean was staggering drunk and in a very ugly temper. Andre persuaded him to go to bed, then he asked me how often Jean had been like that lately. I said that that was the first time I'd ever seen him in such a condition, but that periodically he got into the strangest kind of mood that I didn't understand.

It was then that Andre told me that for years Jean had been a periodic drinker, with the spells occurring fairly regularly every three months or so. Andre said I should just pay no attention to Jean when I saw his mood beginning to change, and not be drawn into any argument with him at such times. Then, if he really went from being moody and strange to actually drinking himself unconscious, to continue to leave him alone. He'd come out of it but wouldn't admit it had happened and it would be futile to try to make him admit it. I was glad that Andre had explained what had been troubling me for so long and I was grateful for his advice. But constituted as I was, how was I ever going to be able to follow it? Yet what else could I do? I felt sick at the thought of the mess I had got myself into, but I saw nothing to do except to grin and bear it. Jean was absolutely darling to Mary Jane and she adored him. That was at least one thing I could start to build on.

IX

Mary Jane was terribly excited by her new surroundings and the fuss Jean made over her when he came home from the office to play her favorite game, Winnie the Pooh. Fräulein cooked our meals for us, but the food was strange and Mary Jane was rebellious about eating it. The only way for her to get outdoors was for me to take her for walks along the lake where we fed the swans. I wanted more space for her to run around in and a chance to cook the kind of meals she was used to. So we decided that she and I would go up to Les Geneveys-sur-Coffrane to the Villa Joliette, which Jean had inherited from his father. Jean would come to visit us on the weekends.

The village of Les Geneveys-sur-Coffrane lies in the Val de Ruz above the city of Neuchâtel in the Swiss canton of the same name. At the time we lived there, it had two small watch factories, two cafés, a butcher shop, a bakery, a general store, and about four hundred inhabitants. In the distance, the snow-capped peaks of the high Alps of the Berner Oberland—the Eiger, Monch, and Jungfrau—loomed beyond the red roofs of the villages nestling in the valley. The buildings were surrounded by fertile fields, carpeted in the spring with wild flowers and in the fall with autumn crocuses. The Villa Joliette, a two-storied stucco house with a sloping roof and glass-enclosed porches, stood opposite the railway station on the branch line winding up from Neuchâtel to La Chaux-de-Fonds.

Jean had warned me that the French-Swiss were notorious for their *méfiance,* their suspicion and distrust. During World War II, it was said that when Hitler had offered Pierre Laval, Foreign Minister of Vichy

France, the French-Swiss in exchange for the French fleet, Laval had said he did not want them; Hitler had retorted, "God knows, I don't want them either!"

The inhabitants of Les Geneveys-sur-Coffrane appeared superficially friendly, calling out "*Bonjour!*" whenever they passed the villa and caught sight of us in the garden. But they never went further than that. Later I learned that at first they had disapproved of my wearing blue jeans. Then the village carpenter, summoned to build extra bookshelves for us, had reported that I not only had a great many books but actually spent several hours each day writing. Obviously I was *une femme savante* ("a scholarly woman"). Everything, even blue jeans, could be forgiven *une femme savante*.

I soon also discovered how superstitious my neighbors were. Anyone who possessed *Le Grand Grimoire*, a book of spells and household remedies, was regarded as a witch. The leading candidate for this designation at the time of our arrival was *La Mère Margot*, who for many years had had a room in the home of Fritz Adorn, the wealthiest farmer in the village. Then Mr. Adorn had evicted *La Mère Margot* for nonpayment of rent. The following day his pigs would not eat or his cows give milk. He consulted an authority on such matters and was advised to take a pitchfork and ram it three times into the manure heap behind his barn at the stroke of midnight when the moon was full. He followed instructions and the next day his pigs ate, his cows gave milk, and it was reported that *La Mère Margot* had been spotted slinking through the village with pitchfork marks on her face and arms.

Before war had broken out in 1870 and again in 1914, wild horses had been heard, but not seen, galloping through the Val de Ruz. In the last week of August 1939 at least a dozen people with reputations for impeccable veracity, heard but did not see these same phantom horses.

On the outskirts of the village there was a botanical garden belonging to a Mr. Droz, an herbalist who had purchased a lion to attract customers for the teas and medicinal herbs that he sold. Each afternoon as the sun began to set the lion *chez* Droz started roaring for his dinner. Nothing delighted Jean more than to assure our guests that it must be the deceptively heady Neuchâtel wine they had been drinking that made them imagine they heard a lion roaring in this peaceful Swiss valley.

Our next-door neighbors, Mr. and Mrs. Dessouslavy, helped me with the house and garden and acted as caretakers when we were away. Mrs. D. appeared each morning, accompanied by her small son, Eric, to help

clean, put up preserves, gather linden blossoms to dry for tea, kill a
chicken or skin a rabbit. I had made up my mind that I would learn to do
anything any other woman in the village could do, although I dreaded
killing a chicken or skinning a rabbit. I shall never forget my horror and
amazement at the ease with which a rabbit's skin came off. It was as easy
as pulling off a glove.

Winters are long and gloomy in the Val de Ruz. *La bise,* the north
wind, blows most of the time and there are seldom any of those warm,
sunny days that have made the resorts of the high Alps so popular. For-
tune-tellers had always told me that I would spend considerable time in
"remote places." I had envisaged myself in Patagonia or Tibet, certainly
not in a small village in the Swiss Jura.

Mary Jane had acquired a group of little friends, but I found myself
with a great deal of extra time on my hands. None of the books in the
villa exactly fitted my mood. Then I remembered a biography that I had
once read, *Portrait of Zelide,* by Geoffrey Scott, about an aristocratic
Dutch girl, Isabelle van Tuyll, born near Utrecht in Holland, who at the
age of thirty had married a M. de Charrière, from an old and noble family
of the canton of Vaud, and settled at Colombier, not far from Geneveys.
M. de Charrière, although a kind and cultivated gentleman, had been
extremely phlegmatic. This characteristic of her husband's, combined
with the tranquil life of a tiny Swiss village at the end of the eighteenth
century, had driven this spirited wife to despair. She had expressed her
frustrations in several novels that had had quite a vogue in their day. I
discovered that not only were Mme. de Charrière's novels still in print
but that it was also possible to visit the De Charrière home at Colombier.
I got the novels, visited Colombier, and left there enchanted.

The house was exactly as I had envisaged it, although somewhat
smaller than I had anticipated. But I was used to having everything in
Europe smaller than I had expected, from the Rhine to the "Mona Lisa."
I also found still available the correspondence that Mme. de Charrière had
carried on clandestinely for fifteen years with Constant d'Hermenches, a
dashing Swiss captain in the service of Holland, a friend of Voltaire, and
a married man whom she had met at a ball and with whom she had fallen
in love. So I purchased these books, as well as a biography of her by
Phillipe Godet, that I set about translating in order to enlarge my French
vocabulary.

Through Mme. de Charrière I got to know Benjamin Constant, the
nephew of Constant d'Hermenches, to whom as a girl she had poured out

her heart. Eventually, Benjamin, much younger than she was but for years her devoted admirer, transferred his affections to Mme. de Stael, an implacable enemy of Napoleon who presided over a brilliant salon in her château at Coppet on the Lake of Geneva. Never has there been a more distinguished group of guests gathered under one roof. All day they argued politics. In the evenings they put on plays and charades, then retired to their rooms to write each other letters, most of which were still available, as well as many personal diaries that their families had published, often as long as a hundred years after their deaths.

Night after night as *la bise* howled around the villa and the village lay in total darkness, I read about the life at Coppet, the plots of Napoleon, Fouché, and their enemies, until that world and those people became more real to me than my neighbors and life in Geneveys.

In spite of the interest of Mme. de Stael and her circle in world events, their passion for politics was balanced by their preoccupation with personal relationships. The scale on which they handled their friendships made me realize that Americans had a great deal to learn, not only about friendship but about the quality of life in general.

Thanks to my total immersion in that particular period of European history, I acquired an understanding of how political intrigues were handled and a grasp of the operation of plots and counterplots that provided a very useful background for the work in which I later became involved.

Eventually, life in Geneveys began to pall. I was not, I realized, cut out to be a hermit. Mary Jane had started school in French and I dreaded shifting her to German if we moved to Zurich. But I was assured that children, if left to their own devices, pick up a new language with remarkable speed. So we closed the Villa Joliette, and Mary Jane and I set off to join Jean in Zurich.

X

had fallen in love with Zurich the moment I first saw it. Over the modern bustle of the Bahnhofstrasse, with its luxury shops and the imposing edifices housing the legendary Swiss banks, hung a sense of history that had instantly captured my imagination: a statue of Charlemagne, like a playing-card king in stone, perched high on the Grossmunster, gazing down on the Limmat, lined with beautiful old houses and flowing out of the Lake of Zurich. Beyond the lake, the snow-capped peaks of the Glarner Alps loomed in the distance. From the old part of town Lenin had set forth for Russia and ten days that shook the world in a train provided by the German General Staff. Not far from there was the Pfauen Restaurant, where James Joyce had written much of *Ulysses* during World War I.

At Joyce's burial service in Zurich in 1941, as his coffin was being lowered into the grave, the city's oldest living inhabitant, who made a practice of attending all burial services whether he knew the deceased or not, inquired in a loud voice, "Who was he?" One of the mourners whispered, "James Joyce!" "*Who?*" demanded the old man, cupping his hand to his ear. The mourner, realizing the old man was deaf, shouted, "*James Joyce!*" "Never heard of him!" muttered the old man, stepping forward and peering down into the grave. "Never heard of him!" I almost expected Joyce to rise up out of the grave with delight.

Eventually I became friends with James Joyce's wife, Nora, and her son, George, who stayed on in Zurich during World War II. Nora said her husband had been shattered by the fall of France and eager to get back to Zurich, where they had lived during World War I—a war that, according to Nora, he had scarcely noticed, so busy had he been with *Ulysses*. Nora, incidentally, didn't think much of *Ulysses*. However, when her husband, in a fit of despair, had flung the only copy of the manuscript into the fire, it had been Nora who had rescued it. "I thought he should have written more poetry," she said. "You know, like, 'The Moon's grey golden meshes make/All night a veil/The shorelamps in the sleeping lake/Laburnum tendrils trail. . . .'

"They tell me my husband is an immortal," Nora lamented. "But I'd rather be getting some royalties from his books than being admired as the widow of an immortal!"

A sturdy, handsome woman with large, liquid blue eyes, a pale complexion, and masses of golden gray hair, always in slight disarray, Nora told wonderful stories laced with the blackest humor, and considered herself an expert in the relationships between men and women. "Girls are fools to believe a word a man says," she informed me one day. "You don't even begin to know a man until you've lived with him for at least twenty-five years!"—a rather startling statement to one of my age at the time. Nora claimed that she and Joyce had been blissfully happy. But when I repeated this to George, his only comment had been, "I wonder what my father would have had to say to that!"

When we first arrived in Zurich from Geneveys, Mary Jane and I stayed briefly with Jean at the Pension Schlichter, then all three of us moved to our own apartment on the Stockerstrasse, where we were joined by Marcelle, a young girl from Geneveys whom I'd engaged to help with the household and take Mary Jane to the park in the afternoons. I joined the American Women's Club, a flourishing organization in those days. There were a surprising number of American women married to Swiss in Zurich, as well as American businessmen and their wives and a large consular corps.

Ever since the Reichstag fire of February 27, 1933, and the subsequent Enabling Act of March 23, giving the German government complete freedom of action without regard to parliamentary or constitutional limitations, the Swiss had watched with growing apprehension the antics of their powerful northern neighbor. What was happening in Germany was a constant preoccupation of everyone we met. And I frequently dropped by the Pension Schlicter to get Fräulein's latest views of what the Nazis were doing.

During the night of June 30, 1934—known as the "Night of the Long

Knives"—the Nazis murdered several hundred people, including former Chancellor General Kurt von Schleicher and his wife, and also Hitler's close personal friend Ernst Roehm, head of the SA, the notorious Nazi storm troops. Roehm, Fräulein informed me, had had a fine record in World War I, but later had gone to Bolivia where his sexual appetites had undergone a most unfortunate change.

The implication was that, in her opinion, anything could happen in South America and, unfortunately, most things did. The SA, it was said, had become a hotbed of homosexuality. However, Fräulein explained, homosexuality was nothing new in Germany. Shortly after World War I she had visited a friend at a private spa in Germany, where she had been greatly impressed by two elegant ladies who spent their days embroidering exquisite pieces of tapestry in the great hall. Imagine her surprise when she had learned that these two distinguished "ladies" were actually a field marshal and his good friend, a general, who always spent their vacations there where they were able to dress as they chose and engage in such nonmilitary activities as tapestry work. Oh, yes, Fräulein said, homosexuality was nothing new in Germany. But under the Nazis it had become vulgarized and was now practiced by the lowest types, instead of being confined to the aristocracy, where, in her opinion, it belonged.

It was many months before the events of June 30 were generally known in all their bloody and gruesome detail, but enough information had leaked out within twenty-four hours to set off a violent reaction in Switzerland. Some weeks later, when Jean asked me if I would like to accompany him on a business trip to Germany, I jumped at the chance. I was eager to see with my own eyes Hitler's Germany, about which we were hearing such horrendous stories.

On the eve of our departure, King Alexander of Yugoslavia and Louis Barthou, the French Foreign Minister, were assassinated in Marseilles. Fräulein Schlichter telephoned me to plead with me not to go. With the memory of Sarajevo still vivid in her mind, she was convinced that war would break out at any moment. But I assured her that even if it did, I'd find my way back to Switzerland somehow.

It was a cold, gray morning and a sense of doom hung over the city as we left for the station. But there was nothing gloomy about our train, the *Rheingold*, with its lush purple and gold interior, its atmosphere of an almost royal splendor. At Basel, however, we were abruptly brought back to reality when German customs officials came stomping through the train, with loud *"Heil Hitlers."* Snapping their right arms up from the elbow in the familiar Nazi salute, they proceeded to confiscate all our newspapers and magazines that contained news of the assassination the previous day in Marseilles. They also demanded to know how much foreign money we were carrying, noted the exact sum in our passports, and warned us that this sum was all the money we would be allowed to take out with us on our return trip. As they departed with more "*Heil Hitlers!*" and the automatic Nazi salute, an elderly gentleman across the aisle from us muttered, "Well, I can still *live,* can't I?" and, picking up a book entitled *Die Kastration,* immersed himself in it.

I glanced at Jean, but instead of the amused smile I had anticipated, I got only a stony stare. I realized he was giving me a coded signal that we were now entering a country where it was wiser to conceal all one's thoughts and feelings.

The train passed through fields where peasant women, in shapeless blue dresses, white kerchiefs around their heads, were digging potatoes and tossing them into large baskets at their feet. Occasionally, a woman would stop her work, straighten up, and wave at the train. But I didn't dare wave back. Already a sense that any human gesture might get me arrested had settled down over me like a thick, black cloud.

In the Mannheim station the faces of the people on the platform had a peculiar pallor. Many of them looked mean and hostile.

Krefeld, where we stayed for a few days before going on to Stuttgart and Düsseldorf, was plastered with posters urging the populace to vote in the upcoming plebiscite for a return to the Reich. I wanted to buy some postcards of Hitler, surrounded by groups of happy, laughing children, but I couldn't help feeling that if I made any such purchase, the proprietor of the shop would report that a foreigner, an American woman, had been buying pictures of the Führer and the game would be up. Neither my American passport nor my Swiss husband could save me. Everyone in the shops, in the restaurants, at the hotel had a curiously furtive manner. If I tried to talk to them, they answered reluctantly and then only in monosyllables.

While Jean was working, I wandered aimlessly through the streets. In school, I had learned about "*Der alte Barbarossa/Der Kaiser Friederich,*" who had been sleeping for centuries in an underground castle. Periodically, he'd rouse himself from his slumbers to inquire of a youth guarding the entrance to the castle if the ravens were still flying overhead. If the answer was affirmative, he returned to his enchanted slumber. Perhaps the ravens had stopped flying and Barbarossa was on the prowl again. . . .

I was amazed there was no mention of the assassination of King Alexander and Barthou in the local press. I had assumed that the confiscation of our newspapers and magazines at the frontier had simply been because Joseph Goebbels wanted to inform the Germans of the assassination in his own way in the Nazi-controlled press. Instead there was a complete blackout of this news. Jean warned me not to mention politics when we dined with his friends, some of whom he had known since his days in Turkey. I found it incomprehensible that none of them even mentioned that President Paul von Hindenburg had died some weeks before. To have mentioned Hindenburg's death, however, would naturally have led to the thirtieth of June and to speculation about the true meaning of that bloody performance. So everyone we met steered clear of anything that might lead toward that snakepit of speculation, and instead chattered about food and wine and about what flowers and vegetables would grow best in our garden at Geneveys.

The way everyone we met—and we met a great many people from all walks of life—had apparently obliterated from their consciousness anything that might have touched on unpleasant reality convinced me that the Germans who later claimed they knew nothing about the concentration camps were not necessarily lying. The real reason they had not known what was happening was quite simply that they hadn't *wanted* to know.

Our departure from Germany was for me personally even more traumatic than our arrival had been. There were the same uniformed officials at the frontier, the same thorough inspection of luggage and passports, the same *"Heil Hitler!"* with arms snapping up from the elbow in the Nazi salute.

Before leaving for the station, Jean had handed me a large roll of German marks, suggesting that I stuff them inside my dress and smuggle them into Switzerland.

"But isn't that wrong?" I asked.

Jean snorted. "Is it wrong to cheat Adolf Hitler?"

"But . . . ," I began.

"But . . . but . . ."

Obviously Jean was about to launch into one of his tirades about American ingenuousness. I didn't feel adequate to conducting a philosophical discussion about right versus wrong or ends versus means in the flurry of departure. So I stuck the roll of money down inside my dress and prayed I would not be searched by some Nazi harpy at the frontier.

When the currency control official came through the train, Jean handed over the form he had been given to fill out and the change he had left in his pockets. The official studied the form carefully, counted the change, glared suspiciously at Jean, then at me, and turning back to Jean, demanded to see the receipted bills for our expenditures in Germany. Jean calmly opened his briefcase and handed over a sheaf of receipts. The official studied them assiduously, comparing them to the form Jean had filled out. Then, just as I felt as if the roll of hidden money was about to burn a hole through my dress, the official handed the sheaf of bills back to Jean, stamped our passports, and with a brisk *"Heil Hitler!"* was on his way.

Jean had carefully altered the receipted bills so that they conformed to the figures on the form he had been given to fill out. When he finally explained this to me after we had crossed the border, I was so relieved to be back in the sane and tranquil atmosphere of Switzerland that I did not have the energy to get into an argument about the morality of smuggling money out of Germany, particularly as I knew Jean would twist anything I might say into a claim that I wanted to make a cash present to Adolf Hitler.

Over the years Jean and I had a great many arguments about what was morally right or wrong, but I found more often than not the arguments I put forward, as well as the positions I took, were much too simplistic. This almost constant reevaluation of long-held beliefs was an important, although often painful, aspect of what I came to think of as my "European education."

To give some idea of the range of these arguments, there was, for instance, the broad general concept that in our country a person is innocent until proven guilty. In European countries where the Napoleonic code prevails, the exact reverse is true. Endless social customs differ, although there is less divergence in customs between people of the same socio-economic class than if a vertical difference is involved. This latter was a complicating factor in my relationship with Jean. His father had been for many years the stationmaster in a small city in the canton of Neuchâtel. He would have had far more in common with a wife from a similar background in this country than he had with me.

I had been brought up to believe that you were kind and considerate to those who worked for you. Jean was convinced that if you were nice to such people, they took advantage of you. He saw ill-will everywhere. If a picture was crooked on the wall, he regarded it as a deliberately hostile act on the part of the girl who worked for us. He would get furious when I said she had probably just knocked it askew accidentally while dusting.

I thought it only considerate to notify Mme. Dessouslavy whenever I planned to go up to Geneveys. Jean thought I should arrive unannounced in order to catch the Dessouslavys doing something they shouldn't, such as taking a bath at our house, which had the only bathtub in the village. Other villagers always took showers in the basement of the schoolhouse on Saturday evenings, but Jean was convinced that the Dessouslavys took advantage of our absence to bathe in splendor at our house.

He had what on the surface appeared to be friends, but basically he saw no reason for wasting time on anyone who could not be useful. I also noticed quite quickly that European women do not have the same type of friendships with other women that American women have. It took Jean quite a while to become convinced that my friendships with several American women, married to Swiss and living in Zurich, didn't have lesbian undertones.

In the beginning, I would argue with him, but gradually I began to see that his way of viewing things had something to be said for it in the sense that it was more closely adapted to human nature than my more idealistic attitudes. What it actually boiled down to was whether or not a person believed in the perfectibility of man. I did. Jean didn't. At one point this drove me to the writings of Jean Jacques Rousseau. The ideals of the French Revolution gave me something to cling to, but it was not easy to apply them to day-by-day living. It was much easier to just shut up than to try to reeducate Jean, particularly when I didn't quite see how Liberty, Equality, and Fraternity could be used to win my argument about how reprehensible I found his trying to catch the Dessouslavys taking baths in our bathtub.

Most Swiss men are convinced that they are superior to women. When I was living in Switzerland, the women had not yet won even the right to vote. In Jean's case, this Swiss attitude was compounded by the fact that he had lived for so many years in the Near East. I had grown up believing that little girls were made of "sugar and spice and everything nice," and little boys were made of "snakes and snails and puppy dogs' tails." The people my family knew left their money in trust for their daughters. Sons were expected to make their own way in this world. Jean was able to accept this as an explanation for why so much of the money in the United States was in the hands of women. Nevertheless, he deplored the situation and was always muttering about how he would like to organize a revolt among American men.

It was certainly lucky that I had developed a much more sophisticated point of view, without losing sight of the basic moral values and ideals I had been raised to believe in, by the time Allen Dulles crossed the Swiss frontier and enlisted my services in his wartime intelligence activities. For if there was one thing my work during the war convinced me of, it was that, in order to engage in intelligence work successfully, it was essential to have a very clear-cut idea of your own moral values, so that if you were forced by necessity to break them, you were fully conscious of what you were doing and why.

I realized quite early in my work for the Office of Strategic Services that I must never have any dealings with an enemy of whatever nationality whom I could not imagine liking as an individual if there had not been a war on. If I didn't like a contact, it might mean, at least in my case, that my judgment of the information I was receiving might be clouded by my personal dislike of the person providing it. An example of this was when a deserter from the German Army, a nasty little man with shifty eyes and a sleazy manner, showed up one day at our apartment with the maps of a dozen German airfields that he wanted to sell to the Americans. My distaste for him was such that I didn't feel able to evaluate objectively either the plans or his motive in trying to sell them to me. Yet, realizing the value of the maps if authentic, I told him I had no idea about such things and gave him the name of the OSS man at the American consulate whom I felt would be far better equipped than I to deal with him.

Not the least aspect of the whole problem of intelligence work revolves around the subtle differences between intelligence work during war or peace. In wartime, of course, the whole issue is greatly simplified. I myself would find such work during peacetime extremely difficult, if not actually impossible. I am not, I fear, sufficiently convinced of the advantages of one set of beliefs over another. At times I have thought I was by instinct an anarchist. Or I'd decide that a benevolent monarchy was the best form of government. I also have had many questions about democracy. In short, I personally would be incapable of engaging in intelligence work in the service of an idea. But when war broke out and my own country was under attack, that solved the problem for me.

The first thing I did after our return from Germany was to give Fräulein a rundown on our experiences. The second was to catch up on the news of the assassination of King Alexander and Louis Barthou in the newspapers and magazines that had accumulated during our absence.

By the time I had finished reading all the political commentaries, biographical sketches, and dire predictions of various pundits, I certainly knew a great deal more about "the powder keg of Europe" than I had ever known before. I also developed an interest in Yugoslavia, which was to continue all during the war, until my file on Yugoslavia actually became second in size only to my file on Germany. I noted with interest that the grandmother of the new, eleven-year-old King Peter of Yugoslavia was Grandpa Barron's friend, Queen Marie, now the Dowager Queen of Rumania, which somehow made me feel quite at home amid all the stories of murder and intrigue.

But a combination of the menacing atmosphere of Germany and all I learned about the hidden antagonisms between nations when reading about the assassination in Marseilles had given me a feeling of apprehension, a vague sense of having swallowed a glass of ice water too quickly, that was to continue until the actual outbreak of war in September 1939. It was a kind of nervous expectancy that couldn't be pinned down to anything specific except the general category of war. But what kind of war? A war that would "destroy European civilization," people said. *Gas* was the scare word on everyone's lips. Actually, by the time we moved from Geneveys to Zurich, people were discussing what kind of gas masks to buy. A few cautious souls had even already purchased theirs.

XI

J ean was traveling almost constantly on business. Often he would be home for only a few days each month. Even I could avoid arguments for a couple of days by just agreeing with everything he said. The net result of such behavior, however, was to build up an increasingly impenetrable barrier between us. His affection for Mary Jane and hers for him continued to make the situation endurable, however. Eventually, having a lot of free time on my hands, I decided to attend the lectures being given at the Federal Institute of Technology by the eminent Swiss psychologist Carl Gustav Jung.

When I had read Jung's latest book, *Modern Man in Search of a Soul*, I had sensed that perhaps his theories could help me discover the source of a curious affliction from which I had been suffering intermittently since several weeks before my first baby had been born.

Suddenly, for no apparent reason, I would sneeze forty or fifty times, then choke up with what resembled an asthma attack but which doctors had assured me was not asthma. It was probably an allergy of some kind.

Allergies were extremely fashionable in those days, so I had been tested for every imaginable allergy from carrots to feathers, all with negative results. Then one day a very perceptive friend informed me that she had noticed I only sneezed when I was among people whom she knew bored me. Could there be, she wondered, a connection between my sneezing and boredom? I had noticed that I never sneezed when I was alone. But I didn't feel it was as much a question of boredom as of trying to please people with whom I had nothing in common. I had not realized, however, until I read Jung, that psychological problems could produce physical manifestations. I had never heard the word *psychosomatic,* neither had practically anyone else in those days. But my friend's comment had rung a very remote bell. *Modern Man in Search of a Soul* rang another.

I had been free of attacks after my marriage to Jean and throughout our time at Geneveys and even after we first moved to Zurich. Then, out of the blue, shortly after our return from Germany, the attacks started again. I was completely baffled as to why. It occurred to me that here I was in Zurich where Jung not only lived but was giving public lectures at the Federal Institute of Technology. Perhaps I should at least go and take a look at him to see how he struck me as a man aside from his theories, which, of course, I didn't really understand but simply sensed might be of great benefit to me personally.

I no longer remember the subject on which Jung was lecturing or even whether the lecture was given in German or English. But I do remember how tremendously impressed I was by Jung himself. Although he was twenty-eight years older than I was, I found him an extremely attractive man.

Tall, with a large, heavy frame and a handsome, rather leonine head, Jung exuded health and vigor. Most of the people I knew considered analysis "dangerous," those who practiced it "witch doctors," and people who paid perfectly good money to be "analyzed," in all probability "mentally deranged." But there was nothing even faintly suggestive of a witch doctor about Jung. On the contrary, with his tweed jacket and pipe, his healthy, ruddy complexion, he seemed wholesomeness incarnate.

What impressed me most about him, however, was his perfectly extraordinary wit. I have often wondered why more has not been made of this particular characteristic of his, although plenty has been written about his hearty, contagious laugh. His wit was often wicked, sometimes even quite cruel, but that did nothing in my eyes to diminish what I felt to be its therapeutically cleansing effect.

I learned that he was holding seminars on *Thus Spake Zarathustra* at the Psychological Club on the Gemeindestrasse. There was much talk in those days of the connection between the Superman philosophy of Frederick Nietzsche and the behavior of the dictators. I was told that in the seminars Jung dealt with Nietzsche's incipient insanity as revealed in *Thus Spake Zarathustra* and how this was connected with an outbreak of what Jung called "the collective unconscious," which he believed was taking hold in Nazi Germany.

I was told that I would have to get Jung's permission to attend the seminars, so I sat myself down and composed a letter to him. It took me over two weeks to produce a letter that satisfied me. When I had finally finished it, it ran to nearly three, single-spaced typewritten pages. In it I pointed out how interested I had been in psychology ever since I had read *The Varieties of Religious Experience* by William James, how fascinated I had been by *Modern Man in Search of a Soul,* how much I had enjoyed his lectures at the Federal Institute of Technology, how interested I was in Frederick Nietzsche, and how eager I was to expand my psychological knowledge. Naturally, I made no mention of wanting to find out why I sneeezed. I felt that was much too trivial a matter to mention in a letter to a man of his reputation. I felt enormously inflated and pleased with myself when I dropped my letter into the mailbox. I was considerably deflated when, some days later, I received a short note from Jung saying that, if I actually thought I would like to attend his seminars, he had no objection. Jung had a marvelous way of cutting through overblown pretentiousness. At one seminar, a woman asked him if he didn't think it basic to remember the second law of thermodynamics. Jung chuckled and replied, "Maybe I would—if I knew what it was!"

The Psychological Club, where the seminars were held, was located in several rooms of a dark, ivy-covered villa, surrounded by dense shrubbery that always seemed to be dripping wet. Zurich may be a lovely city, but its climate certainly leaves much to be desired. One can spend months at a time there without seeing the sun.

The erudition that spilled out during the sessions filled me with awe, as did the originality, even eccentricity, of the various personalities in attendance. Most were doctors, analysts, college professors, or students of esoteric subjects, with only a few being auditors like myself. I was fascinated by those I thought of as handmaidens or Vestal Virgins, Jung, of course, being the Flame.

Eventually I decided I wanted to be analyzed but I didn't want to work with Jung himself, at least not in the beginning. I was so impressed with his intelligence and found him so attractive that I was afraid that if I were not actually tongue-tied when in his presence, I would certainly have difficulty telling him the whole truth. So I decided to work at first with his colleague, Miss Toni Wolff, who seemed to me to be a much more promising prospect. I had the highest regard for her intelligence, but I found her personality so uncongenial that I knew I would pay strict attention to the matter at hand so as to finish as soon as possible.

I worked with Miss Wolff for about a year and a half. Then I had a dream that she said indicated to her that the time had come for me to work with Jung himself.

One day Miss Wolff told me that I was "as curious as a monkey" and was exasperated when I was delighted by the comparison. Later, when I told Jung that Miss Wolff had been annoyed at my delight at being compared to a monkey, he laughed that wonderful laugh of his and said, "Of course! You must realize that she can't understand why anyone should be pleased to be compared to an animal!" He told me that analysis was the American's "shortcut to culture." Analyzing Europeans, he said, was like walking slowly down the stairs into the cellar. But with Americans, after the first few steps, a trapdoor opened and you tumbled down into a cellar filled with rattlesnakes and Red Indians. I don't think Miss Wolff enjoyed life among rattlesnakes and Red Indians.

However, I did learn a great deal from her when she decided the time had come for me to put some order in the vast amount of material I had gathered in my reading at Geneveys about Mme. de Stael and her circle of friends at the time of the French Revolution. She worked with me to whip this material into shape so that I could present it at the Psychological Club in two lectures of two hours each—as the Swiss like very long lectures.

For weeks we struggled over the material, Miss Wolff constantly demanding more dates, more facts, whereas I was interested only in the people and their behavior. Facts had always seemed irrelevant to me for the simple reason that I never used them to orient myself in any way. Besides, I always knew where I could find them if needed. It didn't help that Grandpa Barron had reminded me that "facts are not the truth, but only indicate where the truth may lie."

As a result of my work with Miss Wolff, I began to realize what lay at the bottom of my cavalier attitude toward facts. According to Jung's theory of types, which I have found most useful in everyday life, everyone falls into the two general categories of introverts and extroverts. These two general categories are also subdivided according to four characteristics, which Jung lists as intuition, thinking, feeling, and sensation. Any given individual has these four characteristics available in varying degrees of consciousness. I had long ago realized that intuition was my long suit and that an overuse of intuition, combined with my exaggerated extroversion and gregariousness, was one of the causes of my sneezing fits. Since intuition symbolically leaves the body on the breath, it was

only logical that a respiratory affliction would be the body's way of bringing intuitives back to themselves. Again according to Jung's theory, the
least developed function of an intuitive is the sensation function which
deals with facts, therefore the explanation of my cavalier attitude toward
them lay there.

Jung's theory of types also helped explain my position in my intelligence work of not dealing, on any extended basis, with anyone in the
enemy camp I would not have liked in peacetime. In order to be quite
certain of how conscious one's behavior is—and in intelligence work consciousness is extremely important—it is necessary to line up the functions
in their proper order and use them all. In my case, intuition was my
strongest function, then came feeling, thinking, and sensation. My reaction to the German deserter was based only on my intuition. Therefore, I
did not feel competent to deal with him.

Incidentally, another idea that I got from Jung that has proved most
helpful over the years in its general application is that power, not hate, is
the opposite pole to love. This concept becomes quite clear when applied
to various relationships, even of the most personal kind. When two people cannot get along in a working situation, in a love affair, or even in a
marriage, if they examine the situation closely, they will see that they do
not actually hate each other as may at first glance appear to be the case,
but rather are trying to gain power over each other.

I worked with Jung for about four years. At one point I became infuriated with him because he wouldn't tell me what I "ought" to do with
my life. I didn't realize, of course, that in behaving as he was he
was attempting to throw off what was for me the overwhelming and
destructive father complex that I had projected onto him. I was so
angry with him that I didn't make any further appointments for nearly
a year, but spent the better part of that time writing him insulting letters,
telling him exactly what I thought of him, and basically what a son of
a bitch I thought he was. Then one morning I woke up and began
to laugh in sudden recognition of what I had been doing and what lay behind it. I picked up the phone and called his secretary to ask for an
appointment.

"Oh, yes," she said. "Professor Jung said I should save some time for
you. He expected you would be calling for an appointment shortly!"

It was very instructive to me when Jung asked me if I thought it had
been pleasant for him to receive all those insulting letters. I told him that
it had never occurred to me that he would actually read them. He had

replied dryly that he always read the letters he received, and reading my letters had been a most disagreeable experience.

To realize that he could react to anything I wrote, that he would have any feelings whatsoever about anything I said, that he actually would respond like anyone else to such insults, marked in a way what I think of as the end of my analysis. For if Jung would not serve as the father I always had been seeking, I realized I would never find such an idealized figure in anyone else, but would have to cope myself with all that such a figure represented.

By 1938 I had begun to understand the mechanism that brought on my sneezing attacks, and how it was related to the way I could never say no to anyone who asked me to do anything. Due to the insecurities I felt because of my mother's death, the resulting struggles within the family over me, and my father's suicide, I had always thought if I said no, nobody would like me, let alone love me. Although I understood the mechanism, however, I still couldn't seem to prevent the attacks.

One of the last attacks I ever had was the result of being invited to dinner by a woman I was sure didn't like me, but was only asking me in the hope that I might tell some amusing stories and entertain her guests. When I put down the phone after accepting her invitation, I sneezed myself into a fearsome attack of "asthma." When I told Jung about this, he asked me if it hadn't occurred to me that I could have called her back, saying I had forgotten a previous engagement and that I was sorry but I couldn't come to her party. I said it hadn't and added—it was at the time of the Czechoslovakian crisis—that every time I thought of Hitler marching into Czechoslovakia I also sneezed. Jung peered quizzically at me over his spectacles. "Tell me," he asked, "did you start World War One also?"

That ended my sneezing forever, although for the next year the nameless dread that had brought it on caused my heart to flutter wildly. Then, after "it" had been cornered there, it proceeded to upset my stomach. But by the time war broke out in 1939, I had successfully banished it forever.

I continued to see Professor Jung occasionally and to attend any lectures he gave. When I did see him for an appointment, however, the subject of our conversation was no longer me and my problems but rather what was happening in Germany. In 1936 Jung had published an article entitled "Wotan," which had caused a great deal of controversy. But I felt that his thesis, namely that the archetypes of the old, primitive, Teutonic gods had broken loose and were affecting the behavior of the entire

German nation, was valid. In other words, a whole country had been seized by madness in very much the same way an individual goes insane. This seemed to me then—and still seems to me today—the only possible explanation of such an otherwise incomprehensible and tragic phenomenon.

XII

With the death in 1936 of Rudyard Kipling, followed by the illness and death of George V some days later, the first tiny crack appeared in the world as I had always known it. I had adored *The Jungle Books* and *Kim,* and Kipling's poems of Empire thrilled me.

The death of George V was, naturally, of even more far-reaching significance than Kipling's. During the King's illness, we had been glued to the BBC. Then one evening the words: "This is London"—which during World War II became the signature of Edward R. Murrow—were followed by a bulletin from the King's physician announcing that the King's life was moving peacefully to its close. At 10 P.M., the previous bulletin was repeated, a chorus sang, "The Lord is my Shepherd," then came a prayer for the King, followed by the Lord's Prayer, another hymn, and the announcement that at fifteen-minute intervals further bulletins would be issued. Big Ben's mournful tones marked the passing hours.

At 12:15 grief was obvious in the announcer's first words. "It is with great sorrow that we make the following announcement: His Majesty the King passed peacefully away at a few minutes before twelve."

Edward VIII's abdication crisis and subsequent marriage to Wallis Simpson drove everything else off the front pages for weeks on end. I couldn't even begin to function each day until I had read every word about it in at least half a dozen different papers.

What Kipling's and George V's deaths had started, Edward VIII's abdication had finished. England seemed somehow diminished. Never again, I felt, would there be that "terrible dignity" that had set George V and Queen Mary apart and created such a comforting sense of permanence. I wondered what was ever going to replace those particular symbols of security.

I longed to be able to discuss with someone my own subjective reactions and what the developments might mean. But the Americans in Zurich, although showing some interest in Mrs. Simpson and all the gossip about her, were not particularly interested otherwise. The Swiss, of course, set everything in a historical context, which, in spite of my attempt to master European history, was still quite beyond me. Jean just laughed at my various anguishes, maintaining I was only upset because another American divorcée had succeeded in pulling the King of England off his throne whereas I had had to settle for "a simple Swiss." To this I had retorted that a simple Swiss was scarcely an accurate description of him. The one thing he was *not* was simple.

Actually, Jean was far more interested in France than he was in England. He claimed he had always felt more French than Swiss, and when we traveled, he was usually taken for a Frenchman. In spite of his German-sounding family name, he had been born in Le Locle in the canton of Neuchâtel. French was his native language, as it had been his parents'. He read several French papers daily and I read them, too.

But I found nothing in them to reassure me about conditions in France. France, like England, seemed to be falling apart, although there was much talk about "the great French Army" and of the Maginot Line that would protect France against Germany. It was most instructive to reread all the carefully documented articles about its impregnability after the Germans had made an end run around it in 1940. It would seem that the life of a nation followed the same pattern as the life of an individual. Where consciousness stopped, fate stepped in and the life of a nation or of an individual went careening out of control.

In December 1936 the Stavisky trial was being held in Paris. Actually the case dated from 1934, when the financial shenanigans of Alexandre Stavisky came crashing down around his head implicating in some way practically everyone in French political life.

Faced with exposure, Stavisky fled to Chamonix, where he was tracked down by the Paris police. There was a wild shoot-out, and when it was over, Stavisky lay dead. Whether he had committed suicide or had been killed by the police was an open question. Certainly the French police had good reason to wish him dead, as did practically everyone else in

France except the retired schoolteachers and small shopkeepers who had invested their savings in his schemes and actually continued to believe in him until the end.

After Stavisky's death in 1934, the leftists accused the Radical Socialist government of Camille Chautemps of corrupt dealings with Stavisky and forced its resignation. Edouard Daladier, a recent prime minister, returned to power and used troops to suppress the riots that broke out in the streets of Paris on February 6 and 7.

Jean and I were in Paris at the time of those riots. At the sound of the first shots, I had, much to Jean's annoyance, dashed out of the hotel to see what was going on. There was a wild scene in the Place de la Concorde. A mob made up of people from every walk of life was heading for the Chamber of Deputies and was being fired upon by the Garde Mobile. In the midst of all that chaos, I suddenly thought of how George Washington had said that when he first went into battle during the French and Indian wars, he had been astonished to discover that he had actually enjoyed the sound of bullets whizzing past his head. It had never occurred to him that he might be in any personal danger. That was exactly how I felt in the streets of Paris on that February night.

When I finally returned to the hotel, Jean was in no mood to share my feelings of exhilaration. When I explained to him that apparently I was very much like George Washington in my reactions, he snorted in disgust and inquired sarcastically what country I intended to "mother," since obviously I was not of the proper sex to "father" one.

The Communists claimed the riots had been against fascism. *L'Action Française,* with its Royalist views, blamed the Communists, Socialists, Radicals, Republicans, Jews, and Freemasons. *Le Matin* described the riots as civil war. And the boulevard press was full of the usual horror stories and personal interviews with the rioters. The situation in France was obviously desperate. Yet, at the same time, I felt none of that sense of menace in the atmosphere that had been so threatening in Germany.

My feelings about France and the French were ambivalent and had been ever since Grandma had taken me on my first visit there. I liked everything the French produced: French art, French literature, French wine, French cooking, French perfume, French clothes. I liked the precision and elegance of the French language. I thought Paris a lovely city and the French countryside enchanting. But the moment I set foot in France, I became irritable. Apparently certain French attitudes constellated the residual prejudices of my Puritan ancestors.

I was not amused when I'd turn on a faucet plainly marked COLD and scalding water gushed forth, when I hung up my coat on a hook in a restaurant and the hook promptly fell off the wall, or when I protested to a telephone operator that she had given me a wrong number and she replied blithely, *"Ah! Excusez, Madame! Je vous ai donné juste le contraire!"* ("Ah! Excuse me, madame. I gave you just the opposite!") Actually, I found the French, in spite of their reputation for gaiety, an amazingly grim lot. Their *logique,* which so many others admired, made them overlook all manner of trivia in which I was interested. Whenever I tried to discuss something about the Germans with any of them, I'd find myself cut off at the pass with, "Ah! But *that* is the German problem!" And a wave of the hand dismissed the whole subject as inconsequential. A friend in charge of setting up international conferences for his insurance business told me that he had to be careful to arrange the schedule so that the French delegate spoke last. Once the French delegate had spoken, there was nothing more to be said.

Gradually, my frantic preoccupation with France abated and I was able to turn my attention to other matters. There were certainly plenty of those: not only my work with Jung but the lectures on American literature I was attending at the university and a course in French literature. I had become particularly good friends with two American women married to Swiss—Mary Briner and Carly Goetze—both of whom had sons Mary Jane's age and spent several months each winter in Klosters, where Mary Jane and I joined them for skiing.

A-----

lthough George V's death and Edward VIII's abdication had saddened and upset me, these events belonged to the crumbling of the world as I had always known it—in other words, to the past. My attention turned to the future, not the distant future, but the day after tomorrow. Rumors had been circulating with increasing intensity that Austria would be the first country that Hitler would attempt to annex. After all, he himself had been born there—this man who such a short time before had no job, no money, not even a valid German passport, yet within a decade had become Chancellor of Germany and was now shouting over the radio to his fanatical followers that he was going to see to it that his country, which had been so shabbily treated in "the shameful Treaty of Versailles," was restored to its former glory. To me, Austria was still the land of waltzes and lilacs that I had envisioned as a child. I could not bear the thought that it would be taken over by the Nazis.

Ever since 1931, when the Kreditanstalt, not only Austria's largest bank but actually the most important financial institution in Central Europe, had collapsed, causing other banks throughout Europe to come crashing down "like tin pans down a concrete alley," as one journalist put it, there had been a large and steadily increasing number of unemployed in Austria. Many of them, particularly the younger men, noting the full employment in Germany, had turned to National Socialism. When Hitler restricted travel for all German citizens, a further blow had been struck at the Austrian economy, particularly the tourist trade on which so many Austrians depended for their livelihood. As a result, the ranks of the unemployed had risen in a tidal flood. The Germans were helping to finance a National Socialist movement within Austria itself, and an Austrian Legion had been established across the border in Germany.

The Austrian Chancellor, Dr. Engelbert Dollfuss, when he became Chancellor in 1932 at the age of thirty-nine, was the youngest head of state in Europe. He was only four feet eleven inches tall. Endless jokes were told about him: how, when he was worried, he paced up and down *under* his bed; how he had broken his leg falling off a ladder when climbing up to pluck a dandelion. He was said to be "shrewd as a peasant, charming as a child." I found him an engaging little figure. I loved to watch him in the newsreels, rushing along past troops nearly twice his size drawn up for review, a becoming military cap on one side of his little head and a cascade of cock feathers streaming out behind him in the breeze.

On July 25, 1934, Dollfuss was murdered by Nazi conspirators and left to die a slow and painful death on what, we were told, was "a rose-and-cream-colored Louis XV divan in the room where at the time of the Congress of Vienna magnificent balls had been held." Not only had the conspirators refused the dying chancellor medical attention, but they even refused to summon a priest for whom Dollfuss had pleaded.

Although Kurt von Schuschnigg, his successor, was a singularly colorless figure compared to the spritely little Dollfuss, everyone felt he was doing his best to master the chaotic conditions in Austria. The news we were getting in the press, over the radio, and from the first flood of wealthy Austrian refugees as well as sober-minded Swiss returning from trips to Vienna became increasingly alarming. Eventually it was announced that Schuschnigg had decided to hold a plebescite and let the Austrians themselves decide whether or not they wanted to join Germany.

Then Franz von Papen, who had previously served as German ambassador in Vienna, showed up in Austria "to visit friends." This added to the general feeling of apprehension. Von Papen was universally regarded as a bird of ill-omen because of a long series of incidents that had invariably followed his appearance on any scene. When it was announced that Schuschnigg had been summoned to Berchtesgaden, our hearts sank further. No foreign dignitary had ever profited from a meeting with Hitler.

At Berchtesgaden, Hitler presented Schuschnigg with an agreement to sign. Schuschnigg pointed out that, under the Austrian constitution, the Austrian President was the only person empowered to sign such an agreement. Hitler shouted that Schuschnigg had better see to it that the document was signed or else. Schuschnigg, still hoping to prevent bloodshed, returned to Vienna and continued with plans for the plebescite.

At this point, the German propaganda machine shifted into high gear. We were told that "Communist mobs" were running through the streets of Vienna, "murdering people." Hitler began shrieking that such an insupportable situation could not be allowed to continue.

We'd listen first to the Austrian radio, then switch to a German station, then back again to the Austrian. Schuschnigg resigned. Artur von Seyss-Inquart, a Nazi sympathizer and one of the three men, together with Hjalmar Schacht, former Minister of Economy and President of the Reichsbank, and Hermann Goering, rated as geniuses on the intelligence tests given by American authorities to the leading war criminals at Nuremberg, took over as Chancellor. And German troops crossed the Austrian frontier.

I noted in my journal on March 14, 1938:

> *Germany has marched into Austria. This had been expected, but the decision was precipitated by Schuschnigg's intention to hold a plebescite. So far, however, there has been no bloodshed.*
>
> *Yesterday Hitler laid flowers on his parents' grave at Braunau and, on Saturday night, according to the French radio, "The German troops arrived in Vienna at night in inclement weather. Snow was falling quite heavily and consequently the crowds were small. Opinion is unanimous that Czechoslovakia will be next. There are even those who are worried abut Switzerland."*
>
> *The* Feuille d'Avis de Neuchâtel *said in an editorial this morning, "As for France, 'tis useless to count on her! This nation that formerly imposed her will on all others, offered herself the luxury, certainly rather scandalous, of having no head while the most serious event of the postwar years was taking place."*

Early that summer we went to Venice for Jean's vacation. It was good to be in Italy again—even the Italy of Benito Mussolini—and to smell the salt sea air once more.

We spent our days at the Lido, lolling in our cabana, watching children playing war games on the beach. One side was always Italian, the other German. Jean maintained this was prophetic. No matter what kind of an alliance the Germans and Italians might forge, he claimed, they were basically so different in character that eventually we would see the Germans and Italians fighting each other.

We returned home early in August to find that during our absence the Dowager Queen of Rumania had died. I felt as if I had lost a friend. After all, she was the only queen who had ever talked to me! I would eventually become much more familiar with her country and her people because of Jean's many trips to Rumania during the war, as well as by meeting his Rumanian friends who came to visit us when on their way to Paris or other European capitals.

During the time we had been in Italy, I had not glanced at a newspaper or listened to the radio. Even Jean had neglected buying his usual French newspapers or even the Italian papers which he could have easily read, being as fluent in Italian as in half a dozen other languages. I had not realized until we left Italy and were riding home in the train just how unraveled being out of touch with what was happening in the world made me feel. Once deprived of the effects of the sun, the sea, and delicious Italian food I became aware that my inner life, that mysterious realm that had so baffled me at the Psychological Club, was far more attached to the news than I had thought. That unraveled, floating-at-loose-ends feeling changed with a rush when we got back to Zurich and I plunged into my beloved newspapers and turned on the radio again.

XIV

By the end of August the Czechoslovakian crisis was upon us. Hitler was using the Sudeten German question as an excuse for his *Drang nach Osten,* that expansion eastward that he had written in *Mein Kampf* was essential to German survival.

On September 13 we went to hear Thomas Mann read from his works at the Schauspielhaus in Zurich. I was glad to see in person this distinguished writer who had taken refuge in Switzerland and in whose books I had first sensed the decay eating away at the German middle class. But I found that after listening to Hitler, Goering, and Goebbels shouting on the radio, I had difficulty concentrating on *Lotte in Weimar.* Goethe and his world of values seemed very remote from the world of Adolf Hitler.

The next evening we listened to Goebbels speaking at Nuremberg. We had also listened to Goering's speech that afternoon when he had shouted that he expected the German Air Force to *"Fliegen wie die Vögel, nicht Vögeln wie die Fliegen"*—a play on words in German that translates as "fly like birds, not fuck like flies."

All day Sunday we listened to the Nuremberg rally, and by Monday night when Hitler spoke, we were in a fine state of nerves. He said nothing of importance for the first forty minutes, then began alluding to an unnamed country whose dastardly behavior could no longer be tolerated. With a deafening shout, he finally identified that country: *"Ich spreche von die Tschechoslowakei!"* ("I am speaking of Czechoslovakia!")

The next day Neville Chamberlain sent word to Hitler that he would like to talk with him to see if peace could not be preserved. He would be willing to meet "Mr. Hitler," as Chamberlain persisted in calling him, at any time, at any place convenient to him. Hitler replied he would be delighted to receive Chamberlain at Berchtesgaden. Jean's comment was, " 'Won't you walk into my parlor?' said the spider to the fly." So Chamberlain flew off to Berchtesgaden, and there were those who said Chamberlain should spell his name *"J'aime* Berlin" ("I love Berlin").

My friend Loranda Spalding and her children came helling out of Germany. Her husband was stationed at the American consulate in Stuttgart and Loranda was convinced war was imminent.

When I first met Loranda, her husband had been attached to the American consulate in Zurich. She had all the charm of her Austrian father, for many years Austrian minister in Washington, and all the subtlety and grace of her Polish mother. Of all my friends, she felt closest to the way I did, with the same passionate interest in events. An omnivorous reader with a delightful sense of humor and who spoke several languages fluently, she opened many new vistas for me about life in Europe, particularly in Austria. Actually, I saw the Anschluss, the annexation of Austria, as much through her eyes as through my own. I can still see her face and hear her voice at the time of the Anschluss as she told me, "I wrote something about the Germans going into Vienna. I thought of Vienna as a rose, with all those little brown men like bugs crawling into its heart."

By the time Loranda arrived back in Zurich with her children, we were having a stretch of the unseasonable warm weather that often comes to Zurich in September. The golden leaves of the trees along the Utoquai were fluttering slowly to the pavements and swans glided proudly back and forth along the quay, waiting patiently for their faithful friends who never failed to appear with bags of stale bread to feed them.

We were particularly depressed by the news that Thomas Wolfe had died in Baltimore at the age of thirty-seven. We were both Wolfe addicts and agreed that you had to have longed for the sights, the sounds, the smells of the United States, for all that was beautiful, for all that was ugly, before you could appreciate how much more accurately than any other American writer Thomas Wolfe had caught what was essential to a true understanding of the United States. We both felt that although his books might be exhausting, even sometimes quite boring to read, they were like having a thick, yellow Mississippi flood washing over you, and in Europe one sometimes longed even for that.

On September 17 we were informed that Hitler had demanded that the three-million Sudeten Germans be "returned" to him. Some people commented, "Why not?" Others protested, "Don't be silly! It's not the Sudeten Germans he wants. He's just looking for an excuse to grab Czechoslovakia." Still others said, "He's bluffing. Threaten him!"

On the nineteenth we learned that the English and French were ready, with certain minor reservations, to accede to Hitler's demands. At this everyone, everywhere, felt betrayed. On the twentieth it was reported that "an embittered Czechoslovakia was considering the demands of her erstwhile allies." That same day Hungary and Poland claimed their "rights" to their minorities in Czechoslovakia. The following day, Prague accepted the British and French proposals and Chamberlain made plans to see Hitler again, this time at Godesberg. That the meeting was to be held at Godesberg was regarded as a particularly ominous touch. It was there that Hitler on June 29, 1934, had planned the massacre of the Night of the Long Knives. Superstitious as Hitler was known to be, the choice of Godesberg might well have a sinister significance.

We kept switching our radio to different stations to get various reactions. Occasionally, I would have a rather ghoulish experience, as, for instance, when just after I heard the call for general mobilization in Czechoslovakia, I switched to an English station and heard the British singing:

> *A tisket, a tasket,*
> *A brown and yellow basket!*
> *I sent a letter to my love,*
> *On the way I dropped it,*
> *I dropped it, I dropped it . . .*

Would the radio ever again be anything but an instrument of torture, I wondered. It seemed impossible that we had once played it merely for enjoyment.

During the next two days, word came over the German radio of Czech atrocities and of munitions pouring into Prague from Russia. France was calling up one group of reservists after another. London was telling its people that thirty-five million gas masks were available, that trenches were being dug in the London parks, that the subway had been closed to be bomb-proofed, that gas-proof kennels were available for cats and dogs.

On Tuesday evening, September 27, there was a blackout in Switzerland and the Swiss Air Force droned incessantly overhead. Neville Chamberlain, on the BBC, said in a tired voice that things looked hopeless, although he found it inconceivable that Europe should be plunged into war merely because a small country was threatened by a big and powerful neighbor. He then proceeded to outline the larger principle for which England would fight: to prevent any country from imposing its will on another by threat of force.

Wednesday was once again a beautiful day. The sun was warm, there was no breeze. The city of Zurich seemed to be in a daze. Word had come through that Germany would march at two P.M. England had announced that such a move would be regarded as an act of war. At three the Swiss Parliament decided on a general mobilization for eight that evening. Several people that Loranda and I met in our daily stroll along the quay mentioned that a rumor was circulating that the English pound had strengthened. So we walked over to the Credit Suisse where we were told, "There is talk of Mussolini's intervention." A few minutes later, as we were leaving the bank, we learned that a conference arranged by Mussolini between England, France and Germany was to be held in Munich. Mussolini would also attend.

I had been too emotionally involved with daily developments during the crisis to be able to reflect on its true meaning. Once it was over, I didn't waste any time or energy being angry with Hitler. I didn't expect moral behavior from him or, actually, from the French. But the English? How dare England let Czechoslovakia down! Chamberlain had even informed the Czechs, whose representatives were not permitted to enter the room where the fate of their country was being decided, of what they "ought" to do. Well, I knew what *he* ought to do!

In some curious way, not only I, but everyone I knew, appeared to have little interest in their personal lives. Rather than living in this world, everyone seemed to be living in their radios. It was not easy to withstand the waves of German propaganda that poured over us. People in every stratum of society were affected by this "war of nerves," as it was called. They would say smugly, "Of course, Goebbels believes in the effectiveness of the Big Lie." But no matter how certain they were that, because they were conscious of this, they personally were immune, more often than not they would be sucked in, not only by the Big Lie but by all manner of little lies.

When, before the Anschluss, Hitler had raged about Germans being slaughtered in Austria and "blood running in the streets of Vienna," the timbre of his voice and his hysterical delivery served to convince people that even if what he was saying were not true, he was going to act as if it were. After the Anschluss, German propaganda became even more effective. The fait accompli of the Anschluss tended to authenticate in people's imaginations the validity of Hitler's threats. It was as if words—lying, boasting, ambiguous and loaded words—had become an army of occupation on the battlefront of the mind, preventing people from thinking for themselves.

What is he going to do next? was the question on everyone's lips—on the street, at the market, whenever or wherever you met anyone you knew. They didn't mean only what country was going to be occupied next. So many values had been under attack for so many years that people waited with bated breath for this wild man to haul some new horror out of his bag of tricks—some intangible new horror, something terrifying and weird that had never been used before.

Everything that had been effective at the time of the Anschluss in shaking people up, in causing fights and disputes, not only within different groups and organizations but actually within families, was multiplied a hundredfold at the time of the Czech crisis.

False rumors were a particularly effective weapon. One of those rumors that always caused a minor panic was the implication of large troop movements. Every few days there would be a new one. Somebody had seen someone who had met someone who had just come back from Berlin or East Prussia and he had said that he had seen large troop movements. Sir Nevile Henderson, the British ambassador in Berlin, on one occasion after there had been a particularly persistent rumor of such movements toward the Czechoslovakian frontier, sent two of his aides by car to tour the area where these troop movements were rumored to be taking place. After driving some six hundred miles, covering every part of the district in question, they returned to report they had seen nothing. But this didn't stop subsequent rumors. People's minds and emotions were being consciously manipulated by the Nazi propaganda machine, and the radio was a particularly lethal instrument in these exercises.

In Hitler's case, it was not exclusively Germans who were affected by his speeches. Anyone filled with suppressed envy or rage, anyone economically or spiritually dispossessed, anyone who felt his world of values slipping or anyone harboring a secret will to power was swept along in the wind tunnel created by Hitler's voice.

When Hitler did not declare war at the conclusion of his speech at the Nuremberg Party Rally on September 12, 1938, the world heaved a collective sigh of relief. But few realized that one overwhelming reason for this unexpected restraint was that in the last days of September he had watched from behind the curtains of the Reich's Chancellery in Berlin a long and impressive military parade—bands, tanks, all the warlike trimmings—through the streets of Berlin. The crowds on the sidewalks had virtually ignored the parade. Such a display of apathy on the part of a people who loved nothing better than marching bands and military parades was a clear signal to the Führer that the Germans felt the same reluctance for war as the people of other countries. In short, before Hitler spoke at Nuremberg, he realized that he did not yet have the people behind him. This was a particularly bitter pill for him to swallow because earlier that year, at the time of what became known as the Fritsch-Blomberg crisis, he had finally succeeded in consolidating one important aspect of his power.

When Field Marshal Werner von Blomberg, the Minister of War, and General Werner von Fritsch, Commander-in-Chief of the Army, had been removed from their positions of high command through a series of intrigues staged by the Gestapo, Hitler had assumed both posts himself. In doing so, the German Army lost its last chance to put a stop to the unchecked incursions of the Gestapo that were to have such fatal consequences both within and without the Third Reich.

After the Czech crisis, there was talk in Jungian circles of how this crisis had affected people's dreams. It was regarded as quite depressing that Hitler continued to appear as a positive figure in so many dreams, even in the dreams of those belonging to groups specifically targeted by the Nazis for destruction. If Hitler were really a representative of the inferior side of every German—of those people who liked to describe themselves as "a nation of poets and thinkers"—such dreams would indicate that this madman's power had still not reached its apogee.

Naturally this kind of talk would have been regarded as "stuff and nonsense" by those who knew nothing about the collective unconscious and its power or even refused to believe in its existence. But certainly for me such ideas came nearer to providing a satisfactory explanation than any less esoteric theory. Actually, I did subscribe to the theory that Germany had become possessed, just as an individual falling into madness can be said to be possessed. I was particularly fascinated by how Hitler would throw his tantrums. At such moments it seemed to me he behaved exactly like a woman whipping up a quarrel with her lover. Once I had come to this conclusion, Hitler never again surprised me by his behavior. With this interpretation in mind, I could even figure out his timing, and when he was about to start on his next rampage.

As a result, I felt no confidence in the wishful thinking of so many people that now that he had the Sudeten Germans he would quiet down. No matter what I was doing, no matter how much I tried to convince myself that life had actually returned to normal, a part of me was constantly involved in waiting with a feeling of dread for the curtain to go up on the next act. From the time of the Czech crisis until Hitler committed suicide in his bunker in Berlin, I actually felt as if a part of me was tuned into another world, where other forces that I could not possibly have articulated or explained reasonably were operating. The nearest I could come to describing how I felt was to say that part of me seemed to be encased in a huge whirling cylinder of power—pure, unadulterated, un-controlled—and uncontrollable—power.

In connection with power, Jung pointed out something to me that I did not understand at the time but that later became clear to me, namely that power was my natural element and that I felt as at home in situations of power as a fish did in water. He maintained that this was the result of the fact that, from the moment I had opened my eyes, a power struggle had been waged over me within my family for my affections and loyalties. Consequently, I had been forced in self-defense to become familiar with the rules by which power operated. Jung also said that he believed that as a result of this, I would attract, during the course of my life, extremely ambitious men interested in gaining power for themselves.

However, although I didn't understand what he was talking about at the time, I gradually began to see that he was right. The first two men who brought the truth of Jung's comment home to me were Allen Dulles and Hans Bernd Gisevius, a member of the Abwehr (the intelligence service of the German Army) to whom Allen introduced me. At different times both of these men would discuss with me how they should behave in a situation in such a way as to achieve some specific ambition of theirs. The required behavior was quite clear to me and I would tell them what I thought they should do. They would do it, it would work—and the next time they were baffled, back they would come and the process would be repeated. They might attribute such positive results to my good judgment or even to magic, but to me it was nothing of the kind. The solution was simply obvious.

During the winter after the Czechoslovakian crisis, Mary Jane and I spent our usual two-month ski vacation at Klosters, where she attended the village school. Jean joined us for an occasional weekend, arriving during the day on Saturday and departing late Sunday afternoon. He didn't ski and had no use for the social life I so enjoyed during the week.

He really only joined us so he could claim to have made the conventional gesture of "joining my family for the weekend." But he did enjoy watching Mary Jane ski and skate and loved buying pastries and other goodies for her friends.

The following summer of 1939 we went to Geneveys. Again Jean joined us, not only on the weekends but for a two-week vacation during which he worked in the garden and did not have one of his devastating drinking spells. Actually, it was the nicest time we had had since our marriage and revived my hopes that perhaps we would be able to make a go of it after all.

By the end of August, when we returned to Zurich, the political situation was right back where it had been the previous September, except that now Poland, rather than Czechoslovakia, was being threatened. Although the Czech crisis had been somehow exciting, as any new experience can be, there was nothing exhilarating about this new crisis. No matter how it was resolved, the outlook was grim. Another Munich would be morally very hard to take, yet the only alternative seemed to be war.

Once again people hung on the radio day and night. Some people claimed it was "now or never," that "this thing has got to stop." Others felt that the German-Russian nonaggression pact would open the eyes of the Germans to the way they had been deceived by their government and they would either fall on their leaders or the Germans and Soviets would fall on each other, an ideal solution for those who feared communism more than the Devil himself.

August 25 had generally been regarded as the deadline before Hitler would take some action. But then Sir Nevile Henderson met with Hitler and reassured him that Britain would honor its defense treaty with Poland. Afterward he flew off to report to London. Jean commented that "perhaps this Nevile with one 'l' in his name will be more effective than the other Neville with two!"

The German radio began listing rationed foodstuffs, which was said to be causing dismay in Germany, this because in World War I it had been many months before rationing had been instituted. There were increasingly frequent reports of incidents along the German-Polish frontier and of "drunken Poles careening through the Corridor, refusing to obey the orders of their officers and attacking German nationals."

On August 29 Switzerland called up her frontier troops. All that day planes flew over Zurich, dropping leaflets, urging every Swiss citizen to preserve an attitude of the strictest neutrality. Then, on September 1, German troops marched into Poland at 5:45 A.M., and at 10 A.M., Hitler addressed the Reichstag to tell them that the war against Poland had begun.

On September 3, a stiflingly hot day, Neville Chamberlain—of whom a wag at the Foreign Office had said in 1938, "If at first you don't succeed, fly, fly again!"—had the bitter task of admitting that all his efforts to procure "peace in our time" had been in vain. England was at war with Germany. It seemed as if there should have been at least a clap of thunder or the sound of bombs falling to signal the outbreak of World War II. Instead, there was only a weary old man's voice floating out of our radio and the hum of bees and the fragrance of the last roses of summer drifting through the open windows from our garden.

That afternoon I took Mary Jane out to swim at Mary Briner's at Schooren. On the way we bought an *Extra Blatt* of the *Neue Zürcher Zeitung,* a single sheet printed on only one side for ten centimes; its headline, WAR BETWEEN GREAT BRITAIN AND GERMANY.

At Schooren, the garden was filled with the same roses as our own garden and bees crawled over the tiny blue and white flowers on the clusters of tall autumn asters. Thunderheads were piled high over the snow-capped Glarner Alps at the end of the lake. No breeze was stirring, and in this lovely, peaceful setting it was difficult to realize that Europe was actually standing on the verge of what we had been told would be the destruction of its civilization.

The children played while Mary and I lay in the hot September sun, speculating on what would happen next. Which side would first resort to gas warfare? Gas was still the great fear.

When we reached home around six o'clock, we learned that France had also declared war on Germany. But not a single shot had yet been fired by either side.

The next day the weather changed from the hot, lazy, dog days of the crisis to driving rain and high winds. Winston Churchill got his old job back as First Lord of the Admiralty after waiting patiently for twenty-five years. And the Germans claimed the English, not they, had sunk the British liner *Athenia,* carrying fourteen hundred passengers to America, pointing out that this was just another example of the perfidious way in which England waged war. That evening an Austrian went on the Paris radio, pleading with the Austrians to revolt, claiming the Germans hadn't dared send Austrians against Poles but instead had sent them to the western front, where fourteen Austrians had torn off "the hated uniform" and swum the Rhine, crying, "*Vive la France!*"

In a broadcast from Stuttgart of songs requested by German soldiers on the Polish front, the German announcer suddenly broke in to say that he had just received a request, relayed by phone through Switzerland from those listening on the Maginot Line, asking the Germans to sing "*Parlez-moi d'amour!*"—which the Germans promptly did.

Then the Germans attacked the English for their "keep smiling" attitude. "What," asked the Germans, "does an Englishman do when a catastrophe befalls him? He *smiles!*"

The two songs played constantly on every Allied station were "My Heart Belongs to Daddy" and "Three Little Fishes in an Itty, Bitty Pool."

After World War I, Georges Clemenceau had remarked how none of the nations had behaved as expected: The English, so famous for their calm, had been the most hysterical. The Americans, supposedly so quick, had been so slow, while the French, renowned for their gaiety, had been so grim. I couldn't help wondering what conventional assumptions would go down in this war.

XV

E

ver since the defeat of Poland and no subsequent signs of an invasion on the western front, people had been referring to this curious situation as a *drôle de guerre,* "a phony war."

Then one evening early in April, just as we were leaving the house to see *The Gracie Allen Murder Case* at the local movie theater, my friend Carly Goetze telephoned to say that a special bulletin had just come over Beromunster, the Swiss radio station, to the effect that a hundred German vessels of all kinds were steaming through the Kattegat Channel. She had tried to find out what this meant, but had had no luck.

On the early morning news the following day we learned that Denmark had been occupied, Norway invaded. People said that at last Hitler had made "a fatal mistake," had "spread himself too thin." The BBC called it "the greatest strategic blunder since Napoleon's Russian campaign." Personally, I wished people would stop comparing Hitler to Napoleon and announcing that at last he had made a fatal mistake. Each time that he succeeded in the face of the direst predictions, the dangerous image of his infallibility was strengthened

I had assumed that no one listened to the radio more than I did, but I often stayed up so late that I slept longer in the morning than Carly. Again it was a call from her that alerted me to a far more sinister event than anything that had thus far occurred. In an early morning call on May 10, her first words were, "Well, what about it?"

"What about what?" I asked sleepily.

"Good God!" she cried. "Haven't you heard? They've marched into

Holland and Belgium! Turn on your radio. Goebbels is telling them over Stuttgart why."

The Swiss called their general mobilization at noon. People wondered why the Germans hadn't struck through Switzerland, too. Jean came home early and we spent the afternoon fiddling with the radio without being able to get much specific information.

That evening our friend William Woodfield called from his home on Mt. Pélerin above Vevey to ask if we wouldn't like to come down there over the weekend. He had asked Mary Briner and her son, Robin, to come as well. I had to admit that having the German Army such a short distance from Zurich was making me extremely nervous. So I decided to accept Woody's invitation. Jean said he would stay in Zurich "to keep an eye on things." The weather was absolutely glorious, as it had been the two previous Septembers; "Hitler weather," it was called.

On Monday morning when I phoned Jean from Mt. Pélerin, he said Zurich was "tranquil as a millpond." The city had been deserted over the weekend, but people had now returned and it was business as usual. So we took the noon train home from Vevey.

Never had our apartment looked more attractive, with the afternoon sun slanting through the venetian blinds and the fresh green leaves of the lilac bushes throwing a lovely, soft light into the living room. I was absolutely exhausted from living in possibilities, from thoughts of what was happening in Holland and Belgium. But Mary Jane had quickly revived to recount her adventures to our maid, Hedy, while our dog, Mickey, nearly wagged his tail off with delight at seeing her again. I noticed that Jean had taken out the big atlas and had been sticking colored thumb tacks on the map to follow developments on the western front.

We listened to the seven o'clock news on Beromunster, then I was so exhausted that I fell into bed. I had been asleep for about an hour when Mary Briner phoned to say the situation had suddenly become "extremely critical" and that we should be out of Zurich no later than 2 A.M. She was leaving at once with Robin and would pick us up if we wanted. I knew that because of her husband's position in the Swiss Army, her information was undoubtedly correct. But I still felt too tired to face a trip back across Switzerland in the middle of the night with sleepy and probably cranky children, even if the alternative was the German Army and a thousand Stukas zooming down on us. Still I knew I must not be an ass. So I told Mary to hang on while I spoke to Jean.

I went into his room and said, "That's Mary. She says we've got to be out of Zurich by two A.M. She has it on absolutely reliable authority that they are coming in tonight . . ."

Jean looked up from the detective story he was reading. "Who are *they*?" he asked calmly.

It was beyond my comprehension that anyone at that moment in time could possibly imagine that "they" could be anyone but the Germans. "Why . . . why . . . the Germans, I suppose," I stammered.

"Did you *ask*?" Jean's tone was sarcastic.

"No . . ." I admitted sheepishly, still baffled by his reaction.

"Well," he said, settling a pillow more comfortably behind his head, "you'd be an awful fool to go to Geneva if it's the French!"

I went back to the phone and told Mary to go without us—and promptly fell asleep again. About an hour later, Carly phoned with exactly the same news as Mary but from a different, although equally reliable, source. She and Sven were leaving at once with their two boys, their nurse, and the family dog—and offered to come by for us if we wished.

Feeling less exhausted, I was no longer sure nothing was wrong.

"All right," I said. "When will you be here?"

"As soon as we can get started. Within an hour at the most."

I went in and told Jean. He agreed that with Mary Jane we couldn't afford any longer just to play our hunches, particularly considering the reliability of Mary's and Carly's sources. He was still convinced it was a false alarm, and was determined to stay in Zurich and "shoot some of the invaders, whoever they may be."

I woke Mary Jane and told her we were going back to Mt. Pélerin.

"Are the Germans coming?" she asked excitedly.

I didn't want her to remember all her life that I had awakened her in the middle of the night to tell her that the Germans were coming. So I said that Carly and her family were going to Mt. Pélerin and I had decided we would go with them.

Carly and her family appeared shortly and off we went: four nervous adults, three excited children, and an extremely restless little dog. Our neighborhood was deathly still—no signs of life, no cars, no lights in any of the houses, nothing. But at Bellevue Platz there was a military control checking everyone's papers at the bridge, a sure indication of trouble. Sven asked one of the officers what was up. The officer shrugged. "We don't know," he said, "but it stinks!" Sven asked if we were fools to be leaving. "With children—no!" the officer replied.

On the road to Lucerne there were military controls set up across the road every few miles, where we were stopped to check our papers. When Sven asked what was up, he always got the same answer: "We don't know. But it stinks!" The army had received the order: *Kriegsbereitschaft*, which meant that individual commanders were empowered to take any action that circumstances warranted. A steady stream of cars was pouring in from the border cantons, and the people we were able to talk to all had the same information: The Germans were expected to invade Switzerland any time after 2 A.M.

On that night when as far as they knew their time had come, the Swiss, who are not exactly the merriest people in the world, displayed a charm and friendliness such as I have seldom seen. There they stood, those military controls across narrow mountain roads, all affability and consideration. When we reached Mt. Pélerin, we learned that the Dutch Army had capitulated, but Switzerland, thank God, was still safe.

At first, instead of moving in with Woody and his family, Mary Jane and I stayed at the Hotel du Parc. Although the rumor of the night before had turned out to be a false alarm, I wanted to be alone for a while. I had always known that for me some things were worse than death. Having been caught in a wave of collective panic, I realized how destructive such an experience could be. It was like being sucked under by a very powerful undertow, only on the psychic rather than the physical plane. I couldn't bear listening to speculations about the future, about what was going to happen next. Tacked on to the tail of all such speculations were tiny filaments of fear that led back to that terrible collective panic. I wanted to figure out a way never to be caught in that kind of panic again.

I finally decided that the best way was to be very clear about what meant most to me personally. I asked myself, do you want to go rushing away from something you care about just because you are afraid of death or the Germans? Wasn't it better to stay put, face up to whatever came, and trust a bit in God rather than try blindly to escape, escape, escape, from you knew not what? Wasn't that blind escaping the point at which you became trapped in the collective panic? And couldn't that escaping actually be rushing off to your own particular appointment in Samara?

Eventually I got my nerves under control and no longer felt like a glass being smashed down on a tile floor if anyone even spoke to me, so we moved over to the Woodfields. There was lots of work to be done in the garden, which suited me just fine. I agree with Voltaire that there is nothing more soothing than working in a garden.

Each morning we woke up to Sottens, the French-Swiss radio station. At 9:30 there was Radio Journal de France. At noon, Sottens again. At 5

P.M., the BBC. At 6 P.M., the short waves from America. At 7:30 P.M., an Italian station in English, followed by Sottens and another Radio Journal de France.

The others never listened to Beromunster, but I'd sneak into the den, turn on the little radio there and listen first to Beromunster, then turn the dial a bit further and get Stuttgart. I simply had to hear the German language or I felt as if I were being asphyxiated by some horrible, evil-smelling gas. I had to be reassured that the Germans were only human beings, not all-powerful creatures from outer space. I also think that the comfort I drew from listening to the news in German had to do with a sense of communication. The mere thought that I could not only under-stand, but actually speak, the enemy's language, somehow made the Ger-mans seem less invincible.

On May 28, Woody and his wife, Margery, went down to Vevey early in the morning, so I was alone when it was time for Radio Journal de France.

I will never forget the sound of French Premier Paul Reynaud's voice or his words as he began, "I must announce to the French people a serious event that took place this night. France can no longer count on the cooperation of the Belgian Army . . ."

Reynaud, his voice very deep, very grave, went on to explain what the exact military situation had been when, "like a bolt from the blue," the decision of the King of Belgium to capitulate had come.

When I went to get the milk at Mlle. Volay's, she was distraught. She had also heard the news and kept repeating, "Just think! That King! And without saying anything to anyone!" Mme. Wolff, at the notions shop, was also in a tremendous flutter. What upset her most was how sorry she had felt for Leopold and how she had cried when his Queen, Astrid, had been killed in an automobile accident near the Lake of Geneva when Leopold had been driving. "And to think how we wept for that young King when he lost his wife!" she kept wailing as she shuffled about among the dusty heap of odds and ends that was her shop.

On June 11, Jean spent the day in Lausanne on business and I went down to have supper with him before he took the seven-thirty train back to Zurich. When I returned to Mt. Pélerin, I found Margery and Woody very depressed beause Italy had declared war on France. As far as I was concerned, this was rather a relief. I had found waiting for the other shoe to drop quite nerve-racking.

When I called Jean the following morning, he said he had already known about Italy when we had been having supper together.

"Why didn't you tell me?"

"Because I didn't want to spoil our meal! You would have insisted on discussing what's going to happen next."

"What's wrong with that?"

"Everything!"

"Why?"

"Because *I don't know what's going to happen next*—and neither does anyone else!"

This was a good illustration of Jean's contention that Americans were always living in the future. He claimed that if you eliminated all the purely speculative articles from any American newspaper and left just those reporting something that had already happened, you'd reduce the size of the paper by at least fifty percent.

Mary Jane and I took the two o'clock train back to Zurich on June 12. There was a huge new flower on our pink cactus and I was full of good resolutions about all I was going to do that I'd neglected during the past few weeks. When I thought about how just leaving home, only temporarily, in the middle of the night had knocked me out, I simply could not imagine what the millions who had fled their homes, maybe forever, might be suffering. For the first time I understood what T. E. Lawrence had meant when he had called nomadism "that most biting of all social disciplines."

On Beromunster at noon on June 14, 1940, there was first the local news about a bond issue in the canton of St. Gall, then in the same calm, unemotional tones the announcement that at 8:30 A.M. the first German troops had passed through the gates of Paris.

The fall of Paris was, for me, one of the most emotionally shattering events of the entire war, largely, I think, because of the conflict of values and concepts that it evoked.

I wrote in my journal some of my thoughts and feelings when I heard the news.

> *"Where is that great and friendly nation?"*
> *ask the dead now as they rise*
> *And standing between the crosses, turn dark,*
> *reproachful eyes*
> *Back over the hills toward Paris and farther,*
> *across the sea,*
> *To the nation that bore them and sent them to*
> *die for democracy.*

"Is this why we left Ohio, Mississippi, Arkansas?
To sleep in luxurious graveyards for twenty
*   years or more?*
Only to have our slumber disturbed by the marching
*   feet*
Of the sons of the men we slaughtered going out
*   to meet*
The sons of the men we fought with, all in the
*   same old cause,*
The same illusory nonsense that makes for
*   nations' wars?*
Is this how now you leave us, you there across
*   the sea?*
Alone with our former comrades whose hope we
*   could still be?"*

But only for some short hours do the dead
*   stand watching there,*
While the Germans march into Paris. Then realizing
*   how men care,*
The dead turn back to their crosses, to their
*   graves, to the warm June sky,*
Relieved of their last illusion, indifferent
*   to all that must die.*

For days afterward lines from a poem by Louis Aragon about the surrender of Paris kept running through my head:

On nous a dit ce soir que Paris s'est rendu
Je n'oublierai jamais les lilas ni les roses
Et ni les deux amours que nous avons perdus . . .

XVI

On Saturday, August 24, 1940, Big Ben had just struck 11:30 P.M. when over the BBC came the voice of Edward R. Murrow: "The noise that you hear at this moment is the sound of the air-raid siren. A searchlight just burst into action, off in the distance. . . . An immense single beam is sweeping the sky above me. . . ." The Battle of Britain had begun. For the first time in years, I forgot about Hitler, forgot about that Voice of his, and kept my radio tuned to the BBC.

By now everyone in Switzerland had settled down to his or her own special brand of wartime routine. There were the nightly blackouts and the rationing. Because of the shortage of heating fuel, people were allowed only one fourth the amount needed to heat their homes or offices under normal circumstances. We were permitted to have one room heated by central heating and city authorities appeared to seal off the radiators in the other three rooms, with dire threats of the heavy fines to which we would be subjected if we tampered with the seals. We installed an iron stove in the living room that kept that room so hot that the rest of the apartment seemed like the North Pole by comparison. Being cold part of the time and too hot the rest made me almost unbearably sleepy. Some people found this contrast invigorating, but for me it was one of the most unpleasant aspects of those wartime years.

I was asked with increasing frequency to talk to various groups—always about the United States, its history, its customs, its people. I wrote articles for the Swiss press on the same subjects, as well as a series on the Children's Aid Action, under whose auspices children from the wartorn countries were brought into Switzerland to spend three months in Swiss homes.

This particular form of humanitarian activity had been started in Switzerland immediately after World War I when Austrian railway engineers, switching crews at the Swiss-Austrian frontier, had told their Swiss colleagues of the devastating effect the food shortages were having on the children of Vienna. The first children were brought into Switzerland by the railway workers union. Other trade and professional unions quickly followed suit.

It had been discovered that if children were placed in homes where the family routine resembled as closely as possible that of their own homes, they adapted much more easily. During World War II, it was not always possible to place children in this way. Too many families without any trade union connections were eager to have them. This caused certain difficulties. Children from poor families, accustomed to eating in the kitchen, were baffled by having to sit at the dining-room table and be waited on by servants.

I was told that if I wanted to get the best possible perspective on the work of the Children's Aid Action, I should talk to Frau Kägi-Fuchsman of the Schweizerische Arbeiterhilfswerkes, a charitable union organization. Eventually, through the kind intervention of Nationalrat Opprecht, leader of the Swiss Socialist party, I was able to get an appointment with her.

A short, plump woman with graying hair, alert brown eyes, and a personality that radiated energy and competence, she reminded me of Emma Goldman, the famous anarchist, whom I'd once heard speak at Mecca Temple in New York. Frau Kägi had the same authoritative manner, the same perceptive intelligence, the same type of wisdom based on experience. She was scornful of what she termed the "spirit of Geneva," citing as examples of this spirit various international organizations that had their headquarters in Geneva. "These organizations invariably start out with a good idea," she said. "But a *big* idea. They form a committee of prominent people and start raising funds. Only after they have their committee *and* their funds, do they start looking around to see how—and whom—they can help."

Her organization would see a need, often a very small need, and begin doing what they could on the spot. As the need expanded, so did their activities, and they sought funds as they went along. "We prefer," she pointed out, "to give one child a thousand cups of milk rather than a thousand children one cup of milk, as some ladies have done recently in France! Such a gesture may make the ladies feel wonderful. But it is of very little benefit to the children."

She advised me to take a close look at the Swiss families with whom the French children were staying and the problems they were creating in those families. The children came almost entirely from lower socio-economic groups and many of them were accomplished thieves. But, said Frau Kägi, this had little if anything to do with their backgrounds. Rather it was the result of growing up under an army of occupation when to steal things, particularly food, was regarded as "harassing the enemy." In short, it was considered a patriotic gesture, and consequently not in the least reprehensible.

Pierre, a black-eyed six-year-old from the slums of Marseilles, was the despair of the wealthy Zurich lady of strong Calvinistic beliefs with whom he was staying. Pierre swiped everything he could lay his hands on, squirreling away his loot all over his hostess's large and imposing house. His hostess felt it her Christian duty to make him aware of the moral implications of his unfortunate habit before he became locked into a life of crime. But her daily lectures got nowhere. Pierre continued to steal—from the kitchen, the bakeshop, the market, the neighbors' gardens. Then one day he strolled into the living room, threw himself down on the couch, and announced, "You are right, madame. It is stupid to steal in this house. There is always enough of everything here!"

A brother and sister practiced their skills learned under the Occupation with a slightly more selfless motive than Pierre. On the day of their arrival the family had had meat for lunch. Their hostess, not wanting them to think they were going to have meat every day, explained that meat was heavily rationed in Switzerland. They would not be able to have meat more than twice a week. The children exchanged knowing glances. "Don't worry, madam!" they chorused.

Their hostess thought nothing of this, except to reflect that French children really were more sensitive and understanding than most.

That afternoon, returning from a shopping expedition, she was greeted by the children, dancing about excitedly.

"Please, madame," they begged. "Go upstairs! Look in the bathtub! We have a surprise for you!"

Surprise was right. Tethered in the bathtub was a full-grown sheep.

The children were crestfallen when they had to return it to the farmer in whose field they had found it grazing. They had had no intention of doing anything wrong. They had simply wanted to express their gratitude by augmenting the family's meat ration.

Marcel, whose hostess called him "Grave of Hearts," was a beautiful child with flaxen hair and huge blue eyes; he had been a great favorite of the Germans who had occupied his hometown of Dijon. He had liked to sit on the garden wall at night and watch the flames shoot up when the Germans burned down a house. "Oh, but it was beautiful," he said with a beatific smile. His father had joined the Resistance and his mother hated the Germans. But he only hated girls. A girl had pulled the wings off an angel a German major had given him for Christmas and he had cried all night over his wingless angel. The next day his friend, the German major, had glued the wings of the angel back on. Before Marcel had left Dijon for Switzerland, he and the major had hidden the angel so that while he was away "that girl" wouldn't find it and de-wing it again.

His dislike for girls extended to the little French girl staying with the family next door; he delighted in teasing her by telling her that the hawk circling over the chicken yard was looking for "a little French girl" to carry off and devour. He was only seven, but he was already both a strong antifeminist and a very special type of collaborationist. His affection for the German major was touching. "He's my friend," he said solemnly.

On several occasions I found a similar affection among the children of the occupied countries for some kind soul in the occupying forces. It was one of the few comforting signs of an enduring humanity in a nightmare of horrors.

By 1942 over twenty thousand children had been brought into Switzerland, including a convoy of Serbian children who because of language difficulties had had to be placed together in a *Kinderheim,* a kind of children's boarding house, where they upheld the Serbians' tradition of being the best fighters in Europe. My favorite of all those I met was a twelve-year-old from Lyons—Henri Dupin—whom I had first spotted in a convoy that I accompanied from Geneva to Zurich. During the trip, he had explained to me why the children hid the apples and cookies they had been given and even stopped chewing whenever the conductor passed through the train: "You must never let anyone in uniform know you have something to eat," he pointed out. "They'll think you stole it and will take it away." He was greatly concerned that I might not have enough to eat when the Germans came to Switzerland: "For the Germans always come everywhere, you know!" He insisted that I should, as soon as possible, locate a child small enough to pull up carrots, beets, and turnips, as well as swipe things off of shelves in the stores without stooping down. It was the stooping down that attracted the attention of the authorities. His little brother had been an expert in such matters.

Henri was greatly disappointed to learn that, while waiting for the families with whom they would be staying to pick them up, the boys and girls would be separated from each other. He had his eyes on a girl in the convoy, adding with a wink that although I might regard him as too young for such matters, he had already had a couple of "very interesting experiences." He was one of those bright, friendly children who always seemed to land on their feet, and he helped convince me that personality was the single most valuable asset that anyone, even a child, could have during a catastrophe.

When I went to see him off at the end of his three months' stay with a peasant family near Zurich, it was difficult to believe that the tanned, healthy boy standing at the train window with tears streaming down his cheeks and waving until the train was out of sight was the wan skinny lad I had first spotted three months before in the Geneva station.

Some weeks later there was a small, dirty envelope in my morning mail. Its stamp bore a likeness of Marshal Pétain, and on the back of the envelope was the swastika of the German censor. The letter itself, in pencil on lined paper, had been treated with chemicals to see if it contained any dangerous messages in invisible ink.

Madame:
Today it is three weeks since I said good-bye. Three weeks since I left my little Swiss village. Three weeks since I started on the long journey home. I miss you.

> *Sincerely,*
> *Henri Dupin*

The signature was rather elaborate, and beneath it in lettering like that in a medieval manuscript, were the words A FRENCHMAN WHO WILL NEVER FORGET.

XVII

Eventually, the Germans occupied the whole of France, and Switzerland was completely encircled by warring nations. I was beginning to wonder if I had been a fool not to return to the States with Mary Jane when it still had been possible. But I had grown very fond of Switzerland and the Swiss. To run away just because I was afraid of death or the Germans seemed a rather shabby thing to do. Mary Jane was enjoying her life in Switzerland. Growing up there offered innumerable advantages. As for being killed by the Germans, I figured there was just as good a chance of being killed by an automobile in the United States.

After Pearl Harbor, however, all I could think about was what I might be doing to help in the war effort if I were only back home. Friends at the American legation in Bern thought that eventually something could be worked out so that I might be able to help out there. Then, just as I was getting frantic with impatience, Don Bigelow, First Secretary of the American legation, called to say that a representative of the Office of Coordinator of Information, Gerald Mayer, would be in Zurich during the week and would call me. Don thought I might be able to do some work for Gerry.

I had liked Gerry at once. He had a charming, lighthearted manner and that touch of worldly sophistication that had always appealed to me. Of medium height and prematurely bald, he had a delightful sense of humor and knew Europe well. He was interested in having me write articles about various aspects of American life for the Swiss press, and articles on Switzerland for the American press. Not the usual tourist attraction literature but rather how, for instance, the Swiss concept of neutrality was only a policy of the government, not necessarily a reflection of the sentiments of the individual Swiss citizen. This concept of neutrality was causing a lot of misunderstanding at the moment. Whenever anyone mentioned neutrality to our consul general, he would roar, "*What?* You mean you are in favor of *bombing babies?*"

Gerry was also interested in having analyses of the German press and the speeches of leading Nazis, particularly Hitler, Goering, and Goebbels. What I did not realize until many months later was that Gerry was scouting around among the several hundred Americans living permanently in Switzerland to see if any of them might be suitable to work for the Office of Strategic Services that was to be established in Bern.

In early December 1942, after I had been working with Gerry for several months, he phoned one morning to ask if I could join him that afternoon for a drink at the Baur au Lac hotel to meet the newly arrived special assistant to the American minister, Allen Dulles. He thought perhaps I might be able to do some work for him, too.

I found Gerry sitting beside a man with a ruddy complexion, a small, graying moustache, and keen blue eyes behind rimless spectacles; he was wearing a tweed jacket and gray flannel trousers. As the two men rose to greet me, it flashed through my mind that if anyone imagined this new arrival was anyone's "assistant," they were in for a big surprise. My instantaneous impression of Allen Dulles was that he would never be anybody's assistant—at least not for long.

That evening when I told Jean that I had met the newly arrived special assistant to the American minister, he sighed in mock despair. "Oh, you Americans! Everyone knows Dulles is the head of your intelligence service here—except, of course, you Americans! I assume you will be working for him. That's all right with me. But please be discreet, will you? Remember, the Swiss will know everything you do."

"But won't it be dangerous for you to have me working for American intelligence when you are going back and forth to Rumania on that liquidation you are doing?"

"Certainly not. The Germans know I have an American wife. They will be delighted when they discover she has such high connections. All they are interested in is having me help them get to the States when Germany collapses. Several of them have already sounded me out about this."

Some days later Allen Dulles phoned to ask if I could have dinner with him the following evening in Bern. I accepted eagerly.

I still had difficulty believing that this cheery, extroverted man was actually engaged in intelligence work. I thought of spies as grim-faced, gimlet-eyed characters, wearing gray felt hats with flipped-down brims and belted raincoats with turned-up collars. However, the idea intrigued me. Maybe my childhood dreams of excitement and adventure were about to come true.

I remembered the motto on a set of children's books I had once peddled from door to door in New Jersey:

> *What the child admired*
> *The youth endeavored.*
> *And the man acquired.*

Was I actually to become a spy at last?

I took an afternoon train over to Bern, reaching there about six o'clock. By that time I had unearthed some further facts about Allen Dulles. He was a Princeton graduate, a Republican, the son of a Presbyterian clergyman from upstate New York. He and his brother, John Foster, were partners in the prestigious Wall Street law firm, Sullivan and Cromwell. He had held various positions in the State Department and had actually worked on Woodrow Wilson's famous Fourteen Points at the peace conference after World War I—his uncle, Robert Lansing, having been Secretary of State in Wilson's cabinet. He had begun his career as a teacher in India, but that seemed to be the only exotic touch in an otherwise conventional *curriculum vitae.*

In Bern I went directly to the Hotel Schweizerhof, across from the station, where I'd reserved a room. After freshening up, I went out and walked along under the arcades, past the tower with its clock and the fountain with its *Kinderfresser,* the monster who devoured children, to Allen's ground-floor apartment in one of the beautiful old houses that lined the Herrengasse.

The door was opened by a short, stocky man with pale, watery blue eyes, a bristly, blond moustache, and a rather foxy expression, wearing a white coat and dark trousers. This was Pierre, a French-Swiss, extremely proud of having served as butler "in only the best of homes," according to his own testimony. Later he was to confide in me that as far as the war effort was concerned, "Mr. Dulles has his role. I have mine. You see, madame, he is a gentleman. He understands *nothing!*"

Allen, appearing from a nearby room, ushered me into a study with wood-paneled walls and dark red draperies framing the windows that looked out over a terraced garden that extended down to the river Aar.

Two comfortable armchairs were drawn up in front of the fireplace in which a fire was burning—a luxury that only diplomats could afford in those days. Against the wall opposite the fireplace was a sofa that matched the armchairs and above the sofa, a vitrine in which the most conspicuous object was a large, white porcelain fish. If that fish had been able to talk, he could certainly have told some of the most interesting anecdotes of World War II. On a nearby table was a plate of hors d'oeuvres, a bowl of ice, a cocktail shaker, glasses, and an array of bottles containing every imaginable alcoholic beverage. A picture of an attractive woman with wavy hair, high cheekbones, and a rather classic profile stood in a silver frame on the mantel over the fireplace.

"That's my wife," said Allen, noticing my glance. "She's an angel!"

"She looks awfully nice," I said.

"She's an angel," Allen repeated. "She's always doing things for other people . . ."

As we drank our martinis, Allen kept fussing with the fire, explaining that the wood was not sufficiently dry to make a good fire and that he'd become an expert at making fires at the family property in Henderson in upstate New York, where he'd also become an expert at sailing. Did I like sailing? Yes, but I liked skiing better. He'd never tried skiing. Now, of course he had no time for such "frivolities."

Dinner was announced and we went through a beautifully furnished salon to a large dining room on the other side of the apartment. The food was delicious and exquisitely served, all of which Allen seemed to take quite in stride, just as he seemed quite at home in this lovely apartment with its beautiful and valuable furnishings. He had struck me at first as rather a meat-and-potatoes type, quite uninterested in either food or his surroundings. Actually, as I was soon to discover, he was both a gourmet and a man who appreciated everything beautiful and elegant.

Allen asked how my daughter liked her school. What did I think of Swiss schools? He understood they were the best in the world. He himself had two daughters and a son. I told him about my son, now living with his father so he could go to school in the States. Allen thought that a good idea for a boy who would have to earn his living in the States. Then we discovered we had many mutual friends and talked about them for a while. It was all very easy and pleasant.

I was sure that Allen was not more than ten years older than I was. Yet I noticed certain attitudes in his conversation that indicated to me that because of those ten years he actually belonged to a very different generation from my own. This particular generation gap was something with which I was quite familiar. Men as little as ten years older than I—Jean was fourteen years older—had a very different frame of reference that affected all their attitudes, particularly their attitude toward women. Such men could remember life before World War I, when things were much more orderly and women were treated with deference, as rather fragile creatures who required protection; whose foibles, however charming, were not to be taken too seriously.

Girls of my generation had never been treated with deference or regarded as the least bit fragile. We were supposed to take care of ourselves and do everything the boys did, including sports. Since our early teens, when World War I had ended, we could remember only chaos, flaming youth, the boom and bust of the twenties, the Great Depression, the rising threat of the dictators, and finally World War II. By the time we came along, women had cut off their hair, were smoking in public, and doing all the things men did without thinking anything about it. There was something about the courteous, almost gallant way Allen treated me that made him seem more like a man of my father's generation than my own. This was something I had also felt with Jean in the beginning. I would never have dreamed of swearing, using four-letter words, or even telling a risqué story in front of either of them. And I was very much aware of this inhibition.

At some point later in my association with Allen, we were discussing the notorious Paragraph 175 of the German criminal code, which made homosexuality a criminal offense. The persecutions that resulted were unusually vicious because of the large number of homosexuals in both the SA and SS who took advantage of it to settle all manner of personal vendettas. Suddenly Allen asked, "What do those people actually *do?*"

"Don't you know?" I asked in astonishment.

Allen shook his head.

"Do you want me to tell you?" I asked.

"If you know," said Allen, looking skeptical.

So I took my courage in my hands. After all, wasn't it part of my contribution to the war effort to see that this distinguished spy master was enlightened about one of life's realities of which he was apparently blissfully unaware? We had recently learned that there was a homosexual underground operating among the Foreign Offices of England, Switzerland, Greece, and our own State Department and through which information traveled even more rapidly than by the channels of the Catholic Church and various Jewish organizations. A colleague of my generation had told me how essential it was for us to tap this homosexual underground by having, as he put it, "Washington send us a guy with a pretty behind." When I had suggested that he speak to Allen about it, he had demurred. He was sure Allen didn't know about such things, something I had not believed at the time but which was apparently correct.

"Well," I said, "this little episode that supposedly took place aboard a destroyer in the U.S. Navy will show you that 'those people' do different things just like everyone else!"

When I had finished the tale, Allen, red in the face, exclaimed, "Where did you ever hear such a story? You ought to be ashamed of yourself!" Then he gave a short laugh and added, "Still, I'm glad to know. I've always wondered what those people *did!*"

Such innocence—and it was genuine—probably never would have been found in anyone of my generation.

At certain moments during dinner I had the impression that Allen was attracted to me. But I quickly banished such thoughts. I was not interested in romance; I just wanted him to give me a job.

After dinner, seated in the study before the open fire, I was astonished by Allen's familiarity with every facet of Swiss life. When I asked him how he knew Switzerland so well, he just laughed, that same rather peculiar, mirthless laugh that I'd noticed at the Baur au Lac when he said he'd heard about me and I'd said I hoped he'd heard only good things. Everyone who ever worked for Allen became only too familiar with that laugh. It was a most effective device for turning aside unwelcome questions and very different from Allen's hearty laugh when he was genuinely amused. Later I discovered that he had been in Switzerland during World War I in a similar, if less exalted, capacity, but I didn't learn it from him. It was said that if Allen arrived dripping wet in a raincoat with a soaking wet umbrella and was asked if it were raining outside, he wouldn't answer, but just laugh that particularly mirthless laugh. Not surprisingly, his discretion was legendary.

After we'd talked some more about Switzerland and what I'd been doing since I'd come there, I made some comment about how very attractive the apartment was and how lucky I thought he was to have found it. "It suits my needs perfectly," he said. "But Pierre tells me there's not enough household linen. I understand you have to have coupons for it, as for everything else. I suppose I could get the coupons, but I thought perhaps I could find someone who had some extra linen they could let me have. I'd be glad to rent it from them."

"I can let you have some," I said. "We've closed our place at Geneveys for the duration. I took our linen to Zurich so it wouldn't mildew in the unheated house."

"That would be great," he said. "I expect to be in Zurich next week. I'll get Pierre to give me a list of what we need and send it along to you. Only remember I'm not asking you to *loan* your linen to me. I insist on renting it!"

"All right," I said. "You can rent it if you want!"

Naturally, I would have been delighted to lend him the linen. But I knew that renting it would make a good impression on Jean, who was always growling about how Americans didn't understand the proper use of money.

Then the conversation turned to the work I'd been doing for Gerry, particularly my analyses of the speeches of Hitler, Goering, and Goebbels, as well as of the German press. Allen said he'd read my "stuff" and had found it "most interesting and very useful." He wanted me to continue doing the same thing, but to send it to him rather than to Gerry. He'd also like me to see some people coming from adjacent countries who had to be careful where they went and whom they saw because they would be returning home to occupied territories. Switzerland was riddled with enemy agents. Officially, mine was a Swiss household where such people could visit with a minimum of risk. Or, if I had to meet them in public, I was a journalist and that was an excellent cover.

I mentioned that ever since I'd been living in Europe I'd kept a journal of anything that had interested me.

"Handwritten?" he asked with a frown.

"Yes," I replied, thinking of lifelong complaints about my illegible handwriting.

"Type it," said Allen. "Send me a copy."

"Everything?"

"Everything. I'll decide what's useful."

Useful was a word that was constantly on his lips. He judged everyone and everything by the yardstick of its usefulness in the war effort, even going so far as to wonder why one of the men at the legation was getting married—he didn't consider the girl he was marrying "useful."

In my innocence, I imagined that my new job would be just an extension of the work I had been doing for Gerry plus copies of my journal entries and anything I learned talking with people coming from Germany or the occupied countries, or anything of significance spotted in the large number of foreign publications available in Switzerland. I could also see how I might be useful meeting people that he might not have time for or consider of sufficient interest to meet personally. I never dreamed of the kind of activity I would eventually become involved in, nor what a leap forward I would take in my education as a result.

In spite of the courteous, almost gallant way Allen had treated me when we had been talking about purely social matters, the minute the subject shifted to anything pertaining to work, his whole manner, the tone of his voice, even the expression in his steely blue eyes changed abruptly, and he talked to me exactly as if I were a man. This had made me feel much more comfortable. In any work I'd ever done this was how I'd been treated. I liked working for a man who knew what he wanted and showed a certain imagination in the tasks he assigned. I could see that Allen would be that kind of boss and I was sure that I would be able to work—and work well—for him. One of his greatest strengths was the devotion he was able to evoke in those who worked for him, and this kind of devotion on my part began on that very first evening in Bern.

Several days later I received a short note from Allen, enclosing a list of the household linen he would need and saying he would be in Zurich on Wednesday. Unless I notified him to the contrary, he would come to my apartment at 3 P.M. and pick up the linen then.

He appeared punctually as planned, an old gray Fedora on the back of his head and wearing a rumpled gray overcoat with newspapers crammed into either pocket. He was also carrying a hard-bottomed briefcase that I was eventually to regard as being as much a part of him as his arms and legs. The lock was the kind where you have to spin little wheels to different numbers in order to open it. I noticed he used five numbers, so, after we'd been talking for a while, I said, "I bet I can open your briefcase!"

"Bet you can't! Here, try." He handed me the briefcase. I took it and, spinning the wheels to five different numbers, opened it.

"Well, I'll be dammed!" he exclaimed. "How did you figure that out?"

So I told him that first I'd noticed he used five numbers. Then, since I knew the address of his home in New York, with the street and house number adding up to five figures, I thought that might be it—and it was.

"Are you alone?" he asked. "I thought I was going to meet your husband and daughter."

"Jean's away," I said. "He had to go to Paris. Mary Jane is still at school.'

"Oh, I forgot," he said. "The Swiss keep 'em in school all day, don't they? Good idea! Keeps 'em out of mischief." He laughed.

"I've put the linen out on the dining-room table. I thought you might like to see it first. I'm afraid you're going to have to take two suitcases to get it all in."

"Good," he said. "Have you got them?"

"Yes," I said as he followed me into the dining room.

"My God!" he exclaimed as he caught sight of the linen. "That's enough for a hotel!"

"It's only what was on the list!"

"Where are the suitcases?"

"Here!" I reached under the table and pulled out two huge suitcases.

Allen pushed the linen aside and lifted one of the suitcases up on the table. "Come on," he said. "Let's pack it up!"

When we had finished, Allen turned to me with an expression on his face that made me realize I had not been mistaken when I'd suspected that first evening in Bern that he might be as much interested in romance as in giving me a job. This bothered me, as much for him as for myself. Actually, he didn't know anything about me—about my personal life. My marriage was getting more difficult every day, but I was appalled that Allen was contemplating anything more than just having me work for him. I was sure Jean was right about his being the head of our intelligence service. Even my usual delight in danger was not aroused by the possibilities in this particular situation. So I pretended not to notice Allen's expression and, starting toward the living room, I asked, "Would you like some tea? Or a drink?"

"No, thank you," said Allen, taking his cue from my imperviousness. "I'd planned to take you back to the Baur au Lac with me. I've got a car downstairs. I've a couple more appointments, but they won't take long. Then we can have a drink and some dinner. I've got a suite at the hotel where you can wait till I'm finished."

"I could meet you later," I said, not sure I was quite out of the trap but feeling more self-confident. "The maid's out and I have to wait to let Mary Jane in after school."

"Good," said Allen. "I'll take these suitcases with me. Suppose you meet me at the Baur au Lac around five."

"That'll be fine," I said.

Shortly after five I arrived at the Baur au Lac where the concierge, with a knowing look, told me that Mr. Dulles was expecting me upstairs in his suite. This particular concierge had given me leads for many good stories in the past and was to give me more in the future, being one of those people who understood only too well the value of twenty-franc notes slipped into his hands from time to time. I ignored his insinuating look and took the elevator to the second floor, where I found Allen alone in a large sitting room, overlooking the canal that ran along one side of the hotel. His briefcase was on the floor near a table covered with papers.

"What a nice room!" I exclaimed.

"Yes, isn't it?" said Allen. "Take a look at that sign over there by the window. I've got to have some of those signs. Do you think you can get some for me?"

I laughed as I read the sign he indicated, written in three languages:

Um die kreischenden MÖWEN *vom Hause fernzuhalten, bitten wir die verehrten Gäste dieselben nicht zu füttern.*

Afin d'éviter tout bruit inutile, la Direction de l'Hotel prie sa Clientele de ne pas donner à manger aux MOUETTES.

The SEAGULLS *making too much* nocie, *please do not feed them.*

"I'm sure I can get you as many of those signs as you want!" I said, little imagining how quickly *nocie* was to become a code name between us for the Baur au Lac or anyone staying there.

Allen asked me if I knew of a quiet restaurant in the old part of town where we could get a good dinner. I said I did and we walked over to the Veltlinerkeller.

After a delicious meal, we went down and strolled along the lake, then walked up to a little park behind St. Peter's and sat on a bench for a while. Allen said he was sure we would be able to do some good work together. I replied that I thought so, too. He took out his pipe, lighted it, and then said jokingly, "It *should* work out very well! We can let the work cover the romance—and the romance cover the work!" The idea seemed to delight him. I made no comment. Suddenly he became serious: "Of course, I shall pay you a regular salary. Naturally, I have *millions* at my disposal. But because you're you, I am going to pay you only the minimum. You see, there may be a congressional investigation after the war. There usually is."

"Of course," I said meekly, suddenly feeling like a character in a play. What did he mean by "the romance cover the work and the work cover the romance"? What *romance*? What *work*? And what did he mean by "because you're you"?

I can no longer remember just exactly when I knew the answer to that last question, but I had only been working for Allen for a very short time when I realized not only that he was in love with me, but that I was very much in love with him. He was the second man with whom I had ever fallen completely in love, Leopold, of course, being the first. However, my feeling for Allen was much deeper than my feeling for Leopold had been, partly because I was older and had spent so much time working with Professor Jung to learn about myself, but more importantly because of how perfectly Allen and I could work together. The speed with which he could think, the ingenuity with which he could find solutions to even the most complicated problems, were thrilling to me. I had never before found anyone who reacted as quickly to everything, and this was tremendously exhilarating to me.

Naturally, my feeling for Allen compounded the difficulties of my relationship with Jean, so I decided to get a divorce. But Jean begged me not to until after the war, pointing out how important it was for me to have the protection of my marriage to him in my work with Allen. I realized he was correct in this and put aside any thought of divorce until at least the end of the war. I continued managing as best I could what were actually several very complicated situations.

I knew that even if I divorced Jean, there would be no possibility of my marrying Allen. When we had first faced up to the fact that we were in love with each other, he had been brutally frank with me. "I can't marry you," he had said. "And I probably wouldn't even if I could. But I want you and need you now." I suppose some women would have been put off by such bluntness, but I found it admirable. Allen had put the ball squarely in my court, thus forcing me to take full responsibility for my own actions.

Throughout the war Allen called me every morning at exactly 9:20 and in very few words indicated what he wanted me to do, where I should go, whom I should see. Anyone listening in on our conversations wouldn't have had the least idea of what we were talking about, for they were a combination of American slang and ridiculous names for people and places. If during the day I had to call him because there had been some new development or someone I was supposed to meet had failed to show up at the expected rendezvous, I never ceased to be amazed at the speed with which he caught the drift of what I was trying to convey and how quickly he could exercise judgment about the best way to handle even the most ticklish situations. In short, I had perfect confidence in him and an overwhelming admiration for his abilities.

Yet once the Swiss frontiers opened and people came flooding in from

Washington, his personality underwent what was for me a most disturbing transformation. I never again saw the Allen Dulles I had watched operating with such consummate skill when he was cut off from all outside influence and just acting on his own.

It is rather difficult to describe this personality change except to say that much of the sparkle and charm went out of Allen's personality as I had known it. It was rather like the way an exuberant young person behaves when his parents suddenly show up. I felt that this was largely due to Allen's awareness of various American prejudices and how he felt he should behave in order to circumvent them so that he might achieve his ambitions, whatever those ambitions might be.

I also felt that his attitude toward his older brother, John Foster, played an important role in his soft-pedaling his own personality. I had learned that when his father had been dying, he had summoned his children to his bedside and made them all promise after his death to regard Foster as head of the family. Allen had a very strong family feeling and a genuine devotion to Foster, but there was something subservient in his attitude that infuriated me. I myself didn't care much for Foster Dulles. I considered Allen by far the cleverer and more intelligent of the two brothers. I also felt that Allen was making a miscalculation in acting the way that he was. It might please Foster and it might make Allen himself feel he was carrying out his promise to his father, but I was quite sure that the Allen Dulles I had seen operating so brilliantly in Europe would be more successful in achieving his goals than this other more conventional and almost Rotarian personality of his.

His relationship to Foster was the one sore point between us—the one subject that, after one knockdown, drag-out fight, I never mentioned again. However, I was once strongly tempted to do so when after the war, President Truman offered Allen the embassy in Paris, and Allen, at Foster's request, turned it down. Foster already had his eyes on the State Department when, and if, a Republican administration took over. He didn't think it would help him if his brother had accepted an ambassadorial appointment from a Democratic president. Besides, Foster had other plans for Allen. It has always surprised me that more of a fuss was not made over the constellation of power resulting from Foster at State and Allen at the CIA. Undoubtedly the only reason that there was not more criticism of this particular combination was that Eisenhower was in the White House. The American people had placed their faith in Daddy—and Daddy could do no wrong.

It was a very subtle thing, the difference in Allen's personality when he was operating on his own or under the watchful eye of Foster, either socially or in his work. Alone he never hesitated to show his very real charm, which had so enchanted the European statesmen and politicians who made their way, often incognito, to Switzerland to see him. Of course, in many cases they assumed that what the press was publicizing about him was true—namely that he was "President Roosevelt's personal representative, empowered to accept peace feelers." He felt, and rightly, that this rumor was an excellent cover. He had the background to talk to various Europeans with concrete programs about how peace might be achieved and how various inevitable postwar problems might be handled most constructively.

All these often extremely surreptitious visits were duly noted by the Swiss and the resulting "great man" image filtered down through the bureaucracy. As a result, occasionally some bureaucrat had a rather traumatic experience with Allen, as, for instance, when he wanted to get a Swiss driver's license. The official given the task of administering the test was overpowered by the honor, so impressed in fact that at one point he told Allen to go ahead in the face of an oncoming car because, as the official pointed out, "You have the right of way!"

Allen jammed on the brakes, turned to the official, and said, "Obviously you don't know the story of Julian Gray, 'Who died defending his right of way./He was right, dead right, as he sped along,/But he's just as dead as if he'd been wrong!' " Allen got his license. And the official was still telling the story long after the war when most Swiss had forgotten who Allen Dulles was.

Professor Jung was greatly interested in Allen. After their first meeting, Jung said to me, "Your friend Dulles is quite a tough nut, isn't he? I'm glad you've got his ear." When I asked Jung what he meant, he said that men like Allen, very ambitious and holding positions of power, needed to listen to what women were saying in order to exercise their best judgment and not go off the deep end. Not that they necessarily had to follow anything the women said, but they needed to listen to it and take it into consideration when they made their decisions. To get such a man's ear, he pointed out, was not easy.

I did understand what Jung meant. Allen would often listen to me, puffing on his pipe and staring at me intently, when I'd be explaining something that was to his own personal interest or that of his work. One of my theme songs was about his conspicuousness, how the Swiss had eyes in the backs of their heads, knew everything that was going on, and were particularly curious when strangers showed up in their own neighborhoods, no matter how remote. Another favorite theme of mine was that he must never assume people in public places didn't understand what was being said, no matter what language was used. The Swiss were expert linguists. Even to obtain a job as a waitress in a station restaurant, a girl had to speak at least five languages.

Allen would also listen closely when I'd outline for him various interrelationships between both families and organizations that once had been sympathetic to the Nazis and now had changed sides, as well as the reasons for the change. This was the kind of background material that could be very useful to him, save a good deal of time, and avoid unnecessary gaffes. He understood French and German and thought he spoke them quite well, but it may perhaps be kinder to draw a veil over that latter assumption! No matter how much progress he made in languages, his accent remained atrocious.

I do not speak Italian myself, so I can't evaluate his skill in that language. However, he had many dealings with Italians, particularly with the partisans in northern Italy. He also saw a great deal of a charming Italian countess whom Pierre did not care for, referring to her disdainfully as "*La Cirque*"—"The Circus." On my weekly visits to Bern I'd ask Pierre, when he opened the door, what kind of a week he had had, and if he would lower his voice, shrug, and murmur, "*La Cirque* was here!" I'd know he had had a bad week. A good week was when she had not appeared. When I told Allen this, he laughed. "Am I supposed to have a romance with every beautiful woman I work with?" he asked. To which I replied, "No—just with some of them!"

During the course of his career, Allen worked for eight different Presidents. When I asked him, after his retirement, which one he had liked the best, he grinned. "I'm not going to tell you *that!*" he said. "But I'll tell you this: Harry Truman always did his homework. And he was awfully nice to me."

A few days after Allen had carted those two huge suitcases of linen back to Bern, I received a letter from him enclosing a confirming list of the linen prepared by Pierre and a check for 250 Swiss francs.

Whatever became of that linen I have no idea. I assume that it was used by Allen's successor after Allen himself went on to his job in Germany. But by the end of the war, Jean and I were divorced, the house at Geneveys had been sold, and the linen rental had faded from everyone's memory, including my own.

Jean, Mary Jane, and I had planned to spend Christmas of 1942 in St.

Moritz. I had arranged with Allen to start working for him regularly when we returned to Zurich in January. At the hotel in St. Moritz, I found a huge bunch of massive yellow chrysanthemums, with Allen's card, waiting for me. I was a bit nervous that this might cause a jealous outburst from Jean, but, when on the contrary he seemed pleased, I said, "I should think you'd be jealous."

"Who? Me? Jealous?" he snorted. "Really! You Americans don't understand anything. You assume a husband is jealous when a man pays attention to his wife. It never occurs to you that he is even more annoyed when a man doesn't!"

The skiing at St. Moritz was good that year and the time passed quickly. I sent several reports along to Allen, thinking he might enjoy hearing about some of the international characters, often with rather unsavory reputations, who surfaced periodically in St. Moritz. But I didn't expect to hear from him until our return to Zurich, although for Christmas I had sent him a copy of Benjamin Constant's *L'Esprit de Conquête*. Allen had been interested when I'd told him about Mme. de Stael and her friends and how Constant's book had seemed so relevant at the time of the opening of the League of Nations that it had been liberally quoted in the League's publicity.

On the day after New Year Jean returned to Zurich, leaving me and Mary Jane in St. Moritz for a few more days. In that morning's mail, I received a letter from Allen:

> *Bern*
> *December 29, 1942*
>
> *Dear Mary,*
>
> *It was pleasant last night on returning to find your letter. I am glad the flowers arrived. I wasn't too sure they would as I had the feeling that there was nothing but snow where you were.*
>
> *The trip to the Tessin was planmässig. The weather was foul, but fortunately I never let myself worry about that. It's too futile. In the mornings we played golf—first in a rainstorm, the next day in a fog, and lastly in light snow. But the exercise was what I needed, and as a matter of fact, I played quite good golf. For some strange reason I generally play better the worse the weather. In the afternoons, I visited various acquaintances in the environs which even the weather couldn't spoil.*
>
> *The lake is surrounded by villas tucked away in the hills, full of refugees and lonely souls who have found temporary soulmates or maybe only more corporeal companions.*

I spent a bit of time at Locarno and an evening at Lugano, plus part of a day. At least I now know what the country and people look like, but clearly winter is not the time for a visit.

I am trying to write this on my knees by the fire, here at home. My writing, never of the best, is more heterogeneous (?) than usual. At my side is Benjamin Constant's L'Esprit de Conquête. *I am afraid your beloved author is going to criticize it, but possibly only the Napoleonic type of military conquest.*

My plans are nonexistent. I shall probably be right here for weeks with an occasional visit to the suburbs, including Zurich. Lausanne will see me tomorrow night as someone is giving me a dinner there. Otherwise I am keeping away from the social life—and trying to do a little work and some thinking. There should be plenty of ways to contribute to winning the war. Give me some ideas.

Let me know your plans if ever you leave your mountain retreat.

As ever.

A.W.D

XVIII

We returned from St. Moritz in time for Mary Jane to start school on January 15. I felt marvelously rested and all fired up to dazzle Allen with my first batch of regular reports.

As in my analysis of the German press for Gerry, I took several issues of the *Frankfurter Zeitung*—before the war one of the most respected German newspapers and, even after Hitler's seizure of power, the most serious and reliable—and compared their contents with those of Goebbels's weekly *Das Reich* and identical issues of the *Völkischer Beobachter,* the Nazi party paper. I summarized a few significant articles in each and also reported on the obituaries—how many deaths were of the military or seemed significant in connection with specific bombings.

I'd noticed in discussing Hitler's speeches with Allen his annoyance that "Hitler's got his facts all wrong." I felt that I should at least make an attempt to "enlighten" my new boss about the Nazi theory of propaganda, how it had nothing to do with presenting facts accurately but solely with an appeal to the emotions of the German people. So I translated a few of the relevant passages about propaganda from *Mein Kampf* and included them in the rest of the material. Allen had also suggested that I listen to some German and French broadcasts that the Americans were beaming to Germany and France and let him have my ideas as to their efficacy, so I enclosed a report on some of those, too.

In order to spice up this first batch of material, I also sent along an example of the kind of thing I had been recording in my journal. Our friend Carl Briner, Mary's husband, had just returned from a trip to

Berlin, Hamburg, Cologne, Düsseldorf, and Brussels. What he had to say I summarized in a kind of mood piece. It never occurred to me that there was anything in it that Allen would find "useful." But later he told me that he had been delighted by its confirmation of an attack on Gestapo headquarters in Brussels by an RAF plane manned by a Belgian pilot, and the casualties that it had caused.

Just as I was getting ready to take the large yellow envelope with the reports in it down to the consulate to be sent over to Bern by the courier, Allen phoned and suggested that I bring it over to Bern myself and have dinner with him.

That evening after dinner when we went into the study at the Herrengasse, Allen took out a large legal pad and handed me another. This was the first of many occasions when I helped him prepare his nightly phone call to the States, which went out over a line that was listened in on by the Swiss and presumably also by the Germans. No hard intelligence gathered by American agents could be given for fear of revealing their whereabouts or activities. However, anything published in the European press could be used along with items attributable to "a well-informed source," such as Carl's report on the raid of the Brussels Gestapo headquarters. After the war I learned how eagerly these nightly calls had been awaited in the States, although when I listened to them at the time, they seemed to me quite bland. Those of us living in Switzerland were well aware of the information they contained, and I failed to realize that the type of thing that Allen would be reporting was actually hot news to the people back home.

After we'd finished the material for the phone call, Allen handed me a copy of a Swiss magazine, on the cover of which was advertised an article "*Zurück zu Wilson?*" by François Bondy.

"Do you know this fellow Bondy?" he asked.

"I don't know him personally. But I know of him . . ."

"I wish you'd get in touch with him for me," said Allen. "I've been asked by Washington to contact him. He's been writing brilliant letters to friends in the States about the political situation in different countries. The censors in Bermuda have been so impressed that they suggested to Washington that I try to contact him. They believe I'll find him very useful."

François Bondy was a Swiss journalist, and I myself had often been impressed by his articles. I'd imagined him as an elderly, rather professorial type, but when we met at the Pfauen Restaurant, I was amazed to find him a soft-spoken, gentle, almost timid young man in his mid-twenties, with large blue eyes, a pallor I associated with scholarly activities, beautiful, slender hands, and a slight stoop, as if he spent his days poring over rare manuscripts. He had an encyclopedic knowledge not only of Europe but actually of the world, as well as a familiarity with the history of various nations and cultures that was dazzling. He also presented his ideas in a very witty and original way, often saying things that would start me thinking along entirely different lines than I had ever thought before. I have seldom met anyone less restricted by conventional wisdoms. After the fall of Mussolini, when there was so much talk about whether the use of the phrase "unconditional surrender" was a help or hindrance to the Allied cause, François remarked that one reason it was a hindrance was that conditional surrender was actually what the Allies were seeking. Since the dissemination of truth is the best propaganda, he felt the Allies should have asked for conditional surrender—and then stated their conditions.

Having François as a friend was better than having a library of reference books and a team of researchers. It was certainly much more agreeable. His knowledge was based on solid scholarship. When he wrote about current events, he did so either as an eyewitness or from information provided by an impeccable source with whom he had talked personally. He never indulged in flights of fantasy when writing journalistically about real situations. If he labeled a report "an eyewitness account," that was precisely what it was. He spoke fluently at least six languages and could write equally well in most of them.

At the very beginning of our friendship, François insisted that I meet his friend Bob Jungk. Bob, who had been born in Czechoslovakia and had grown up in Berlin, was a very different type. Unlike François, he was not a Swiss citizen but in Switzerland legally as a student without permission to work. This led to endless complications, for to work was all that Bob ever wanted to do. He had written a splendid and informative series of articles, signed F.L., about Germany for *Die Weltwoche,* that had increased the circulation of that Swiss weekly until, as the ads for it said, "It circulates in twenty-seven countries and is forbidden in Rumania." Bob's articles for other Swiss papers were signed by various combinations of initials and handled by an agency that he had established so that the editors of Swiss papers would not know that his articles were the product of one person working illegally, but would assume them to have been written by many people from various occupied countries whose lives might be in danger if their true identities were known.

During the first year of this arrangement, Bob had sold articles under seven different sets of initials to *Die Weltwoche*. At Christmas the editor had sent seven bottles of wine to the lady who ran the agency, begging her to distribute them to his seven contributors as a token of his appreciation of their fine work. Bob got them all.

His sources within Germany and his knowledge of the intrigues within the Nazi party itself were extraordinary. He was what for want of a better name might be called an "intuitive" journalist. He could write about anything, whether he actually had been an eyewitness or not, with an amazingly high degree of accuracy and was the envy of many of those who did not possess that gift. At the time of a meeting of the Soviet Presidium, the *Neue Zürcher Zeitung* commented sarcastically that since the meeting of the Presidium had been a closed and secret session, they could not say what had transpired but would have to wait until either an official statement was issued or "until Bob Jungk informs us what happened behind those closed doors."

For a considerable time his illegal activities had been successfully concealed from the Swiss. Then, in true soap-opera fashion, he was denounced to the authorities by "a woman scorned." Although the Swiss were obliged to throw him in jail, the soap opera continued. Swiss editors might officially frown on anyone producing articles illegally, but still they wanted Bob's articles. So even in jail, he didn't stop writing. He even wrote to the authorities about conditions in the jail. Later he wrote about the conditions in the camp to which they had transferred him, believing they were doing him a favor.

None of this endeared him to the authorities or made it easier for those who were trying to help him. The Swiss imposed fines, which, with his sources of revenue cut off, he couldn't pay. When a group of colleagues, secretly rather pleased to have his articles, always so much better than their own, eliminated, raised money to pay his fines and get him out of jail, Bob, instead of remaining quiet, rushed about, in and out of coffee houses and restaurants, expressing himself at the top of his lungs about anything and everything that annoyed him. Eventually, the authorities would spot an initialed article, unmistakably from his pen, and he would be thrown into jail again.

At one point Allen commented that it certainly was a reversal of values to throw someone in jail for working. However, he understood—and sympathized with—the Swiss. Still, Bob was too useful a person to be kept out of circulation. With a certain amount of discreet help from Allen, Bob eventually trickled out into more or less permanent circulation, ostensibly to finish his doctorate but actually to continue writing for the Swiss press and rendering valuable services to the Allied cause.

Everything in Bob's life took the form of a crisis through which he moved, running, never walking, carrying half a dozen papers, dropping things, losing things. Yet always out of the chaos and confusion poured a steady stream of brilliant articles and useful information.

Once Allen asked me, "Do you think Bob Jungk ever really talked to Tito?" My answer was, "Do you suppose Tito believes Bob Jungk ever talked to you?" I felt there was nothing Bob couldn't do, no place he couldn't go, nobody he couldn't see—if he wished.

Once I had met François and through him, Bob, I not only had two sources of an incredible amount of extremely diverse and useful information but also two of the best teachers of European political and cultural history that any American, ravenous to learn about such matters, could possibly have had.

The first person Allen asked me to see for him, Anna Siemsen, was typical of those who had useful information, who needed to be listened to at some length, and who required a bit more "stroking" than Allen had time to give. Anna Siemsen had been a Socialist all her life and, although she looked much older, must have been in her mid-fifties when I went to see her at her chalet at Chexbres.

She wore her snow-white hair in a tight bun at the nape of her rather long neck and her skin had that translucent quality so many vegetarians seem to acquire as they grow older. Tall, spare, plainly dressed, with the kindest eyes imaginable, she was also quite deaf and, as she modestly put it, "formerly a teacher." Actually, until 1933 she had been professor of pedagogy at the University of Jena, at which time she was dismissed for signing a protest against the firing of another professor. (The University of Jena was one of the first German universities to come under Nazi control.) After her dismissal, she had gone to Switzerland hoping to find, as she put it, "people on our side interested in overthrowing the regime in Germany. But I was too naïve!"

Her contacts among European Socialists ran through lifelong personal relationships. She and her friends had worked out a code so that they could write to each other as if they were writing about personal and family matters when actually they were communicating politically. First names referred to nations or public figures. "Thomas," for instance, meant the British.

She claimed the trade unions were still strong and thought it might be possible to organize the workers in West Germany, particularly in Hamburg.

In their letters her friends complained about the "primitiveness" of the Allied broadcasts to Germany and had asked her if she could not get word to the Allies to make their propaganda more positive. Her friends, she said, would like to know specifically what Allied postwar "intentions" were. They were fed up with present conditions, but felt it would be helpful to know what kind of a world they would be going into after the war. This was precisely the point on which the Russians had an advantage. According to her, "Every politically minded person admires Russia. This does not mean they are Communists. Quite the contrary. However, it is impossible for anyone capable of thinking politically not to admire Russia. Add to this the German's admiration of military prowess as such and it is easy to understand the psychological impact of Russia's present military successes."

She claimed that not only her Socialist friends but the German people as a whole feared that the Allies might hold back indefinitely and let Russia "crush" Germany. This would be a great mistake, for "under these circumstances Germany would turn Communist at once." However, she and her friends would infinitely prefer to have Germany turn Communist to having the Nazis remain in control.

She told me a delightful story about why the Germans liked the English better than the French. After World War I, a German was asked which of the two nationalities he preferred. "The English, naturally," he replied. "An English officer comes to my home and asks if I have any guns. I give him my word of honor as a gentleman that I do not have any guns. He accepts my word of honor and leaves. A French officer appears, asks me the same question. I give him the same answer. And the dirty rat goes down in my cellar and takes my guns away!"

She asked me if I could get her a book, *My Boy Franklin* by Sara Delano Roosevelt. She was writing an article for a German woman's magazine and wanted to use a picture of FDR as a baby being held by his mother, which she saw in that book. I happened to have the book, so I promised to send it to her. The caption under the picture she wanted to reproduce was: *At the outset Franklin was plump, pink and nice. I used to love to bathe and dress him.*

She thought that would appeal to the German women—and I was sure it would, too.

It may seem to those nourished on the exploits of James Bond, the spy novels of John Le Carré and Graham Greene, to say nothing of factual postwar memoirs of feats of derring-do, that the journalistic activities of Bob and François and the views of Anna Siemsen have little to do with intelligence work. But intelligence is a mosaic. General material about background and people's interrelationships can be both illuminating and important. Quite often missing pieces of the mosaic emerge that make a previously incomprehensible picture unexpectedly clear.

I very quickly learned the importance of personal relationships, how important it was to win people's trust and confidence. Once this trust and confidence had been established, their own contacts would be opened up to me. In a way, such work followed the same pattern as establishing good sources in journalism. However, a great deal of time and energy had to be devoted to it. What was so exhausting and time-consuming was doing incidental favors, such as shopping for family back home or imparting all manner of information about where to go, who to see, and what to do in Switzerland. Providing Anna Siemsen with a picture of FDR as a baby was actually about the easiest task I had to perform when "stroking" the people I saw for Allen.

D uring the next few months of 1943 I did an increasing amount of work for Allen. In fact, that was just about all I did. Jean was away frequently and Mary Jane was busy at school. I had cut out completely all purely social contacts, partly because I no longer had much time for them, but more so because in that way I could be sure that I didn't let anything slip inadvertently that would give someone a clue as to the kind of work I was engaged in.

Allen was reputed to be not a very good administrator and I could believe that. In my opinion, one of his greatest assets was his ability to win the loyalty and enthusiasm of those who worked for him and to whom he granted what was for a man in his position remarkably easy access. I am not sure if those people would have worked with the same enthusiasm for anyone else. Part of his hold on them was his ability to direct their activities imaginatively, indicating to them various possibilities that they might not have otherwise seen if left to their own devices. And, of course, this dealing with people personally rather than delegating authority may well have been why he was not regarded as a good administrator.

He was first and foremost a pragmatist, who could usually tell at a glance what would or would not work and what facet of any activity could be used to further the work of his organization. The speed of his reactions, in personal as well as in professional matters, never ceased to amaze me.

On my weekly visits to Bern, our evenings together usually followed the same general pattern: drinks, dinner, then a discussion of my reports and the preparation of his nightly phone call to the States. When all the business was out of the way, we'd engage in a bit of dalliance before I made my way back in the blackout to my hotel. On those occasions I was impressed by how we were never disturbed. No phone calls. No visitors. He might not have been a good administrator, but he obviously knew how to protect his privacy.

But one evening just as we had finished with business and had begun to thoroughly enjoy ourselves, the doorbell rang. Allen put his left hand over my mouth and, reaching for a pad and pencil on the night table at the head of the bed, he scrawled, DON'T MOVE. DON'T MAKE A SOUND. The doorbell rang again. There was a pause, then another ring and another at increasingly frequent intervals. After the fourth ring, I looked at Allen and raised my eyebrows inquiringly. He shook his head and scrawled on the pad again, smiling delightedly: PERSISTENT BASTARD, ISN'T HE?

More minutes passed until there was banging on the door. I was becoming quite apprehensive, but Allen seemed to be enjoying our dilemma. Another ten minutes or so passed and there was the faint sound of the outside door to the vestibule closing. But still Allen did not move. Eventually, after what seemed to me an unconscionable amount of time but which was probably not more than another ten minutes, he jumped up. "I guess he's gone," he said. To which I countered, "How do you know it was a 'he'?"

This broke the tension. Allen laughed his genuine, hearty laugh, not that hollow laugh that so effectively held people with whom he did not wish to communicate at a distance. And that was that.

A footnote to that little episode occurred after the war when one of my colleagues confided in me that he wished he knew what the "Chief," as he called Allen, had been up to when he had gone to see him late one night. He had known that Allen was home, but although he rang the bell repeatedly, he couldn't get Allen to answer the door. "Not even when you pounded on it!" I interrupted. My colleague, who both liked me and was the soul of discretion, exclaimed, "Oh, my God. So it was you, was it? Congratulations!"

Sometimes in our relationship Allen took what to me were hair-raising chances. One morning he rushed into my apartment in Zurich. He knew Jean was away and that Mary Jane would be in school. By chance, the maid was out at the market. His hat pushed back on his head, his pockets stuffed with newspapers as usual, he said, "Quick!" Without any further

My mother,
Mary Agnes Cogan Bancroft

My father,
Hugh Bancroft

My grandmother,
Mrs. William A. Bancroft

My grandfather,
Gen. William A. Bancroft

M.B.
("Precious Doll")

Clarence W. ("CW") Barron

M.B. with Nolan
("This is
Miss Mary's own pose.
She requested to
be photographed thus.")

My daughter,
Mary Jane

Mary Jane and M.B. at Gstaad

Mary Jane
at St. Moritz

My son,
Sherwin

M.B.
at Weissflujoch

M.B.
in Ascona

Henri Dupin
("A Frenchman who will never forget")

Gisevius testifying at Nuremburg

M.B. and
The Hon. Elizabeth Scott-Montagu
working on the translation
of Gisevius's book

Hans Bernd Gisevius

Allen Welsh Dulles

M.B. and Clover Dulles at Ascona

Jean G. Rufenacht

Carl Gustav Jung

On the Liechtenstein
frontier as Germany collapsed
(M.B. is in foreground
of photograph to right of man with
black broad-brimmed hat.)

M.B. with Prince Constantine
of Liechtenstein

**M.B. with OSS colleague
Paul Blum in just-liberated Paris**

preliminaries, he added, "I've got a very tricky meeting coming up. I want to clear my head." Feeling it was too risky to go into my bedroom, we settled in on the living-room couch. In scarcely more time than it takes to tell the story, he was on his way again, pausing in the doorway only long enough to say, "Thanks. That's just what I needed!"

Within seconds after his departure, the maid returned from the market and I found myself looking over the vegetables she had bought, vowing to myself that the next time I saw him, I was going to tell Allen that in the future I was not going to cooperate in "clearing his head," no matter how tricky his upcoming meeting might be.

Toward the end of May, on one of my trips to Bern, Pierre, obviously feeling increasingly important in his position of trust, served us the usual delicious meal. After dinner Allen and I retired to the study to work on material to be used in Allen's regular call to the States.

Allen seemed preoccupied. He did not, as was his custom, reach for a pad and hand me another, but instead sat puffing on his pipe. Suddenly, he looked up and, fixing me with a very stern expression, said, "Contrary to general opinion, *I* think you can keep your mouth shut."

"Thank you," I said meekly, realizing I had just received what, coming from him, was a rare accolade. "I try to, but it's not easy!"

"I have been very satisfied with your work," he continued. "But now you've *really got* to keep your mouth shut or five thousand people will be dead."

Suddenly, I saw five thousand people lying in their coffins—and said no.

"Nonsense," said Allen. "You've *got* to do this job for me. I've got no one else." He puffed on his pipe for a few moments, then said, "There's this German . . . I've known an awful lot of people in my life, but never anyone quite like him. He's a member of the Canaris organization—the intelligence service of the German Army known as the Abwehr. He's brought me a fantastic story. My office is piled high with denunciations of him as a double agent. But he can't get anything out of me; I don't know what's being planned at Allied headquarters. . . . I'm inclined to believe his story, but you can never be sure. He's not the kind of person to whom you can offer money; money doesn't interest him. But he does have one weakness: He has written a book about his experiences in the Third Reich. He wants this book translated so that it will be ready for publication the minute the war ends. I want you to translate it."

"But I don't know German well enough. I can speak it, yes, but—"

Allen cut me short. "You can write English, can't you? Besides, translating the book is not the point. That's only an excuse, a side issue. Your
real job is to establish such a good relationship with him that he talks
freely to you. I want you to report to me everything he says to you—
everything. With you working on his book, he may be off his guard and
say things to you that contradict the story he is telling me. That's what I
want to find out. He will call you as soon as Jean leaves for Rumania next
week. He'll say he's Dr. Bernhard. That's not his real name, but it's
better you don't know who he is until you get the relationship established."

This waiting until a personal relationship is established before any
mention is made of who a person actually is is customary in intelligence
work. Awareness of who a person is or what position he holds, in a
worldly sense, can warp an objective evaluation, particularly within the
high-intensity field of power in which an intelligence service operates—
and not just in wartime.

Later, walking back to my hotel in the blackout, my mouth felt dry,
my hands icy. What, I wondered, was I afraid of? The answer, of course,
was of myself, of my ability to keep a secret, the responsibility for the
lives of five thousand people. Who were these five thousand people anyhow? In my panic, I had forgotten to ask Allen and he had not seen fit to
enlighten me. Well, I'd probably learn soon enough after I'd met Dr.
Bernhard.

The night was threatening and overcast. Occasionally there was a flash
of lightning and the rumble of thunder in the distance. As I hurried along
under the arcades extending out over the sidewalks in the old part of
Bern, I was aware of footsteps approaching behind me. The eerie blue
lights at the curb crossings made it impossible to see more than the feet
and legs of the passerby. I quickened my pace. So did the footsteps.

Suddenly, someone materialized at my side. "You have *such* pretty
legs!" a man's voice murmured softly, suggestively, in French. "Aren't
you afraid to be out alone so late at night?"

"Young man," I snapped, "when a woman has reached my age, she is
afraid of *nothing!*"

I have no idea why I seized on old age as a putdown, particularly when
I had been addressed in French. But it worked. The poor man's confusion
was almost tangible.

"*Pardon, madame! Pardon!*" he murmured, falling back into the
shadows.

At the next crossing he turned off and I heard his echoing footsteps receding in the distance.

For some reason, this absurd incident made me forget those five thousand endangered individuals and I was able to get a good night's sleep.

The next morning, however, riding home in the train, my panic returned. I simply *had to* talk to someone in whose judgment I had confidence and whose discretion I could trust. Jean was discretion itself and he certainly understood the need for secrecy, but pride held me back from confessing to him my feelings of inadequacy for this new task Allen had set me. I could just hear Jean's snort of disgust, his comments about Americans and how little they knew about life, his mocking, "Oh, my poor Europe!" He claimed that at least he had one advantage over other Europeans, having suffered from "an American occupation" since he'd married me.

Fortunately, I had one person I could turn to: Professor Jung. If Allen discovered this, as he seemed ultimately to discover everything, he certainly couldn't object to my having selected so distinguished and trustworthy a confidante. He himself might not have been a believer in analytical psychology, but he had been interested when I had expounded some of Jung's ideas to him. He said that although he had personally never found any need for analysis, he realized that it could be helpful to others. Actually, *useful* was the word he had used. His wife, Clover, he said, had often been to analysts over the years.

When I walked into Professor Jung's study the next day, he was sitting in a comfortable armchair by a window, looking out on the Lake of Zurich.

"Well?" he asked, peering over his glasses with a quizzical, slightly ironic expression. "What's the trouble? I understand it's very important that I see you."

When I told him about the job Allen had given me and my concern about being able to keep secrets, he threw back his head and laughed, but quickly became serious. Yes, he, too, thought I could keep secrets: "Although probably only the prospect of five thousand corpses if you didn't would ever make you do it!"

Jung's confidence in my discretion assured me somewhat, but still I was extremely nervous. He might have been a world-famous psychologist, but even he could make a mistake.

On the morning after Jean's departure for Rumania, Dr. Bernhard phoned asking when he could come by "to pay his respects."

"Now, if you'd like . . ."

"Splendid! I'll be right over . . ."

Within the hour he walked through the door, a giant of a man, fair-haired, blue-eyed, with a healthy tan and wearing tortoise-shell spectacles. His light gray suit made him seem even larger than he actually was, but his manner was so engaging, his smile so beguiling, I didn't feel in the least intimidated by his size. Yet there was an enormous tension in the air. After all, he was a member of the famed German Abwehr, "a German spy."

We both began talking at once, neither paying the slightest attention to what the other was saying but rattling on about how delighted we were to meet, what a lovely city Zurich was, what we liked in art, literature, music. There was scarcely a subject we didn't touch on, leaping from peak to peak like a couple of mountain goats, all the while eyeing each other appraisingly. He had not brought his book with him. He would return with it later—"This afternoon, if you'll permit me."

When he returned that afternoon, my heart sank when I saw his manuscript: 1,415 pages of double-spaced typing in a very involved and difficult German. How was I ever going to translate that mass of material, establish a good relationship with this living dynamo, report everything he said to Allen, and at the same time keep up with all my other work? Obviously I would have to have someone help me. But who? That was the question uppermost in my mind as Dr. Bernhard insisted that I read at least the table of contents of his beloved book. The manuscript was bound in three thick volumes, clearly labeled in the best German tradition: *The Burning of the Reichstag, The Thirtieth of June, The Fritsch-Blomberg Crisis.* But on the table of contents that Dr. Bernhard handed me a fourth volume was listed: *Reinhard Heydrich: The Story of a Futile Terror.*

"There are four volumes on this list," I said. "You brought only three."

"Don't worry," he said. "I'll bring you the other volume soon."

There was something in his tone that implied that, because I was an American, I was interested only in what was undoubtedly the most sensational section.

"Of course, parts of the manuscript read like a detective story," he continued. "But I assure you that the sensationalism is only incidental. It may help sell the book, but it interests *me* least of all. You'll see what I mean when you read the manuscript. Promise me you'll begin at the beginning and read straight through. Please don't pick out just the sensational parts. I want to get your overall impression."

That evening Allen was on the phone. "Did you see the doctor today?"

"Yes. . . . Actually, I saw him twice."

"What's the prognosis?"

"Good—but the treatment will take longer than we'd anticipated."

"Why don't you come over to dinner tomorrow night? We can discuss it in detail then. . . ."

The next evening, settled in the study after dinner, I gave Allen a play-by-play account of my meeting with Dr. Bernhard.

"It's clear that he expects me to have a great many pages of translation ready each day to work on," I said. "And it's equally clear that he intends, at least for the present, to appear daily. I'll simply have to have someone to help me with the translation."

"Have you anyone in mind?" Allen asked. "Remember, you'll have to guarantee discretion."

I did have someone in mind—my friend Mary Briner, who unlike myself just loved to keep secrets. Allen thought this might be a good solution. "I didn't expect to have to put *two* people on this job," he said reproachfully. But fortunately he understood the problem.

I then went on to tell him that Dr. Bernhard had said that it would mean a great deal to him to be able to discuss his ideas with a woman. During the previous ten years, his relationships with women had been "purely physical," because he had not wanted "to compromise a nice woman." "You see," he had said, "everyone thinks I am in the Gestapo. . . . Even here in Switzerland. . . . That's because I began my career in the Geheime Staatspolizei [Secret State Police] in Prussia which later— after I had been transferred to another department—developed into the Gestapo. . . . But I don't expect you to understand any of this—not until you have read my book."

"That's what he claims when talking to me," said Allen.

"Maybe it's true."

"Maybe," said Allen. "Let's see what you think after you've read his book."

"He also said that unless a man could talk to a woman about what interested him most, he couldn't get the spiritual sustenance provided by *etwas weibliches*."

"What the hell does that mean—'*etwas weibliches*'?" Allen demanded.

"Whatever women have that men don't. Actually, it's untranslatable. Anglo-Saxons don't express themselves that way . . ."

"I'll say they don't!"

"Incidentally, when he was talking about women, he said he thought that when he married, he ought to marry a woman that he was in love with but who wasn't in love with him. He thought that was the only kind of woman who could manage him or that he could remain faithful to. . . ."

Allen snorted. "I never heard such rot! What a man wants is a woman who thinks he's wonderful." He gave me a sharp, penetrating glance. "I guess there is more to you and Dr. Bernhard than meets the eye. I was afraid of that. He's a very attractive fellow. Are you sure you can handle that angle of it?"

I assured him I could, although I wondered if those were famous last words. I had been enormously attracted to Dr. Bernhard, and unless I was greatly mistaken, he had been equally attracted to me.

As I was getting ready to leave, Allen said, "Wait a minute! You haven't told me what you think of him. Do you trust him or not?"

I didn't want to say anything that might create a false impression. I had seen Dr. Bernhard for only a couple of hours. He was obviously a very complex character.

"Well?" asked Allen impatiently.

"So far I'm sure of only one thing: He wouldn't do anything that *you* wouldn't do!"

"My God!" said Allen. "I don't know if that's so good!"

I've often thought of that remark. Allen had a keen sense of moral values, a clear perception of the difference between Right and Wrong. He knew that every tree throws a shadow in proportion to its height, and was quite aware that he himself was a rather tall tree.

Sir Kenneth Strong has said that Allen was "the greatest United States professional intelligence officer of his time," that "he might without disrespect be described as the last great Romantic of intelligence—the last of a dying breed that dealt in mystery and intrigue and was to be replaced by quite a different type of man, as technological advances invaded every branch of intelligence work."

In any case, when in the course of his wartime work he had seemingly to violate any of the generally accepted ethical or moral values, Allen knew precisely what he was doing and took responsibility for it. In my opinion, this characteristic helped to make him so effective and to win such a degree of loyalty from those who worked for him.

During the following days Dr. Bernhard appeared regularly to go over the few pages of translation that I had managed to prepare with Mary Briner's help. My curiosity as to his real identity was rising to a fever pitch. We were having a hot spell and he would take off his jacket before settling down to work. My eyes would zero in on the tiny H.B.G. embroidered on his shirt. H might stand for Hans or Heinrich. B for Bernhard. But what about G? I was dying to ask but restrained myself.

By now I was beginning to trust Dr. Bernhard. He seemed so open, talked so freely, never asked me anything even faintly resembling a probing question. I couldn't believe that he was interested in anything more than having his book translated. Still, I realized that I must continue to maintain a suspicious attitude toward him until I was absolutely convinced that the translation was his only interest and that he was not using our relationship as some kind of an elaborate device to penetrate the American intelligence service.

Not yet knowing his true identity, I was baffled by what he was actually doing in Switzerland. Why should a member in good standing of the German Abwehr, as Allen had said Bernhard was, have so much free time on his hands? Could he be acting as a spy master for the Germans in Switzerland? Was he spying on the Swiss? But that was no concern of mine. I knew that in this war, just as in World War I, the Swiss let the intelligence services of the belligerents on both sides go about their business as long as it didn't touch on purely Swiss interests. At first they had tapped the phones of all the embassies, legations, and consulates, with members of an organization known as Department Ear listening in. But the diplomats engaged in so much "love talk" and exchanged such trivial gossip that more often than not those listening fell asleep. So after some months the Swiss just kept track of who telephoned whom and when. This allowed them to plot on graphs the various networks.

Because Dr. Bernhard had insisted that I read his book straight through and not skip around, I found that the translating consumed so much of my time that my reading went very slowly.

About two hundred pages into the manuscript, I came to the following passage:

My partner in the sleeping compartment on the train turned out to be one of the cleverest Gauleiters Hitler had ever had. . . . Erich Koch, satrap of East Prussia, later of the Ukraine. . . . A first-class demagogue, an adventurer, at home in both the highest and lowest classes of society, in ability he towered above his fellow Gauleiters. Possessed of a vivid imagination, he was always ready to confide—in whispers and under a promise of absolute secrecy—utterly fantastic stories. . . .

During that ride through the night, Koch consumed the entire stock of alcohol in the sleeper, his loquaciousness increasing proportionately. Finally our conversation turned to HIM. We began talking about the 30th of June, speculating on when and how the next series of murders would occur. I asked when he thought his turn would come. . . . He said he hadn't the slightest doubt that "they" would be coming for him soon. . . . Suddenly, giving me a confidential nudge, he hissed in my ear: "Believe me, Gisevius, he will kill us all, one after the other! Believe me, I know the perfidy of the Hapsburgs!" Delighted with this bon mot, he repeated it: "I know the perfidy of the Hapsburgs!"

So G stood for *Gisevius!* At last I knew "Dr. Bernhard's" identity. My curiosity was satisfied, but I didn't feel exactly comfortable. Some weeks before I had been told by one of those "well-informed sources" that were so helpful to the Allied cause that a member of the Canaris organization, stationed under the diplomatic cover of vice-consul at the German consultate in Zurich, was regarded by the Nazis as "unreliable." If Hitler should decide that he wanted to invade Switzerland, he would have this man killed. Then he would proclaim that, since the Swiss were unable to protect the lives of German citizens on Swiss soil, he would have to march in and do it for them. The name of this man had been Gisevius. Naturally, I did not mention this to Dr. Bernhard, but it certainly did nothing to allay my nervousness. I even had fantasies of his being murdered in our living room.

Gradually, I became familiar with the contents of Gisevius's book. In 1933, after passing his bar examination and planning to make a career in government service, he had applied for a position in the Prussian Ministry of the Interior and had been recommended by Undersecretary Grauert, whom he knew slightly, to Rudolf Diels, the newly appointed chief of the Prussian Geheime Staatspolizei. It had not taken Gisevius long to discover that extraordinary things were happening in this department, and he had set about getting himself transferred out of it as quickly as possible. In the meantime, he had become friends with Arthur Nebe, his immediate superior and a noted criminologist, whom the Nazis had retained when they had discovered that their own thugs were incapable of professional police work.

One day Gisevius and Nebe had learned that Diels, encountering a colleague in a department store, had remarked jokingly that he was buying a new hunting jacket because, "Somebody important is going to be bumped off." After that, Gisevius and Nebe kept an even closer lookout for any suspicious activities within their own department. Eventually, they uncovered enough evidence indicating that the Nazis themselves, not the Communists as the Nazis had proclaimed, had set fire to the Reichstag. A young Dutch Communist, Marinus van der Lubbe, with a record of arson, had been in the building on the night of the fire, apparently quite by chance. However, Van der Lubbe's presence in the building had given the Nazis a splendid excuse to stage a spectacular trial, which Gisevius was sent in an official capacity to observe. He had also been, again in the company of Nebe, an eyewitness to many of the events of June 30, 1934.

The outside world was aware of much of the substance of what he had written about the burning of the Reichstag and June 30. But his written testimony, coming as it did from an official of the Third Reich, was important confirmation of information that until then had appeared only piecemeal in the underground press.

Gisevius's detailed account of the way in which General von Fritsch had been removed as Commander-in-Chief of the Army on a trumped-up charge of homosexuality was a first. So also was his description of how Field Marshal von Blomberg had been dismissed as Minister of War after the Gestapo had produced the record of the woman he had married, showing that she was a convicted prostitute. But what made Gisevius's manuscript such dynamite was his description of the many attempts by various generals and highly placed civilians to organize a coup d'etat. Initially, these conspirators planned their putsch to take over the government simply by removing Hitler from office. Later they realized that they would have to kill him if anything as complicated as a coup d'etat were to succeed.

Within the group of conspirators were such men as Dr. Hjalmar Schacht, president of the Reichsbank; Ulrich von Hassell, German ambassador in Rome; Carl Goerdeler, former mayor of Leipzig; clergymen like Dietrich Bonhoeffer; lawyers; labor leaders; professors; a group of young idealists known as the Kreisau Circle gathered around Count Helmuth von Moltke and various military men like Field Marshal Erwin von Witzleben, General Ludwig Beck, and General Franz Halder, chief of the German General Staff. The conspiracy had the blessings of Admi-

ral Canaris, head of the Abwehr, although his subordinate, Colonel Hans
Oster, acted as the coordinator of the activities of the conspirators. A
small number of Abwehr members served as couriers. This Abwehr connection was absolutely essential. The Gestapo did not dare to touch the
intelligence service of the German Army and Abwehr members could
travel freely.

After Heinrich Himmler had coordinated the police of the Reich,
Nebe was made an SS general and played an extremely important role in
the conspiracy. He was able to warn the conspirators of the activities of
the Gestapo and to prevent anything that might arouse suspicions being
brought to Himmler's attention.

By the time I had finished reading Gisevius's book, had gotten to know
him better, and had realized that there was actually an active opposition at
work within Germany itself, I could understand what he was doing in
Switzerland. I told Allen it all made sense to me. Difficult as it might be
to believe, the conspirators actually hoped that if they got rid of Hitler,
they would be able to take over the whole country and to negotiate peace
with the Anglo-Americans. Their hopes went even further: They envisaged the western Allies joining them in a crusade against Russia—and
communism. Gisevius had been sent to Switzerland to get in touch with
the western Allies. Other emissaries were making similar contacts in
Sweden and elsewhere.

XX

G isevius was very anxious to meet Jung and have Jung read his book.
He had been greatly impressed by Jung's "Wotan" article published in
1936, and felt that some of his own conclusions about the Nazi madness
would fit in with Jung's concepts. I told this to Jung and a meeting was
arranged.

After Jung had met Gisevius, he told me that Gisevius and I were
going to have an interesting experience working together because we
were exactly the same psychological type. He warned me that if I wanted
Gisevius to "spill," I must never ask him for a "fact." If I did, his reaction
would be exactly like my own under similar circumstances: He would be
thrown off-balance and that would be the end of our freewheeling, asso-
ciative way of communicating, during which I might be able to learn so
much.

I told Jung that whenever I wanted Gisevius to phone, all I had to do
was to think about him for about ten minutes. Then the phone would
ring and he would ask, "Yes? What is it? I just got your message to call!"
Jung was very interested in this phenomenon and asked me to keep close
track of it for him. Allen, of course, thought it crazy. On one occasion
when I was telling him how I had contacted Gisevius and how interested
Jung was in our ability to communicate in such an unorthodox fashion, he
snapped, "I wish you'd stop this nonsense! I don't want to go down in
history as a footnote to a case of Jung's!"

One day Jung asked me if I'd heard the rumors that he flew regularly
to the *Führerhauptquartier* to "advise" Hitler. Of course I had, and they

had amused me greatly. He chuckled and said he'd been the subject of the wildest kind of rumors all his life, and that it was probably "only natural, considering my line of work!" I told him I'd also heard the wife of one of Switzerland's leading physicians, who was very proud of his international practice, say that her husband had a recurring nightmare that Jung had "stolen" his practice. Jung chuckled again and pointed out that this particular man had always been jealous of him, denigrated his work, called him a charlatan and, "being such a fine gentlemen, could not explain his recurring nightmare by admitting a possible psychological basis."

Jung thought the stories about his flying to see Hitler had been started when Dr. Ferdinand Sauerbruch, the famous Berlin surgeon who was supposed to be treating Hitler, had first begun coming to Switzerland. They had met on several occasions. "That was enough for my enemies!" said Jung.

He asked me if the Americans had heard that Hitler had begun to drink heavily. He had been told this by "a usually reliable source." He had often been struck by how Hitler ranted and raved about "the drunkard Churchill." Churchill was known to be a heavy drinker, but he was certainly no drunkard. Hitler, on the other hand, in the course of his career had frequently associated with genuine drunkards. If he himself had now begun to drink, it could be a psychologically significant development.

I told Jung how I'd never succeeded in persuading anyone to read *Mein Kampf*. I could get them to buy it, even begin to read it, but they'd toss it aside, announce the man was crazy, and refuse to continue. They wouldn't even listen to his speeches for the same reason. It was no use pointing out to them the insane asylums were full of people, none of whom had ever caused the havoc Hitler had. I found *Mein Kampf* fascinating, not only because it contained Hitler's plan of action that he seemed to be carrying out to the letter, but also because it showed such a shrewd understanding of how to manipulate the psychology of the German people. Jung said the Germans were as clever about their own psychology as they were stupid about other people's. Certainly one of the best ways to learn about them was "to study them at work on themselves."

He said that the difference between the French and the Germans was that a Frenchman would say, *"Enchanté de faire votre connaissance!"* ("Delighted to meet you!"), when what he actually meant was, "I hope the hell I will never see *you* again!" And he would not feel in the least guilty about such hypocrisy. A German would sell you a pair of suspenders, expect you to pay him for them, and then be hurt because you didn't love him for having made the sale. The Germans, who so yearned to be loved, simply could not understand why they weren't. The French didn't give a damn whether anyone loved them or not.

He also said that Goering could never exercise the same "magic power" over the Germans as Hitler. The Germans were too well aware of those qualities in themselves that Goering represented, whereas Hitler spoke to their unconscious.

Allen was always interested in Jung's opinion of the effectiveness of Allied propaganda. Jung never ceased to point out to me the futility of negative propaganda. He constantly emphasized the fact that the Germans would not be likely to turn on their radios at the risk of their lives simply to be scolded and told what a terrible people they were. They would much rather listen to their own radio playing Beethoven or Wagner and recounting deeds of German military prowess.

When the Allied armies were entering Germany, Eisenhower issued a series of proclamations that Jung said were excellent. When I told Allen this, he asked me if I thought Jung would be willing to write him to that effect so that he might pass on such a letter to Eisenhower. Jung said he would be delighted to do so. The idea of "bucking up headquarters" rather appealed to him! He would send me a copy of his proposed letter and I should feel free to make any suggestions I thought might "improve" it.

When the copy of his letter arrived, I knew it was precisely what Allen had hoped for. I did suggest, however, that Jung address Allen as "My dear Dulles" rather than as "Dear Mr. Dulles." Jung, who was considerably older than Allen, always called him "Dulles" when talking about him to me. He was a world-famous psychologist. Allen was "only" a spy master. This amused Jung, and he wrote me that "it is refreshing to see that you understand these trifles which poison so many Anglo-American relations and cause trouble between Americans and Europeans."

Allen was delighted with Jung's letter and asked me if I would write a suitable letter to Jung to thank him. This I did; Allen signed it and I carried it back to Jung. At the same time I wrote a covering letter for Allen to send off to Eisenhower with Jung's letter enclosed, and Allen signed that letter to Eisenhower, too. Shortly, a letter arrived from General Walter Bedell Smith, Eisenhower's Chief of Staff, saying how pleased Eisenhower was with Jung's letter and asking if Allen would please see that Jung was so informed. Allen told me to write an appropriate letter to Jung and another to Eisenhower's Chief of Staff, which I did. Again Allen signed both letters. Off went one letter to Eisenhower's headquarters and I trotted out to Küsnacht with the one for Jung.

Then, suddenly, this whole ridiculous rinky dink, all this corresponding with myself, as it were, became too much. I sat down and wrote the entire story to Jung, as I was sure it would amuse him greatly. And it did!

XXI

Late one evening the phone rang. In Zurich where everything shuts down so early, any late-night sound can be ominous, particularly the telephone. I picked up the receiver. A voice said, "This is the overseas operator. We have call for you from Boston, Massachusetts." I froze. I knew this could only be bad news—and it was. My son, Sherwin, had fallen off a tractor on which he was riding and the tractor had run over him. The doctors were trying to save his life, but they doubted if they could save his leg. This was not going to happen to me again. My first son had died. Sherwin was not going to die too, and he was *not* going to lose his leg.

For three days I sat by the phone. I couldn't eat; I couldn't sleep. I just sat there praying and concentrating on the fact that he was going to be all right. I refused to accept even the thought of anything else.

At the end of the third day a second call came through saying that not only was Sherwin going to live, but the doctors had performed a miracle and saved his leg. He might have some bad scars, but that was all. Not even a limp. Years later he would get great mileage out of those scars. After serving as a Naval officer in the Korean War, he let girls assume the scars were the result of war wounds. But I never enjoyed this little pretense as much as he did. I couldn't forget those seventy-two hours sitting by the phone in Zurich when I had been unable to get to him. And that experience made me feel a particular obligation to write at length to the families of the flyers who crashed in Switzerland, some of them so badly wounded that they eventually died.

As the months went by, there was a steadily increasing number of American flyers whose planes had been shot down over enemy territory and who made their way into Switzerland. Those who had crashed in Italy told of being knocked unconscious when they crashed and waking up to find themselves surrounded by a group of excited peasants, counting their money and quarreling about how much should be allotted to which family members willing to risk their lives by hiding a flyer until all his money was exhausted and he could be conducted by night to the Swiss frontier and then pushed across into safety.

Each weekend two or three of the flyers would come to stay with us—I had signed with the authorities that I would be responsible for their "safety." Could I help it if they "escaped?" The American authorities blinked. The Swiss authorities blinked. And flyer after flyer escaped to take various underground routes through France, over the Pyrenees into Spain and Portugal, and eventually back to their units in England.

Each memory of those months evokes another, such as that unforgettable evening when, having missed the regular Swiss news report, I was twirling the dial of my radio and suddenly over Radio Belgrade came the voice of Lale Andersen singing "Lili Marlene."

That song was not just *the* song of World War II, but in contrast to World War I which produced so many catchy popular tunes, it was the *only* song, eventually sung by the soldiers of many nations and after the war to Americans by another and more famous Marlene, known to all filmgoers as Marlene Dietrich. Written in 1938 by Norbert Schultze and Hans Leip, rejected by more than two dozen music publishers before finding its way into the repertoire of Lale Andersen, "Lili Marlene" was made into a record by her. Even then it did not catch on until one evening when the newscaster on Radio Belgrade at 9 P.M., unable to locate the record of the station's usual theme song, grabbed the first record he could lay his hands on. The right girl had appeared at precisely the right moment and Lili Marlene became every soldier's sweetheart. John Steinbeck called her "the enemy alien who cannot be interned." She became so popular with the British in North Africa that General Bernard Montgomery had to issue an order forbidding his troops to sing the song of the enemy.

Everyone knows how a piece of music can evoke a whole era. All I have to hear are the opening bars of "Mack the Knife," "The Horst Wessel March," "Lili Marlene," and the theme song from *The Third Man,* with its wailing zither, and I'm right back in the Europe of the thirties and forties.

But popular songs were not the only background sounds of those hectic years. There were also the views and opinions of Maria, who had joined our household after Hedy, Annie, and Roseli had departed in rapid succession to marry and I had begun to feel that I was running a marriage bureau.

Maria, a devout Catholic of enormous respectability, had been born in Germany just across the Swiss frontier. When I began working for Allen, I asked him if he thought I should let her go. He thought not. "It's better to know you have a German in the house rather than a girl of some other nationality who might perfectly well have a Gestapo boyfriend." When I told him that Maria had several brothers and a brother-in-law in the German Army who wrote her regularly, that clinched it. "Get her to show you their letters," said Allen. "That's just the kind of stuff we need."

So Maria stayed on. When the whole world was holding its breath as the Germans bogged down at Stalingrad, Maria brought me a letter from her brother-in-law, Fritz. From Stalingrad he wrote that he wished Maria would send him an aluminum spoon. He had lost his in the snow. He had written his wife to send him a new one, "but there are no more aluminum spoons in Germany. I guess the Russians have mine. But better my spoon than me!" He closed his letter by saying he hoped to see Maria in the spring, when he came "rolling into Zurich in a tank behind Field Marshal von Bock. I've walked across Norway and France and half of Russia and I'm not walking anymore!" he wrote.

Allen was delighted to learn that there were no more aluminum spoons in Germany. I was not so pleased at the thought of Fritz and Field Marshal von Bock rolling into Zurich in the spring.

Maria was an authority on communism. She could reel off the names of churches that had been burned by the Communists until Hitler had appeared and put them in their place. In one village during the inflation, 115 people out of 200 voters had voted Communist. Most of these Communists had since disappeared into the Party. People called them the Beefsteaktroops—"outside brown, inside red." It was said the older men in the Gestapo were mostly drawn from this group. There was no question but what there were Communists everywhere. Some came from good, even noble, families and should have known better. Unfortunately, there were bad Germans, just as there were good British and possibly a few good, or at least sensible, French. Dreadful catastrophes happened from time to time. Nothing could be done about this. It was just God's will.

When Maria returned from her vacation in the summer of 1943, she reported that the mood in her village had changed completely since she had been home the previous summer. People no longer cared how the war ended, just as long as it ended. They didn't care who won. Everything was getting worse every day, but nobody expressed any hate. That was what was so wonderful about Germans. They never expressed any hate. In the three weeks she was at home, she heard only one person pass any kind of judgment on anyone else, and that person was from Hamburg, where she had lost everything in the bombing.

This woman said the phosphorous bombs were so devilish that God would surely punish those who used them. Maria herself didn't know what kind of bombs the Luftwaffe had dropped on London, "but surely we Germans were more humane!" People said that if you got even a tiny bit of phosphorous on your clothing, you could put it out with water, but the minute it dried, it started burning again. These firebombs had burned the asphalt right off the streets. People were cooked alive in the air-raid shelters, and "balls of fire blew around in the air." In Hamburg, after two days of this firebombing, you couldn't even see your hand in front of your face. The animals in the Hagenbeck Zoo got loose and "ran around, tearing people to pieces." At Cologne, where firebombs had been used, people threw their burning children into the river, but they just went on burning, even in the water. Leaflets had been thrown down over Cologne saying that, although the city would be bombed, the cathedral would not be touched. People took refuge in the cathedral, but it, too, was hit—"by mistake, they claim, but who knows?" They still hadn't finished digging out the corpses, which had been burned to a crisp.

Terrible stories were circulating in the village about how badly the people in the cities were behaving. People in the country always behaved much better anyhow. The cities in the Rhineland had been evacuated and these city people had been quartered all over in the country. They were impossible; nothing was good enough for them. They refused to do any work, wouldn't even help the peasant families who, "out of the goodness of their hearts," had taken them in. They just strutted around, "playing ladies and gentlemen" and complaining about the food.

Fritz had been home on leave while Maria was there. He said everyone in the army was "swindling." Army cooks were in league with the officers and gave them food that they sent home to their families. Fritz had actually been swindled out of his leave. He hadn't had any leave for twenty-three months. But then his company got a new captain, "a decent man, not a swindler like most of the lower ranks." It was the lower ranks in the army and the lower functionaries in the party who were doing the swindling. This captain looked up the records, and when he saw how Fritz and other men in his company had been swindled, he gave forty-five of them leave the next day, saying that when the war was over, "Plenty of accounts would have to be settled."

While Maria was home, an aunt had died. The funeral had been beautiful, she reported. Family and friends from three surrounding villages, all sharing the same Catholic church, attended the services. Even the policeman in one of the villages came, although nobody liked him. He was, it seems, a Prussian. "In our part of the country, nobody likes Prussians." There was another Prussian in the village, but he was in jail, even though he had been sent to the village by the Nazis "to keep an eye on things." Someone in the village who hadn't liked his Prussian ways had broken into his room one night when he was out and found two hundred cans of meat.

Hans, a friend of Fritz's, did something Maria found wonderful. Hans was sitting in the village café, having a glass of beer, when a Gestapo man from the village came in. "Well," said Hans in a loud voice to the proprietor of the café, "I guess I'll go home now and listen to the English radio!" He paid for his beer and departed. Shortly after he reached home, the Gestapo man knocked on his door. When Hans opened it, the Gestapo man brushed by him and started looking for the radio.

Actually Hans didn't have a radio. The man demanded, "Why did you say you were coming home to listen to the English radio when you haven't got a radio?" "Because . . . ," said Hans, going over to open the window, "I don't have to have a radio to listen to London." And sure enough, through the window of the house next door—which was Gestapo headquarters in the village—floated the voice of the BBC! The Gestapo man flushed scarlet and strode out of the house, banging the door behind him. "The Gestapo doesn't like it when the people make fun of them! But Hans had them this time. There was nothing they could do."

One of the most interesting items in Maria's report was her contention that the people in her village admired the Poles. We had heard similar opinions about the large number of Poles who had been fighting with the French and had crossed the Swiss frontier with units of the French Army at the time of the fall of France and then had been interned by the Swiss. The French troops had been returned to France after Swiss negotiators, working out an arrangement whereby Swiss neutrality would be preserved, had first delivered the French weapons and ammunition to the Germans. But the Polish units had remained in Switzerland, where they had established their own university, worked on Swiss farms, and produced an amazing number of Polish-Swiss babies.

This latter activity so intrigued the Swiss authorities that they had interrogated many of the Swiss women involved. To their surprise, an overwhelming number of the women said that it was the nice manners of the Poles that had first attracted them. The Poles would offer to carry their parcels home from the market, something a Swiss man would never dream of doing. What Maria had said about how the Poles were admired in her village, the report of the Swiss about the Poles' good manners, and the fact that in the intelligence community Poles were regarded as top-flight agents have combined to make me wonder about those Polish jokes that imply the Poles are stupid and loutish. My own experience has been that they are apt to be clever, sensitive, highly intelligent, and very sophisticated about human nature.

Just before Maria left to return to Switzerland, a clandestine radio station had been discovered in the village. Earlier, one of the man's children had announced in class, "Papa goes into the oven every evening and talks!"

She also brought back a joke told by a comedian in Munich that delighted her. A stooge comes out on the stage and says to the comedian that he must do military service. But because the comedian is such a famous man, he can choose whether he wants to go into the army, navy, or air force. The comedian says, "I don't want to go into any of them. I want to be Deputy Führer!" "Are you crazy?" demands the stooge. "Is that a requirement?" asks the comedian.

Maria was a self-starting talker. I had to be careful not to give her too many opportunities to express her opinions. Since she approved of orders, I ordered her never to begin to talk to me when I was reading or writing. The result was that whenever I was doing anything else, she would suddenly materialize and inquire, "Is Madame's head empty now?" If I assured her it was, she launched forth in some recently formed opinion or recounted some incident she had heard about at the market, interpreting things first in terms of world affairs but ultimately attaching the whole to religious beliefs or her favorite, "God's will."

My colleagues, including Allen, were vastly entertained by her stories and her views. They christened her the "Wehrmacht" and were always begging me to ask her what she thought of this, that, or the other thing.

Her reports of what was happening at home or what she had heard from German friends were frequently a confirmation, in primitive terms, of more sophisticated information reaching us through other channels.

She thought Gisevius was a Dr. Lubbe, a Dutchman who had written a book on European history that I was translating. But as the months passed, she observed with increasing frequency that she thought Dr. Lubbe must have studied in Berlin for he had such a remarkably good Berlin accent. She would then cock her head to one side and look baffled. Wheels were obviously spinning, but no train of thought moved forward.

XXII

People unfamiliar with Europe and unaware of the comparatively short distances between different countries are apt to think that because we were in Switzerland, we were in no position to learn much about any country that did not share a frontier with the Swiss. But the constant flow of travelers that in peacetime made tourism one of the country's chief industries continued, although naturally somewhat restricted, throughout the war. Many of these travelers, coming for vacations or to do business with the Swiss banks, were eager to get in touch with the Americans there. There were also many refugees living in Switzerland, who kept track of their political enemies with an ingenuity and skill far superior to any possible surveillance that we ourselves would have been able to maintain. Any information they gleaned was passed on to us.

Although my work with Gisevius took up an inordinate amount of time, I was also meeting a procession of visitors from just about every country in Europe. I remember vividly two Rumanian friends of Jean's, unusually colorful characters, even for Rumanians, and wonderful storytellers. They did not know each other and came to see us some ten days apart. Both had been enchanted when they discovered that Jean, whom they had first met in Rumania, had an American wife. Of course, their own hearts, they both explained enthusiastically, were with the Allies, although they added with helpless shrugs, lifted eyebrows, and expressions of extreme distaste, what else could they do but cooperate with the Germans?

One of the men traveled frequently on economic missions for the Rumanian government. I can still remember the stories he told us when he came to see us in August 1943; how, for instance, because Bulgarian women would have nothing to do with either the German or Rumanian soldiers, carloads of Rumanian prostitutes had been shipped to Bulgaria, where they were paid fifteen thousand lei a month, a sum that had bedazzled them and made them reluctant to return home.

This man was incensed by the tremendous number of horses killed in the war—"twelve thousand in the first two weeks of the Bessarabian campaign"—a disaster for the Rumanians and a figure that he had learned through a close friend of his who owned a large leather factory. He punctuated his stories with marvelously descriptive gestures, indicating how the Russians had recoiled, then sprung forward to crush the Rumanians in an enormous bear hug. Very few Rumanian soliders, he claimed, ever returned from the Russian front.

Seven and a half divisions of well-equipped Rumanian troops were stationed on the Hungarian frontier. The tremendous hatred between the Rumanians and the Hungarians was something I had not realized until Jean had explained it to me, apropos of how trains running between Berlin and Bucharest bore no indication that they passed through Budapest. And trains leaving Budapest for Bucharest never mentioned the latter city as a destination, but were simply scheduled for Istanbul. On one trip, the train Jean had been waiting for in Budapest to travel to Bucharest had arrived so crowded with German soldiers and high German officers that he had just about given up hope of getting aboard when he spotted a German railway official he had known for many years. This man found a place for him among the German officers. When Jean reached Bucharest, the only civilian among highly placed military men, he was treated with the greatest respect by Rumanian officials, who assumed he *must* be Gestapo. They were the only people who traveled in civilian attire in such exalted company in those days. Many courtesies were extended to him on that assumption, which greatly facilitated his business on that particular trip.

Our Rumanian friend who was so disturbed by the loss of twelve thousand horses also told us how the Rumanian troops were encircled at Stalingrad, how other Rumanian troops had broken through to help them and had sent for more troops that had never arrived. The point of this story was that the Germans had deliberately intercepted the orders and "allowed" the Rumanians to be taken prisoners. Many rumors of this kind were circulating in Bucharest. He didn't know how true they were, but the effect was to convince the people that any Rumanian "failure" was the result of German treachery.

The Russian breakthrough at Stalingrad, he said, came first against the Rumanians, followed by similar breakthroughs against the Italians and Hungarians. The Germans "often stole away in the night without a word to anyone." They "borrowed" artillery which they never returned and stole trucks, pitching their rightful drivers out into the streets and "allowing" them to fend for themselves.

He pleaded with me to tell the Americans not to bomb Bucharest. And he gave me the name and the precise location of an electrical works and an airplane factory that should be bombed "to show the Rumanian people that you are not against them, just against the Germans!"

The asphalt roads in Russia ran north and south. Those running east and west were "purposely" left in the muck for the Germans. Russian organization made German organization look "pathetic." Russian prisoners were working in the mines and were being very well-treated "intentionally." They were splendid workers, but contemptuous of Rumanian mining equipment. At first, they were supposed to work only eight hours a day, but they said they preferred to work by output and were now putting in fourteen hours a day. It was incredible how much work they could turn out. The same was true of the Russians working on the farms.

The other Rumanian who visited us that August, and whose stories I remember equally vividly, was a minor Prince who traveled regularly with the diplomatic courier. On this particular occasion, he was on a wheatselling mission for the Rumanian government.

He talked glibly about "the people" and their troubles. Intellectually, he was able to grasp the people's problems and say all the right things about them in order to sound liberal. Actually, he didn't give a damn about anything but eating in the best restaurants, sleeping in the best hotels, and wearing the best clothes.

He had been in Paris just before coming to see us. When he had first arrived there, he had hunted in vain for lodgings. This had infuriated him, being on such an important mission for his government. So he had gone to German headquarters and demanded, as a representative of a German ally, that he be given a room at the Ritz—he was "not accustomed to sleeping in just any hotel." At first the Germans were reluctant—the Ritz was where their own headquarters staff was billeted—but finally they had acceded to his request.

He claimed that in Paris the women were more beautiful than ever, that he was able to get excellent food "without coupons in the chic restaurants at prices much lower than in Bucharest." The Germans went about Paris "looking slightly embarrassed." His French friends had told him that they had no complaints about the German Army, either officers or men, but the party officials and the Gestapo were quite another matter.

Whenever there was an air raid, everyone rushed out to look at the planes. No one took to the shelters. It was possible to live far better for the same money in Paris than in Berlin. Actually, Paris had astonished him. He had expected it to be like a tomb. He had met a German officer with whom he had been at school. They had made the rounds of the night spots together and found business booming. He assumed, of course, there "is another side to the Paris story," but he personally had not seen it.

The Prince was convinced that the Russians would eventually occupy Bucharest. When that unfortunate moment arrived, he intended to open a brothel, figuring that was the best, if not the only, way for a person like himself to earn money under a Russian occupation. He was quite annoyed that he had not thought of it before. "There has been a great need under the Germans for a chic, modern brothel, centrally located and run along imaginative lines." He had already selected the house he intended to use. On the street floor he would have a hat shop—"I just adore hats!" On the second floor there would be several large, beautifully furnished salons for the entertainment of the patrons. The three top floors would be given over to the women.

He described how, when the Germans marched into Paris, the windows of one of the large bookstores had displayed pictures of both Mussolini and Hitler, with the rest of the windows heaped with copies of only one book: Victor Hugo's *Les Misérables*. And he told us the story of a German officer, dining alone in a Paris restaurant where, at a nearby table, two French couples were making loud and unflattering comments about *les Boches*. After the German officer left, the headwaiter presented the two French couples with the officer's unpaid bill, to which was attached a note that read, "A German pays his bills. A *Boche*, never!"

In addition to Rumanians, I was also meeting with a considerable number of Yugoslavs. My interest in Yugoslavia, had continued after being aroused at the time of the assassinations of King Alexander and the French Foreign Minister, Louis Barthou, on the eve of the trip to Nazi Germany I made with Jean. I had been intrigued to discover that King Alexander and I were the same age, and that he had the distinction of having been sent to military school in Russia at the age of *one!*

Allen was already thoroughly familiar with both the history and present conditions in Yugoslavia, having at one point in his State Department career been in charge of the desk that dealt with the affairs of that
part of the world. He apparently knew the name of every city, town,
river, bridge, railway line, and personality in the entire country. One day
I gave him a slip of paper on which one of my Yugoslav contacts had
written a name which not only I but the general public had never heard
of at the time: Josip Broz, known to his followers as Tito. The name that
everyone then was familar with was that of the man with whom the
Allies, particularly the British, had been dealing, General Mikhailovich.
My contact said the Allies should forget about Mikhailovich and work
with Tito, whom my contact described, certainly with no exaggeration,
as a leftist.

I found the Yugoslavs I met extraordinarily interesting as individuals—
often fanatical and always with fiery personalities. I both enjoyed them
and admired them. The problem was that very few of them spoke English. Those who did spoke it almost imcomprehensibly. Their French
and German were apt to be a little better. Yugoslav names, both of
people and places, difficult enough in themselves, were different in every
language. My head would ache as I tried to decipher what my contacts
were telling me. Keeping track of the various languages spoken within
Yugoslavia itself compounded my difficulties. The Croats and Serbs
spoke different dialects of the same language and consequently could
understand each other. But the Serbs used the Cyrillic alphabet in writing
and the Croats, Latin characters.

The Serbs belonged to the Greek Orthodox Church, the Slovenes and
Croatians were Roman Catholics. In Bosnia and Herzegovina, there were
large numbers of Muhammadans left over from the Turkish conquest of
that part of the world in the days of the Ottoman Empire.

Most of the reports I received from Yugoslavs were absolutely hair-
raising: the activities of the secret police of the various factions—the
Ustachi and the Chetniks—the mass murders, the concentration camps,
and the increasing activities of various partisan groups, known as "the
men of the woods," who were receiving secret help from the populace of
the countryside. Yet, no matter how bloody the report or in what danger
the individual bringing it might be, after making his adventure-filled way
to Switzerland, he was eager to return as quickly as possible to his own
country and participate in the general slaughter.

XXIII

After the fall of Mussolini in the summer of 1943, Gisevius spent several of our working sessions berating me for the way the Allies had handled the situation in Italy, as if I were in some way responsible. He thought that the minute Mussolini fell, we should have made peace with the Italians and followed this up with peace offers to the Rumanians, Bulgarians, and Hungarians, all of whom, he claimed, had been watching how we treated Italy just as Hitler and Mussolini had watched how the League of Nations had dealt with Manchuria. He believed if we had made such peace offers, those particular Balkan countries would have fallen into our arms "like ripe fruit." This, he said, would have been so devastating to German morale that Germany would have collapsed "within seventy-two hours."

He never ceased to insist that everyone always overrated the Germans. I had difficulty believing that until I realized that what he meant was that no one understood precisely where German weaknesses lay and consequently really did tend to overrate them in some respects while underrating them in others.

Allied bombing of German cities, he claimed, was creating an enormous pool of people who had lost everything. In addition, there were twelve million foreign workers and prisoners of war in the country to augment this "proletarian mob." In Russia there were over five hundred thousand German prisoners of war, including thousands of officers and at least thirty generals whom the Russians had been indoctrinating and on whom they could impose any conditions they wished before permitting them to return home to Germany. The Freies Deutschland ("Free Germany") committee, established in Moscow after Stalingrad and headed by Field Marshal Friedrich von Paulus and General von Seydlitz, should not, he insisted, be taken lightly. The Russians held one trump card: They could offer the Germans the prospect of retaining their army intact, and that would have a very powerful appeal, particularly to the young officers for whom the German Army was the only remaining source of pride. In short, a great many factors already existed for making "an eastern solution" both possible and appealing. This was causing difficulties for the conspiracy of civilians and officers who wanted to get rid of Hitler—particularly the older men who, like Gisevius himself, favored "a western solution."

The Allies, he claimed, had said they were fighting fascism, Mussolini, and Hitler. Their behavior in Italy was proof they were doing nothing of the kind. Churchill had already said that he was fighting not just Hitler but Germany, and demanded unconditional surrender—"that stupid phrase with its overtones of revenge that will only make the Germans fight more desperately than ever." Actually, he considered the Russian *Mensch* admirable and claimed that the Russian women were the only virgins left in Germany. But no matter how admirable the individual Russian might be, Gisevius felt the Germans were much closer to us than Asiatics, and he considered the Russians Asiatics. If we didn't watch out, if we—and the British—"disappointed" the Germans, they might well fling themselves in the arms of the Russians, and the resultant terror would mean "the end of Western civilization."

I was beginning to get as sick of hearing that phrase—"the end of Western civilization"—as I was of "unconditional surrender." Throughout the thirties the threat held over our heads had been that this war, when it came, would mean "the end of Western civilization," particularly because of the availability of new and terrible poison gases. But as the war had dragged on and no gas had been used, the threat had been shifted to whatever horror the person considered the most devastating. This was more often than not the menace of Russian communism.

One evening Gisevius phoned around ten to ask if, in spite of the lateness of the hour, he might come by at once, he had something important to tell me. He insisted that I ask Jean, who happened to be at home, if such a late visit were all right with him. Jean, who made it a rule to be at his office every morning by seven-thirty, and invariably took to his bed with one of his beloved French detective stories when the clock struck eight, had already retired. But he said it was all right by him if Gisevius came by.

Within half an hour Gisevius appeared to tell me I must take an early-morning train to Bern and tell Allen to fire his cook. When he had been at the German legation earlier that day, someone had shown him a report that "a tall, heavy man" had come in the back way to Mr. Dulles's apartment and spent over an hour with him. This "tall, heavy man" had left his hat in the hall. In it were the initials H.B.G. Of course, Gisevius himself, being in the Abwehr, had a perfect right to see Allen, but certainly Allen couldn't have a cook who was a German agent working for him.

Ironically, although the lady in question was fired on the spot, she continued to hand in reports to the Germans and collect her pay. The person to whom she gave her reports naturally did not know she had been fired and Gisevius was not about to tell him. However, he continued to read the reports, which, he told me, were "occasionally surprisingly inventive."

When Gisevius was leaving our apartment that evening, he slipped on the outside stairs and dropped his briefcase, making a tremendous clatter. When I went in to tell Jean what Gisevius had told me, he listened without comment, then observed; "I advise you to tell Gisevius to learn to walk downstairs quietly before he tries to kill Hitler!" and promptly returned to reading his French detective novel, *Le Pot des Confitures (The Pot of Jam)*.

XXIV

For a time Mary Briner continued to help me with the translation of Gisevius's book. Then, because of other responsibilities, she had to abandon the project, but I still needed help.

Gisevius and I were no longer attracted to each other as we had been in the beginning. Things had settled down into a regular routine without any of the strong physical attraction that we had at first felt toward each other. This meant that Gisevius was no longer as inspired as he had been to tell me fascinating stories about his experiences in the Third Reich in order to impress me. But it was those stories that Allen was most interested in. I thought perhaps the storytelling might start up again if a new personality were injected into the situation. If Gisevius and I were the same psychological type, as Jung had told me we were, namely, extroverted intuitives, he, like myself, needed constantly new possibilities looming on the horizon in order for a situation to retain its zestfulness.

During the first weeks of my work with Gisevius, when the attraction between us was like that of a high-tension power line, he would often grab my hand and say, "Let's go to Lucerne for a couple of weeks and work on my book. I know just the place. Surely you can work something out."

The temptation was enormous, for he was right. I could have worked something out. Jean was still in Rumania; our maid was thoroughly reliable, and I had no qualms about leaving Mary Jane with her. Besides, at that moment I felt it would have served Allen right for all the work he was heaping on me and the difficult position he had put me in. But then my common sense, or actually what I thought of as my patriotism, would come to my rescue and I would resist.

One day, however, Gisevius begged me to go to Lugano with him, where he claimed to have at his disposal "a beautiful apartment" and where he would be meeting the first chief of the Gestapo, Rudolf Diels— and I nearly succumbed. Martha Dodd, the daughter of the American ambassador to Germany in the late thirties, had had an affair with Diels and I knew him to be a terrific ladies' man, despite his now being married to a relative of Hermann Goering, who kept a close eye on him. The dangers inherent in this expedition were nearly irresistible. But resist I did and felt very proud of myself for doing so. But when I told Allen about it, his only comment was, "Why the hell didn't you go? It might have been very interesting."

I had asked Professor Jung why he thought Gisevius had been able to survive in the Third Reich as long as he had. Jung's reply was that he imagined that it was at least partially because Gisevius's unconscious was tied into the German unconscious. Consequently, when he was with the Nazis, they didn't sense a foreign presence. Gisevius was fully conscious of his anti-Nazi sentiments and extremely clever about concealing them, but Jung pointed out that what other people "see" in a person is his or her unconscious. I had followed this up with a query about whether Jung didn't think that Gisevius was "close to the edge of being homosexual." And Jung had exclaimed, "Close to the edge? He *is* the edge!"

After that remark, I began to pay more attention to what Gisevius told me about various personal relationships within Germany. For instance, he claimed that the real bond between Himmler and Heydrich was that they had once been "involved" with each other, adding that if this type of involvement survived the breakup of the original affair, the relationship, just like a similar heterosexual relationship, was indestructible.

Sometimes Gisevius would bring me bits and pieces of information gathered by other intelligence services working with the Germans. He was particularly pleased when he reported that the Hungarians, in despair because they had been unable to document with whom Allen was sleeping—for, of course, in their eyes everyone had to be sleeping with someone—had concluded that Allen and Gero von Gaevernits, his assistant, must be having an affair because they were constantly together and Gero was so extremely handsome!

I realized then that if I were going to have someone replace Mary in helping me entertain Gisevius, it must be a worldly, sophisticated person, as well as someone with impeccable discretion. So I suggested to Allen that we ask the Honorable Elizabeth Scott-Montagu, whose cousin, Lord Lothian, had been the British ambassador in Washington to join us. Allen thought this an excellent idea.

Elizabeth had been driving an ambulance in France in the spring of 1940 when her unit had been cut off by the Germans racing toward Paris and she had fled into Switzerland with the Gestapo at her heels. She had first worked in the propaganda section of the British legation in Bern, then had moved to Zurich to form the Anglo-American Players and stage several plays as a kind of oblique Allied propaganda at the famous Schauspielhaus. When she had been looking for people to join her group, she had phoned me and suggested we meet.

Our meeting was a huge success. Elizabeth had a marvelous sense of humor, and we laughed over some of the absurdities of various situations in our respective legations, including well-meaning attempts at "oblique" Allied propaganda. She had had some experience in acting and eventually played the lead in two of the plays the Anglo-American Players staged. Later, she and I had worked together for the Praesens Film Company on a multilingual film, *The Last Chance,* about a group of refugees finding their way over the Alps to Switzerland from Italy, that was to win worldwide acclaim. So, before I even suggested to Allen that she join us, I knew that she and I could work well together.

Gisevius was enchanted at the thought of having a titled English lady working on his beloved manuscript. He knew all about Elizabeth, even informing me of something that I had not known, and that was that on her mother's side she was a direct descendant of Mary, Queen of Scots. He was as impressed by this touch of royal blood as all Europeans are by such connections.

Ever since we had been working together, he had been in the habit of sending me beautiful plants. On the morning of the day that Elizabeth was to join us, a huge blue hydrangea with blossoms at least eight inches in diameter arrived, purchased, I was later to learn, with Abwehr funds, as all similar offerings had been.

Elizabeth and I lunched together and Gisevius appeared around 2 P.M. I find that in my reports to Allen of those days I wrote up this first session with Elizabeth in some detail. It set the pattern for many subsequent sessions!

After Gisevius joined us, there was a certain amount of banter, then I suggested we have some coffee before getting down to work. Himmler

had just been made Minister of the Interior. Elizabeth asked what significance this might have. Gisevius replied it didn't have any particular
significance; Himmler had already had the power implicit in that office
for some time. The psychological effect on the German people would be
the same as on those in foreign countries: It would shake them up
considerably. But the most interesting recent shift in governmental posts
had involved Kurt Daluege who had gone insane from syphilis. Naturally this had not been disclosed. Good Nazis simply did not get syphilis. Daluege had handled all the police work for Himmler after
Heydrich's assassination, and losing both Heydrich and Daluege had
been a tremendous blow to Himmler, particularly since it had been
Himmler who had suggested to Hitler that Heydrich be replaced by
Daluege. Poor judgment on the part of his subordinates infuriated
Hitler.

"Why did Hitler make Himmler Minister of the Interior if it doesn't
mean anything?" Elizabeth asked.

"Because he always likes to have a cover for what he is actually
doing," Gisevius explained. "He had been looking for a figurehead to be
governor of Bohemia and Moravia, someone who would not necessarily
go there but would have the title of governor. Baron Konstantin von
Neurath, who has held that position until now, is finished. Frick, who
has been Minister of the Interior, is sixty-six. Himmler did Frick's work
anyhow, so Frick was the ideal choice. He'd never go near Prague.
Frank, a real swine, does all the dirty work there anyhow. Now Frank
will be promoted. Shifting people around like this preserves appearance.
And the German people can still be sucked in—if appearances are
preserved."

"Have you discussed any of this with Allen?" I asked.

"No . . ."

"Why not?"

"I don't find it particularly interesting. . . . Besides, he knows it
anyhow. You can't use this kind of thing on the Allied radio broadcasts
to Europe. This interpretation, I mean. The Germans wouldn't believe
it. . . . They'd just dismiss it as Allied propaganda. . . ."

"What about General Jeschonnek?" Elizabeth asked. "Did he really
commit suicide? There's a rumor he was murdered, you know . . ."

"Yes, I know. . . . I have no definite information. . . . But I have the
impression that something is not in order about his death. However, the
true story is probably not as dramatic as murder. Nothing ever is. . . ."

"Did Wolff kill Heydrich? We've heard that rumor, too."

"No . . . Wolff has been in trouble. But for a mésalliance. . . . Nothing else."

"I wish you'd tell me about yourself," said Elizabeth. "I know from your book that you were in the Gestapo until 1933 and that now you're in the Abwehr, attached as vice-consul to the consulate here. . . . But I've no idea what you do, either at the consulate or in the Abwehr."

"You wouldn't believe me if I told you."

"I'll believe you if it's true!"

"Well, I don't do anything. I hardly ever go to the consulate. . . . If I do, they all quake in their shoes. They think I'm Gestapo. Von Bibera— the German minister in Bern—can't make up his mind about me. Am I just an agent provocateur? Or am I actually Gestapo? If he'd ever voiced his suspicion to Himmler or Heydrich, my goose would have been cooked long ago. My Abwehr boss has the rank of colonel . . . I'm just a simple private in the ranks. . . . The last two times my boss tried to send me somewhere—first to Bordeaux, then Berlin—I refused to go. By the mere refusing, he decided I must be Gestapo, with enormous power and influence."

"Don't you have to send in any reports to keep your Abwehr job?"

I was glad Elizabeth had asked this question. It was something I had long wanted to know.

"Of course, I get orders to send in reports, but actually I haven't done a stroke of work for more than three years. . . . When I first came here, I expected it would be all over within six months. . . ."

"You actually never send in a report?" Elizabeth asked.

"Maybe sometimes a fantasy . . ."

"Like what?"

"Oh, the kind of thing Hitler likes for bedtime reading. . . . How Dulles had been in trouble years ago for cutting up babies and putting them in ashcans . . . that kind of thing."

"Don't be silly!" said Elizabeth, laughing. "Do you really never send in a report?"

"Never! No sheet of paper exists in the Third Reich on which I have written anything that could possibly be construed as of the slightest use to the Nazis. I've had some very narrow escapes. . . . Last March, for instance. They had me up before a court then. But you've no idea what I'm like when I'm mad. . . . How I can scare people. . . . They had in my dossier a verbatim description of a row I'd had with Canaris as a result of which Canaris didn't speak to me for three months. Everything

in my dossier was true, but for some reason they didn't believe it."

"I believe that you can scare people!" I interjected. "But you'll still have to convince me that the Nazis are as stupid as you make them out to be."

"All right," said Gisevius. "Have it your way! But I assure you they are stupid."

At this point I suggested that we might do a bit of translating. The passage we selected had to do with how Heines, police chief of Breslau, had "knocked down a waiter" when leaving a restaurant.

Gisevius interrupted. "Not knocked down," he said irritably. "He pulled out his gun and shot the man."

I couldn't help laughing at his expression of disgust.

"You may laugh," Gisevius said indignantly, "but the waiter didn't!"

After about an hour of translating, Gisevius left us.

"I can certainly see the problem," said Elizabeth. "I do think the best way to work is to get as much translating as possible done when he is not here. Then we can concentrate on entertaining him when the three of us are together. If we come to a place in the manuscript that is just sheer drivel, that horrible German philosophical fog, we can gang up on him. Try to persuade him to cut it or, better yet, just throw it out entirely. Otherwise we can just flatter him. I suspect that vanity is not one of his lesser characteristics!"

So that was the way we worked from then on. Gisevius no longer had the escape hatch of claiming my objections were simply those of a "sensation-loving American." England was now backing me up. Once the translating was out of the way, Elizabeth and I would focus our entire attentions on the author, and off he'd go into his fascinating stories that were so useful in giving helpful insights into the personalities and intrigues of the Nazis.

Once Elizabeth asked him where he drew the line so that he didn't feel like a traitor.

"That's comparatively easy," he said. "For instance, if I knew German troops were going over the Brenner Pass to Italy on a specific day, I wouldn't tell Dulles so he could order an Allied raid and get another feather in his cap. But if I learned a piece of political news, for example, that an invasion of Sweden was being planned, I might alert him to that, because something might be done to put a stop to it."

XXV

When Jean returned from his fifth trip to Rumania since the outbreak of war, he brought with him four loaves of white bread, four kilos of bacon, a huge salami, two kilos of pork fat, and three kilo tins of foie gras. He had had a good trip home, leaving Bucharest at 2 P.M. Wednesday and reaching Zurich at 3 P.M. Friday. The Germans at the frontier hadn't even bothered to open his bags, saying, "What? You here again?" The man who was supposed to make him undress to be searched simply took him into the room reserved for such purposes, offered him a cigar, and spent the whole time explaining how he must go to the United States as soon as the war was over and that Jean must help him get a visa.

Allen had been beside himself with eagerness for Jean's return. On August 1, Allied planes had raided the Rumanian oil fields at Ploesti, and Allen, realizing that the railroad ran by these fields, knew Jean would be able to give him a firsthand report of the damage caused by the raid. He even suggested that I go up to meet Jean at the frontier and that we go directly over to Bern from there. But I knew this wouldn't sit too well with Jean. After such a long trip, the one thing he looked forward to was a hot bath and a good night's sleep. I planned not even to bring up the subject of going to Bern to see Allen until the following day, but Jean knew me better than to assume that I had no such plan.

"I suppose I'm to go over to Bern tomorrow to see His Highness," he said as we were having dinner.

I laughed. "You're right," I said. "But, please, don't do it just for me. I don't want you to have any difficulties just because of the Americans . . ."

Now it was his turn to laugh. "You forget my Germans on the frontier," He said. "They probably won't be able to sleep tonight because I'm not already in Bern!"

So I gave Allen a call to say we'd be over for dinner the following evening, then handed the phone to Jean. His end of the conversation was not very illuminating. "Yes! Yes!" he said. "Yes—a fine trip. Yes, of course. We'll be delighted." And that was that.

During the course of the evening, Jean told me he had found the atmosphere in both Vienna and Munich certainly no worse than on his last trip. The trains were overcrowded but ran on time. However, the feeling in Rumania was less anti-German than on his previous visits. The Rumanians were feeling much more kindly toward the Germans because they were defending them against the Russians. The Germans had thrown sixty divisions against the Russians—at least that was the talk in Bucharest. German staff officers had stayed in the city during this period and had given the people great confidence because they had looked so competent.

The Rumanians were greatly upset by the bombing of Sofia. They couldn't understand why Sofia had been bombed and not Bucharest. Their pride had been hurt! What the Rumanians themselves called their adaptability, but which others referred to as their opportunism, had begun to surface in various ways. Some were now explaining that they actually had Russian blood or Russian relatives. Russian prisoners had recently been released. And Rumanians born in Bessarabia, or who could speak Russian but had previously pretended they couldn't even understand it, now chattered openly in Russian. Yet even they still clung to the Germans, praying to be spared what everyone in Bucharest recognized as probably inevitable—a Russian occupation. The American prisoners were being treated like lords. When some of them had wanted to go to the movies, the adjutant asking permission was told by the Rumanian officer in charge, "For God's sake, let them do anything they want. Only don't come asking my permission or I'll have these damn Germans on my neck!"

Shortly before Jean left Bucharest there had been a trial of two Rumanian officers accused of shooting a German SS officer. When the Rumanians were acquitted, there was great rejoicing. The incident had involved a regiment of Rumanian soldiers who had adopted a little eight-year-old orphan girl, very bright, very pretty, whom the soldiers adored.

In the barracks one evening, the German SS officer had asked her what her name was. She had told him an obviously Jewish name. The SS officer then said, "Open your mouth and shut your eyes and I'll give you something to make you wise." The little girl opened her mouth, shut her eyes, and the SS officer shot her dead. The story was the talk of Bucharest and was published in all the newspapers.

The next evening in Bern, Jean gave Allen a detailed account of the devastation at Ploesti. The oil fields, he said, were now very heavily guarded with antiaircraft guns mounted on flat cars, and a new railway siding had been built on which tank cars were hidden among the trees. Jean had been standing at the window of his compartment in the train, trying to memorize every last detail of the damage Allied planes had done, when a drunken German officer had appeared beside him and had proceeded to lament the terrible things that were happening, insisting that Jean take repeated drinks from a whiskey bottle he was carrying. Jean, not wanting to argue or have his reactions dimmed by whiskey, would tip the bottle up to his lips, pretend to take a swallow, and hand it back to the German, whose maudlin lamentations continued until he collapsed on one of the seats in the compartment and snored until the train reached Budapest. At that moment he had jumped up, glared at Jean with no sign of recognition, and to Jean's intense relief descended from the train without another word. It was not often, Jean pointed out, that one saw a drunken German officer—in fact, he had never seen one before. He considered his traveling companion's behavior indicative of a deterioration in German morale.

Gisevius continued to come to our apartment to work, but he and Jean had not yet met. Then one afternoon when only Gisevius, not Elizabeth, was there, Jean suddenly appeared—charm incarnate. Gisevius made a speech about "having enjoyed the hospitality of your home for so long and being so very appreciative."

Jean, all smiles, murmured, "Please! Please!"

Almost at once they discovered mutual friends, Jean having over the years worked with many Germans. Then Jean said he had received two phone calls from Rumania that afternoon: "The situation there is very dark," he said.

Gisevius agreed. "I imagine they will make their last stand in the Carpathians," he said.

Jean imagined so too.

They discussed the "stupidity" of the English and the Americans for not landing in the Balkans after the fall of Mussolini—and again they agreed. They shared the same views about how bitter the Yugoslav partisans must be and what a trump card their "deception" would be in the hands of the Russians. They went into ecstasies over the beauties of Split and the whole Dalmatian coast and agreed they would take me there the minute the war was over.

I said I'd rather go to Berlin.

"Ach, Berlin!" they exclaimed in unison, and Jean went on to tell us about his first trip to Berlin when he was twenty-one, how he had had his picture taken in a bus, and had treasured it over the years.

Gisevius found this "touching."

Gisevius said how much he appreciated my work, how difficult translating was. Jean said nothing was harder than translating. Gisevius agreed and said he thought English a beautiful language. Again Jean agreed.

I saw no reason to point out that they had both told me repeatedly that English was a "terrible language." Gisevius said English would soon be the "world language." Jean thought so, too. They discussed Winston Churchill's vocabulary, both claiming to admire it, although both had previously complained to me about Churchill's "purple prose."

Gisevius said he was looking forward to visiting the United States. He liked Americans so very much. Jean said that was fortunate.

"Why?" asked Gisevius.

"Because it makes certain death easier!" said Jean.

Shouts of mutual laughter.

After Gisevius left, Jean, having done his bit for the Allied cause, hung up his charm-incarnate cloak and would only say that he liked Gisevius, adding, "He is *not* a Nazi . . ."

I thought it easier to let it go at that. Both Jean and Gisevius had behaved perfectly from my point of view. I was not actually surprised that Jean had behaved so well for I knew he had been sincere when he had told me I could do anything within reason to help the Allied cause. But I was lost in admiration of Gisevius's behavior. At every moment his reactions had been very subtly calculated to make the best possible impression on Jean. No wonder, I thought, that the conspirators had picked him as an emissary.

Some days later Allen telephoned to ask if it would be all right with Jean if he and Gisevius met at our place that evening. I said that Jean had left on an audit, but that it would be all right with me.

"Fine," said Allen. "Will you set it up for eight-thirty? Get some cold cuts. I'll provide the coupons. Gisevius knows I'm phoning you and he will be calling you later."

When Gisevius called, I told him I was expecting him at 8:30 and I was providing supper. "Fine!" he said and hung up.

At 8:45 neither of them had appeared. I had no idea where they were or what they were up to. By 9:15, still no show. Ours was a very dark street. One or both of them could have been murdered in the blackout, for in spite of Swiss neutrality and a very strict control of foreigners on Swiss soil, on occasion the Gestapo infiltrated people into the country and an assassination was not beyond the realm of possibility.

I went downstairs, opened the front door, and peered out in the darkness. It was deathly still. What could be keeping them? My heart was going like a trip-hammer, my mouth felt dry, my hands icy. I went back upstairs, tried to read, couldn't concentrate, went out into the kitchen and looked at the cold cuts and salad in the icebox, then paced around for another fifteen minutes.

Suddenly I was filled with an overwhelming rage. How dare they upset me like this? What right had they to disrupt my life? I wished I had never met either of them. The angrier I got, the more detached I felt until I reached a point where it was a matter of indifference to me whether they had both been murdered in the blackout.

At that instant, the front doorbell rang. "Sorry to be late," said Allen, charging into the hallway, his hat on the back of his head, his coat pockets stuffed with newspapers. "Where is he?"

"He hasn't come yet . . ."

"He hasn't? Perhaps he's been killed!" Loud laughter.

"Perhaps."

"Good! Then I can eat all the cold cuts . . . I'm starved." More shouts of laughter.

Another ring at the front door and Gisevius rushed in. "Sorry," he said. "I was detained . . . I . . ."

"Never mind. . . . It doesn't matter," said Allen. "I just got here myself . . . Get the food, Mary!"

So I got the food and for nearly two hours I sat there listening to those two saying nothing—absolutely nothing—of the slightest importance about anything pertaining to the war.

At one point Allen asked, "How is the coast of France fortified?" To which Gisevius replied icily, "I think the Gaullists have the correct information about that!" But aside from this abortive sortie, nothing. All I could think of was what the American press would have said if they had known that the chief of the OSS in Switzerland and an Abwehr officer were devouring cold cuts together in the apartment of an American woman after arriving separately and secretly in the blackout.

XXVI

Early in July Gisevius phoned to say he was going away for a few days. "Homer" would drop by to give me some pages of the manuscript that he had been reworking. Homer was Eddie Waetjen, Gisevius's friend and Abwehr colleague who was also attached to the German consulate in Zurich under the usual diplomatic immunity. The reason for the selection of his particular cover name for Eddie had been that he was translating the *Odyssey* from the original Greek for his own amusement. His mother was an American, and he had a sister married to an American and living in the States. He had a delightful sense of humor, was very easy to talk to, and a person of whom I had grown extremely fond.

When he arrived that afternoon, he seemed curiously distrait. He laid the manuscript on the table without making any comment about it.

"Why didn't Gisevius bring that back himself?" I asked.

Eddie hesitated. "I hoped you wouldn't ask," he said. "Actually, he's gone back to Germany . . ."

Gisevius had told me repeatedly that he would not go back to Germany again until the moment he and his friends had been waiting for in order to kill Hitler had arrived.

"Does Allen know?" I asked.

"Yes," said Eddie.

Because of my feeling that to talk about something was apt to put a jinx on it, I quickly changed the subject. Where were Eddie and his family planning to spend the summer?

"In Ascona," he said.

I myself had rented a house for me and Mary Jane in Ascona for six weeks beginning July 15. Jean was going to be doing a lot of traveling; the lease on our Zurich apartment was running out. We were moving into a new apartment in September. And before that Maria was going home on vacation. Besides I myself felt badly in need of a vacation. Eddie was delighted with this news. I'd been working much too hard, he said. Several weeks in Ascona would do me good and I could take advantage of Gisevius's absence to make some progress on his book.

Ascona, in the Tessin, on the shores of Lake Maggiore and a short distance from the Italian frontier, was an ideal place to relax, the one place in Switzerland that had anything even remotely resembling a bohemian atmosphere, the only place to pick up a few extra eggs, some butter or salad oil, besides the minuscule amounts of such essentials provided on our rationing cards. I was determined to get the maximum benefit from no translating, no entertaining of authors, no meetings with foreign nationals with complicated stories to tell or mysterious axes to grind. In fact, I had told Allen, "No work, and above all no excitement of any kind!"

My natural instinct had always been to flow out toward people, without an *arrière pensée* in my head. The work I had been doing, with its necessity of regarding everyone I met with suspicion and mistrust, had put a terrible strain on my nerves. And, of course, having to sit down and write up each meeting as factually as possible, while selecting facts in such a way as to give the correct impression, was no small task, granted my own particular way of "seeing" things not necessarily visible to the naked eye. I had, it was true, developed a special kind of shorthand for communicating with Allen and with some of the other people with whom I worked. But because this shorthand was different in each instance, it often complicated rather than simplified the process.

One of my colleagues, Bob Shea, would become frantic whenever Henry Hyde, who did such splendid work with the French *Résistance,* and I would be discussing a situation. Henry, witty and intuitive, had been educated abroad, spoke French like a native and fluent German. He thought and spoke with the speed of light and had immense charm.

Neither Henry nor I needed to finish our sentences when communicating with each other. A conversation between us would go something like this:

"You see, the point was that if he could get to Lyons . . ."

"Precisely! But that's why I told Pierre . . ."

"I know. That's what I pointed out to Helene when . . ."

"But she could have taken . . ."

"No. The seven-fifteen P.M. was all right in case . . ."

"But he didn't . . ."

At this point, Bob, who had been getting increasingly red in the face, would explode, *"Why can't either of you finish your sentences?"*

The house we had rented in Ascona was not much larger than a child's playhouse: two small rooms, a minuscule kitchen, and an equally diminutive bathroom. It didn't even have a telephone. It was set in a tiny garden filled with flowers, with a mother cat and three kittens in residence. There were several toads in the garden, as well as butterflies and bumblebees, all of which intrigued the kittens.

The weather was perfect the first four days we were there, but on the afternoon of July 19, huge thunderheads started piling up around the lake. By the time I was ready to prepare dinner, the sky was black as night. There were flashes of lightning and rumblings of thunder in the distance.

Mary Jane had put out a saucer of fresh milk for the cat and her kittens; they were lapping it up contentedly when there was a flash of lightning, a tremendous clap of thunder, and in through the kitchen window sailed a small, black, cross-eyed kitten with a huge toad in its mouth. The mother cat and her kittens scattered in alarm. The black kitten dropped the toad and, with hisses worthy of an animal ten times its size, made for the milk.

Mary Jane and I were as startled as the mother cat and her kittens. That flash of lightning, that violent clap of thunder, made us both feel as if this tiny ball of black fur had literally arrived from heaven—or more likely—hell. I felt goose pimples rising on my arms. When either of us approached the kitten, it would arch its back, stare at us with a wild expression, and hiss like a tiny dragon.

When the kitten had finished the milk, it accepted another saucerful. The other kittens and their mother had taken refuge under one of the beds and nothing would persuade them to come out. In the meantime, the toad had recovered sufficiently to hop out the door and disappear into the downpour.

We got very little rest that night. If there came a lull between the moment when one thunderstorm retreated and another arrived, there would be hissings and scamperings, punctuated by growls that sounded more like those of a lion than a kitten.

The next morning it was still raining and thundering. The black kitten kept the mother cat and her kittens terrorized under the beds. If Mary Jane tried to catch it, it would start racing around the room at such a rate that I expected it to dash up a wall and across the ceiling. This was no normal kitten. Could it be some kind of evil omen?

Just as I was starting to scramble eggs for our lunch on the twentieth, the clock in the village struck noon. Mary Jane reached over and switched the radio to Beromunster. Over the air came a special announcement: An attempt had been made on the life of the Führer. The attempt had failed. A number of high officers had been arrested. . . .

I looked at Mary Jane. She stared back at me. She understood as well as I what had happened.

We kept the radio on for the rest of the day, turning the dial constantly. One version would be given by one station, a different version by another. It was impossible to get a clear picture of what had actually happened. One familiar name after another came over the air as having been arrested or executed by the Gestapo. Gisevius was not mentioned, but that didn't mean he was safe. There were continuing reports of massive arrests and executions, of conflicting orders to different army groups.

After supper, Mary Jane and I went down to the village and I called Allen from a public phone. "You've been listening to the radio?" he asked.

"Yes . . ."

"Well, I don't know anything more than you do. . . . You might drop in on our friend up on the hill. He'll be in touch. . . . How's the weather down there?"

"Terrible."

"Well, cheer up. Things will work out somehow. . . ."

Not exactly an enlightening or reassuring conversation, but it did make me feel better. The reference to "our friend on the hill" was, of course, to Eddie Waetjen. We found Eddie and his family gathered around the radio, knowing little more than we did.

During the following days, bits and pieces of information came trickling in. Occasionally, there would be some good news, but on the whole it was all bad for the conspirators. My plans for a calm and restful vacation were shattered.

I felt a curious sense of unreality, just as I had when I had listened to Neville Chamberlain announcing that England was at war with Germany. All I could think about was that enormous expenditure of time and energy by the conspirators, all those complicated and dangerous intrigues. And now this fizzling failure. . . .

XXVII

We returned to Zurich on the first of September with our furious black kitten, who refused to stay in the basket we had purchased for his transportation. He clawed, hissed, and growled until the conductor took pity on us and moved us into a first-class compartment with a door that could be closed and the kitten could be let out of his basket. Once installed in first-class splendor, he was satisfied and sat gazing quietly out the window all the way to Zurich.

Before Gisevius left for Germany, he had given Allen a memo, which Allen sent me to translate on my return from Ascona. The memo was nearly twenty pages long, much of it a rehash of the ideas that Gisevius had been hammering on ever since I had known him. It had been written on the assumption that the assassination attempt would succeed and that Hitler "would end as a political and military failure, so that this time there would be no stab-in-the-back legend as there was after World War I."

The entire memo was a warning against such a possibility. It strongly urged that the Germans be allowed to punish the war criminals themselves, to conduct their own "general housecleaning." Although fully justified feelings of revenge might—and probably would—make the Allies wish to do this themselves, it was far more important, he pointed out, that the trials and general cleanup be handled in such a way that in ten, twenty, or even a hundred years, it would all seem "equitable and morally justified, not only to the outside world, but above all to the Germans themselves."

The memo concluded with some rather bitter comments about the skepticism with which the outside world had always regarded the German opposition. And it emphasized the importance of the role the opposition could play in the work of reconstruction, not so much because most of the conspirators came from the more privileged classes, but rather because they were among the most competent men in Germany and the best suited to accomplish the tremendous tasks ahead.

It was disheartening to read this memo after what had happened and to realize how many of the men identified as among the most competent and "certainly the best friends of the West in Germany," were already dead. I was reminded of the colloquy in the film *La Grande Illusion,* between Jean Gabin, as the French officer, and Erich von Stroheim, his German counterpart, when they agreed that the real loser in the war of 1914–1918 had been the European upper class, the true bearer of European culture and tradition and the class to which they both belonged in their respective countries.

Elizabeth Montagu and I speculated constantly about the chances of our ever seeing Gisevius again. We'd take out the manuscript and run through it, checking those places where we thought a few more facts or the inclusion of some of the stories he had told us would make it livelier and more interesting. We occasionally even indulged in a bit of gallows humor, planning, if he never returned to shape the manuscript as we thought best and publish it ourselves, prefaced, of course, by an extremely moving tribute to the author.

Then one day in late January 1945, the phone rang, and I heard the familiar, "*HALLOO!* When can we meet?" he asked. "There is *so* much to talk about! Could you possibly come to my place? I'm not feeling too well . . ."

"How about two o'clock?"

"Good! I will be expecting you!"

When he opened the door of his suite in the hotel, I was shocked. He looked at least ten years older. His hair had turned gray, and he had lost a tremendous amount of weight. He made a valiant effort to be his old, enthusiastic self, but shortly tiny beads of sweat appeared on his forehead and he looked as if he were about to faint. He was obviously in no state to talk about his experiences.

I pretended that I had a lot of work to do and had only rushed down to see him because I was so delighted he was back. He seemed greatly relieved. Could I perhaps come back tomorrow or even the next day?

There was really nothing wrong with him physically. He just felt "*kaput*—like a broken spring.*"

When I returned two days later, he plunged at once into the story of all that had happened to him since we last met. At times even I, familiar as I was with all the people involved, had difficulty following him. What made it so confusing was to keep in mind that what the conspirators were attempting was not only to kill Hitler, but to use this as a signal to start a military putsch to take over control of Germany and to install a temporary military government under General Beck. Then, as soon as order had been restored, this military government was to be superseded by a civilian government under Carl Goerdeler, the former mayor of Leipzig, as Chancellor. The conspirators had hoped that this civilian government would be acceptable to the Allies for negotiating peace.

During the next two weeks, I went to see Gisevius at his place for a couple of hours each day, during which he talked without stopping. Then, as he began to wilt, we'd break off and I'd go home to write up what he had told me for Allen. Eventually, Gisevius left Zurich for a house he had rented on the Lake of Geneva, where he had installed his mother and his fiancée, Gerda, in whose house he had hidden in Berlin. There he set to work writing up his experiences on July 20 as well as the events leading up to it and following it. This meant that once more Elizabeth and I were back at our job of translating, with Gisevius appearing periodically in Zurich to go over what we had done and telling us further anecdotes about his ordeal.

In the weeks immediately preceding July 20, the war had been going very badly for the Germans. The Russians were pushing rapidly forward in the east. German generals by the dozen were surrendering virtually without a fight. In the west, the Hitler-Rommel strategy of forcing the Allies into a holding position had failed.

Elizabeth and I had noticed how extremely nervous Gisevius was. He was constantly on the move—Basel, Bern, Geneva, the Grisons, back to Zurich again, telephoning occasionally but no longer appearing regularly to talk or work on the book.

He had been at Davos when he got a call from Theodor Struenck. Struenck was a member of the Abwehr through whom Gisevius had previously sent an urgent message to General Beck that since there would be no help from Britain and the United States, there was no point in negotiating further with those countries. The conspirators must go ahead on their own, and the sooner, the better.

Gisevius had assumed that Struenck was bringing him word that the conspirators were finally going to act. Instead, on arriving in Zurich, he learned that Struenck had come to warn him of his own great personal danger. There had been an "indiscretion," and Gisevius had come under suspicion. Nebe and Colonel Georg Hansen, a friend of the conspirators who had taken over the remnants of the Abwehr after Admiral Canaris, its former chief, had been ousted, had been questioned by Obergruppen-führer Ernst Kaltenbrunner, chief of the Security Office under Heinrich Himmler. Himmler had ordered Gisevius brought back to Germany and intended calling him to the colors so that he could be arrested as an army deserter if he refused.

"Aren't they ready to act yet?" Gisevius had demanded somewhat irritably.

"They claim the assassination will take place any day now," Struenck replied. "But you know how often we have been disappointed. Actually, sometimes Hansen seems doubtful of Stauffenberg."

Colonel Count Klaus von Stauffenberg, of the German General Staff, who had agreed to place the bomb in Hitler's headquarters, was a deeply religious man who equated the salvation of the nation with the salvation of the army. Extremely ambitious, hoping one day to command the army himself, he had been seriously wounded in combat, having lost an eye and part of one hand.

"Does he at least still claim to want to do it?" asked Gisevius.

"He says he is going to do it," Struenck replied. "But some of the Stauffenberg group are apparently still suffering from religious scruples about actually killing the Führer!"

However, the personal messages Struenck had brought Gisevius from Beck, Goerdeler, and Hansen satisfied him that matters had at last pro-gressed beyond the stage of purely theoretical discussions. Only two questions remained open: Would Stauffenberg lose his nerve? Would the Gestapo get wind of the conspiracy before the attempt could be undertaken?

Gisevius decided not to fake an illness as Hansen had suggested but to return to Berlin with Struenck. Everything went smoothly at the frontier. Apparently, it never occurred to the officials there to look at their list of wanted persons, on which, of course, Gisevius's name already appeared.

Struenck went straight through to Berlin, but Gisevius changed trains at Wannsee, got off at Zehlendorf, and walked the few hundred yards to the home of Count Helldorf, figuring the last place the Gestapo would look for him would be in the home of the Berlin police chief.

But when he reached Helldorf's house, he found gaping ruins on either side and the house itself badly damaged. A servant still on the premises told him that Helldorf was staying at a hotel in the city. Gisevius called Helldorf from a pay phone and Helldorf suggested that Gisevius come to see him at once.

When Gisevius arrived at Helldorf's office, Helldorf, debonair as ever, inquired if Gisevius had guessed that the assassination planned for the previous day would be called off. Goering and Himmler had not shown up, and Stauffenberg had been unwilling to set off the bomb unless there was a chance of getting them, too.

The conspirators, Helldorf continued, were still sticking to their original plan: Once the bomb was set off, General Olbricht, Deputy Commander of the Replacement Army, would summon Helldorf to German Army headquarters and declare the Berlin police subject to German Army orders. Helldorf would then order the police apparatus paralyzed for the next few critical hours. The police would resume their functions under military control only after tanks had surrounded all government buildings. Nebe had been informed of the entire plan and had taken the necessary measures for handling the criminal police.

Gisevius had been disturbed by Helldorf's apparent lack of enthusiasm. Helldorf admitted that he was concerned, but he urged Gisevius to talk to Nebe. Nebe, he said, was extremely pessimistic. This disturbed Gisevius even more. After all, Nebe, with his close Gestapo connections, might have sensed more than Helldorf.

After leaving Helldorf's office, Gisevius made his way to the Struencks'. There, he learned that Colonel Hansen would come by that evening, but Nebe would not be able to make it until the next day.

After lunch, Gisevius decided to visit General Beck, whom he found working at his home in Lichterfelde.

"At last!" Beck exclaimed when Gisevius was ushered into his study.

Beck appeared outwardly as calm and optimistic as ever, but he cautioned Gisevius not to expect too much "afterward." The situation in the East was desperate. The Center Army Group no longer existed. The front in the west was still holding, but Field Marshal von Kluge, commanding in the west, had sent word that there would probably be a breakthrough within two weeks. And Field Marshal Erwin Rommel's estimate was only a week longer.

Beck suggested that Gisevius get in touch with Stauffenberg as soon as possible. Stauffenberg recently had been of tremendous help to the conspirators at headquarters, having actually taken over most of the work.

By six o'clock, Gisevius was back at the Struencks', where Goerdeler arrived shortly.

"What's going to happen now?" Gisevius asked as soon as they had taken their places in the Struencks' sitting room.

Goerdeler shrugged. "Apparently the attempt is going to be made at last, but . . ." He shrugged again. "Beck thinks very highly of Stauffenberg," he added.

"But how do *you* get along with Stauffenberg?" Gisevius asked.

Goerdeler tipped his head back and stared at the ceiling. "Well," he said finally, "if he were not a young man and if I were not so much older, I would not be able to take the way he cuts me off short. . . . As it is . . ." Another shrug.

At first, Goerdeler said, the original plan for the division of work had been strictly followed. The military men had dealt with the technical strategy of the putsch, the civilians had worked on the political end. Beck had been the strongest advocate of this viewpoint, entrusting all political preparations to Goerdeler.

Recently, however, Stauffenberg had refused to abide by the original agreement and had insisted on taking over the political as well as the military direction himself. He felt that Germany's hope lay in the military and he wanted to retain all the militaristic and socialistic elements of National Socialism. He had even tried, Goerdeler said somewhat bitterly, to get two different labor leaders to oppose him for Chancellor in the new government.

It was nearly midnight when there was a knock at the door and Mrs. Struenck opened it to admit Hansen and Stauffenberg. Stauffenberg was wearing a black patch over one eye and in the course of the evening frequently lifted it to dab at his eye with a wad of cotton.

As he sat there with his arms hanging limply at his sides and his legs in their heavy boots stretched out in front of him, Gisevius reflected that he certainly didn't look like the ardent disciple of the poet Stefan George that Gisevius knew him to be. His voice, too, was in contrast to his massive build. Hoarse, but at the same time, soft.

Stauffenberg said that Gisevius undoubtedly knew how grave the situation was, but he, as Chief of Staff to the Commander of the Home Army, would be glad to fill him in about anything with which he was not familar. Of course, Gisevius had just come from Switzerland, where all manner of information was available. What were his impressions of the situation?

Gisevius explained the radical shift that had taken place in Allied attitudes during the past few months, and how, after the invasion, there had been absolutely no chance of persuading the Allies to help the conspirators. Gisevius personally felt there was no longer any chance of avoiding a total occupation of Germany with all the consequences implicit therein. Actually, the only subject left for discussion was whether the Germans themselves would take matters into their own hands and get rid of Hitler or wait for others to do it for them.

"Isn't it altogether too late for the West?" Stauffenberg asked when Gisevius had finished.

Hansen gave Gisevius a significant look. Gisevius had said nothing about the West.

Stauffenberg said that he didn't want Gisevius to misunderstand him. He had not yet decided this West-East question in his own mind.

Then Gisevius and Stauffenberg began arguing about whether or not the Russians would actually take Berlin within a few weeks. Stauffenberg could back up his arguments with a technical military knowledge that Gisevius did not possess. And he took Gisevius's comment that, until now all military prognoses had proved erroneous, as a personal insult.

"How do you know that I will even set off the bomb?" Stauffenberg demanded suddenly.

"Why else have you come here?" Gisevius retorted, and the subject was dropped.

Stauffenberg insisted that after the assassination the question of purges must be handled with extreme care. He had no objection to punishing the Nazi and Gestapo killers, but he would not permit any of the field marshals to be condemned because of their spineless attitude toward Hitler's invasions.

Gisevius said that only a broad purge would convince the Allies that there had been a fundamental change rather than merely a tactical shift. Stauffenberg asked how the honor and reputation of the army could possibly be preserved if the pettiness and recklessness of its leaders were revealed? And he added, much to Gisevius's dismay, that Gisevius's book, with its attacks on the generals, would naturally have to be banned.

Gisevius let this pass, and asked Stauffenberg to give his regards to Olbricht, who he would be glad to see if he so wished. Stauffenberg became extremely agitated. He said Gisevius knew quite well that the Gestapo was looking for him. Gisevius replied that he had no intention of doing anything rash. He planned to see no one except Beck, Goerdeler, Nebe, and Helldorf.

Hansen, apparently deciding that it served no useful purpose to have Gisevius and Stauffenberg quarreling, pointed out that it was nearly dawn. He and Stauffenberg had better leave.

As Stauffenberg was bidding the Struencks good-bye, Hansen took Gisevius's arm and said in a low voice, "We must talk. . . . I'll come by tomorrow morning." He gave Gisevius a meaningful glance and murmured under his breath what Gisevius said would always remain for him the final verdict on July 20: "This whole thing strikes me as so frivolous! . . . It . . . simply . . . cannot be . . . done . . . this . . . way!"

On the morning of the thirteenth there had been an Allied air raid that had lasted an hour. Afterward, Gisevius had gone to see Helldorf to give him his impressions of Stauffenberg. Later, Nebe joined them, complaining as usual about the incompetence of the generals.

Gisevius returned to the Struencks', where he found Hansen, who explained that when he took Stauffenberg home the night before, they had quarreled furiously, so loudly, in fact, that the chauffeur must have overheard what they were saying. This was something for which both the Struencks and Hansen were to pay heavily later. Nevertheless, Hansen insisted, no matter what disagreements he and Stauffenberg had had, he still admired Stauffenberg's superb talents as a military man and his gift for organization as well as his culture. It was quite an experience to hear Stauffenberg recite Stefan George's poems as he often did for hours on end. He was certainly superior to his colleagues in many ways, but it was quite impossible to discuss politics with him. In recent months he had definitely changed—become increasingly secretive and subject to whims, even quite tyrannical at times. Hansen attributed these changes to the terrible wounds he had received rather than to any pressures resulting from his involvement in the putsch. Actually, he could still talk to him when they were alone together. He just felt ill at ease with that "debating club" that Stauffenberg had gathered around him.

Those debates, about the justification for the assassination, about what could be done in the East, and about socialism, went on continuously. It was impossible to get down to basics, to discuss with Stauffenberg or with anyone in his circle the technical details of the putsch. Just a few weeks before, Stauffenberg had been talking about playing off the West against the East. Recently, there had even been talk of a joint march of the German and Russian armies against the plutocracies. The military disaster on the eastern front had only served to accelerate this radical reorientation.

After lunch, Gisevius hurried off to see Beck. Beck wanted to go over everything from the beginning and insisted on putting it all down on paper, this being the only way he could work. Men of Beck's generation had no conception of how, under a terror, everyone, including one's own children, must be regarded as potentially dangerous spies. Nor did it occur to such old school gentlemen that any slip of paper, even if only written for one's own private information, might find its way into the hands of the Gestapo with devastating results for all concerned. Gisevius was only too aware of this problem.

Finally, the discussion had turned to the technique of the putsch itself. Stauffenberg would get a chance to plant the bomb at the next conference at Hitler's headquarters, probably on the fifteenth, Beck pointed out. It was still an open question, however, as to where this conference would be held. It would undoubtedly be attended by various high officers, so there was a chance of some innocent victims. Immediately after the bomb exploded, the headquarters' communications center would be put out of commission. This would insure that headquarters would be cut off from the outside world for several hours and prevent the issuance of counterorders should there be any survivor with the authority to issue them.

As soon as the code word, Valkyrie, was given, the troops stationed around Berlin would start moving in. During the first three "stagnant" hours, the conspirators would have to rely on the battalion under the command of Major Otto Remer. An attempt would be made to draw General Friedrich Fromm, Commander of the Replacement Army, over to the side of the conspirators, which would greatly facilitate matters. Olbricht thought it likely Fromm would accept a fait accompli. Field Marshal von Witzleben was to take general command of all the armed forces.

Beck had worked out a careful plan for preserving the civilian character of the putsch: The troops would be subordinate to him as Chief of State. He also intended to place the police under his jurisdiction so as to be able to coordinate them with the army in the early stages of the putsch. Because of Gisevius's police experience, Beck was counting on Gisevius to work directly under him in connection with the police. Beck told Gisevius that he thought he shouldn't be too upset by Stauffenberg's talk. He hadn't the slightest doubt of Stauffenberg's loyalty or of his own ability to handle him.

When Gisevius returned to the Struencks', he found Nebe there, as gloomy and pessimistic as ever. Nebe expected that at the very least he himself would be killed during the course of the putsch. The assassination attempt would take place between noon and 2 P.M. Each day at 2 P.M., the department heads of the Security Office—Mueller, Schellenberg, Ohlendorf, and Nebe—lunched with their chief, Kaltenbrunner, at Gestapo headquarters on the Prinz Albrechtstrasse. This had previously presented Nebe with an excellent opportunity to check on how things were going. But on the day of the putsch, he said, he would much prefer not to be there. However, not to be would be too dangerous. The others might draw conclusions from his absence.

Gisevius pointed out that, by two o'clock, it would all be over and the guards' battalion would have already surrounded the Gestapo building. Nebe shook his head. The news would undoubtedly burst in on them during lunch. He could just picture the scene and how unpleasant it would be to be shot in the company of such gangsters.

July 14 was a comparatively quiet day. On Saturday, July 15, Goerdeler and Gisevius visited Beck in Lichterfelde. Unable to keep their minds off what was probably happening at Hitler's headquarters, their conversation was desultory. By two o'clock the waiting had become a torment. The bomb, Beck said, had been scheduled to be set off between eleven and one. What could have happened? By six o'clock, when they had still received no word, they realized that something had again gone wrong. There was certainly no point in letting the Gestapo catch them all together. Gisevius left first to phone Helldorf, arranging to meet Goerdeler later.

The minute Helldorf heard Gisevius's voice, he said with amazing calm, "You know, of course, that the celebration did not take place?" He then indicated that he would drop by the Struencks' that evening.

Helldorf arrived at the Struencks' just as they were finishing supper. He had gone to the Bendlerstrasse at 1 P.M., as prearranged, where he had found Olbricht, General Hoepner, and the Stauffenberg group. They had not had to wait long for the expected call from Stauffenberg at the Führer's headquarters. Stauffenberg signaled, in a kind of code, that Goering and Himmler were not present. He asked if, under the circumstances, he should go ahead anyway. The group agreed he should. But within fifteen minutes, Stauffenberg had called back again to say that when he had returned to the conference room the meeting was breaking up. Hitler had already rushed away.

Helldorf said that Olbricht had looked visibly relieved at this news. He locked the papers pertaining to the putsch in his safe and left, observing jocularly that now at least they could all enjoy a quiet weekend!

Gisevius had been greatly disturbed by Helldorf's report. Why had Stauffenberg felt it necessary to phone? The previous Wednesday, the assassination also had been called off because Goering and Himmler had not been present. Why hadn't Stauffenberg and his friends decided what to do if that situation should repeat itself?

In fact, Gisevius was so disturbed that he began urging serious consideration of the western solution, trying to persuade Field Marshals von Kluge and Rommel, both of whom had been in touch with the conspirators, to refuse to obey any further orders from Hitler but instead to surrender to Eisenhower.

After Helldorf's departure from the Struencks', Goerdeler wanted to discuss the situation further, but as usual the discussion went around and around in a circle, until finally about 2 A.M. they were all so exhausted they decided to turn in. Not before Goerdeler, however, had made Gisevius promise to go to Beck the following day and try to persuade him to accept the western solution.

The next morning Gisevius bade Goerdeler a sleepy good-bye. Only later did he reflect that sometimes fate kindly spares us the realization that we are seeing a dear friend for the last time.

That afternoon Gisevius went to see Beck, and urged him to seriously consider the western solution. But Beck said he could not make a decision until he had talked with Stauffenberg, who was coming to see him later.

During the night of the sixteenth and seventeenth, the air-raid sirens sounded constantly and the raids continued well into the morning. Nevertheless, Gisevius managed to make his way between raids to Helldorf's office. Helldorf asked if Beck had agreed to the western solution and appeared both irritated and disappointed when Gisevius said he had not. Gisevius, knowing that Hansen was coming to the Struencks' that evening, called to suggest to Mrs. Struenck that Helldorf join them. Mrs. Struenck, accustomed to getting such calls, quickly replied, "Of course!" When they reached the Struencks', they found not only Hansen, but Dr. Hans Koch, lawyer to the famous theologian Pastor Martin Niemoeller and an old friend of Gisevius's, already there.

As they sat down to talk, a pair of feet in high black boots was suddenly seen pacing on the sidewalk outside the cellar window. Struenck rushed out, returning quickly, to say that Nebe was outside but refused to come in. He wanted to speak to Gisevius privately. Gisevius left the room to find Nebe, obviously upset, waiting in a dark corner of the vestibule. Nebe said that at lunch that day the Gestapo chiefs had decided to issue an order for Goerdeler's arrest.

On hearing this news, Hansen suggested that Gisevius take his car to report this latest development as quickly as possible to Beck. Gisevius found Beck very much disturbed by his meeting with Stauffenberg the night before. Stauffenberg claimed that General Helmuth Stieff had been to blame for the fiasco. Stieff, one of Hitler's youngest generals and a brilliant staff officer, had for the past six months been one of the chief activists in the Stauffenberg group. He had kept the bomb locked in his safe awaiting the great hour. But, according to Stauffenberg, Stieff had suddenly lost his nerve. While Stauffenberg had been making his first call to the Bendlerstrasse, Stieff had picked up the briefcase with the bomb in it and carted it out of the room.

This, however, didn't explain to Gisevius's satisfaction, nor apparently to Beck's, why Stauffenberg had felt it necessary to call the Bendlerstrasse at all. Nevertheless, Beck still seemed confident that next time the assassination would come off. If that next attempt, on Thursday, July 20, failed, Beck admitted he would then be willing to consider the western solution. "But mind you," he added, "Kluge will not take the hurdle then either. At the last moment, he'll back down."

When Gisevius told Beck that the Gestapo had issued an order for Goerdeler's arrest, Beck agreed that Goerdeler must go into hiding at once.

As Gisevius started to leave, Beck took his arm. "You must understand," he said, "what a bundle of nerves Stauffenberg is. He has already threatened twice not to set off the bomb."

Gisevius claimed that this was the worst moment so far for him. Was the fate of so many people to depend on a man who, according to Beck, was a bundle of nerves?

XXVIII

On the morning of July 19, Gisevius saw Beck again. Beck suggested that Gisevius stay with Helldorf while awaiting the signal the following day and then accompany him to the Bendlerstrasse.

That evening Helldorf and Nebe dropped in at the Struencks' to go over once again the police measures that were to be taken. Helldorf said that he realized that during his term of office, he had been too compromised by his association with the Nazis not to have to resign within a few days after the putsch had succeeded. But until that moment, he was determined to do everything he possibly could to help. However, he expressed a certain pessimism about the explosive effect of Stauffenberg's bomb. Since the mass bombings, everyone had a story about the peculiarities of bombs, such as how a bomb had knocked down a whole block of houses and yet left plaster casts standing unharmed in the midst of the destruction. When Helldorf and Nebe began to speculate on what form Hitler's famous Providence might assume to protect him the following day, Gisevius cut the discussion short, suggesting that they all get some rest. He felt that even mentioning Hitler's famous "Providence" might bring on bad luck.

July 20 was an almost unbearably hot day. Gisevius arrived at Helldorf's office at the appointed hour, where they were joined by Count Gottfried von Bismarck. Shortly after twelve the sergeant on duty reported to Helldorf that a major was outside with a message from General Olbricht. Could this be news of the assassination? Their spirits rose.

The major, a small man of about thirty, ghastly pale and obviously nervous, entered clutching a black briefcase. He raised his hand instinctively in the Nazi salute, but apparently decided that under the circumstances he should omit the otherwise automatic *"Heil Hitler!"* With a suspicious glance at Gisevius and Count Bismarck, he asked if he might speak to Helldorf privately. Helldorf said he could speak quite openly, the other two gentlemen were entirely trustworthy.

The major, opening his briefcase, produced maps of Berlin. He was, he said, on the staff of the District Command. General Olbricht had given him the maps on which the buildings that were to be occupied had been marked, and had ordered him to go over the maps with Helldorf once more.

At the sight of the maps, Gisevius's heart sank. These were the maps that he and Nebe had prepared at the time of Stalingrad, when the conspirators had also hoped to make a putsch. Many of the buildings marked on them had since been destroyed with no indication of this on the maps. In short, the maps were useless and there was no time to update them.

The major wanted to know what help might be expected from the police. Helldorf explained that it had been agreed that the police would be immobilized for the first few hours and would not undertake any action until the occupation of all important buildings by the army had been completed.

The major seemed baffled. Wouldn't he at least have Nebe's detectives to make the necessary arrests? No, he was informed, not until after the army had occupied all government buildings. The major began to argue, and Gisevius intervened to ask Helldorf if perhaps the arrangements couldn't be changed. But Helldorf was adamant: The police would remain immobilized until the government buildings were secured. The major was expected to carry out Olbricht's orders and occupy the buildings already marked on the maps. At that point, he would undoubtedly receive a new set of orders.

Finally, the major left, unhappy and confused. Helldorf's comment was: "Not exactly a promising collaborator!"

By two o'clock, the tension had become such that Gisevius decided to risk a call to Nebe. Nebe answered the phone and said that unfortunately he was too busy at the moment to join Gisevius. Something "extraordinary" had happened in East Prussia—where Hitler's headquarters was located. He had to brief two detectives who were leaving within thirty minutes to fly to the Führer's headquarters with Kaltenbrunner to begin an investigation of "this extraordinary happening."

Had the bomb already exploded? Was that what Nebe was trying to convey? The communications center at the Führer's headquarters was to have been put out of commission the minute the bomb went off. Could the conspirators be setting a trap for Kaltenbrunner by luring him to East Prussia? Such thoughts and many others raced through Gisevius's head as he continued to plead with Nebe for a meeting, however brief. Finally, Nebe acceded, but through an idiotic misunderstanding which Gisevius claimed could only have happened on a day like this, he and Nebe missed their rendezvous.

The hours dragged by. Then, around four o'clock Helldorf rushed into the room where Gisevius and Bismarck were still waiting. "It's starting," he exclaimed excitedly. "Olbricht has just phoned that I should hold myself in readiness. There will be an important message shortly!"

They didn't have to wait long. Just before four-thirty Helldorf reappeared. "Gentlemen, we're off!" he exclaimed triumphantly. "Olbricht has just ordered me to report to the Bendlerstrasse. He says the Führer is dead, a state of siege has been declared, and he has urgent orders for me from his superior, General Fromm!"

At the Bendlerstrasse, nothing unusual seemed to be happening. No troops. Nothing. Gisevius was not surprised that the guard at the entrance admitted Helldorf, dressed in his police general's uniform, without question, but he was disquieted by the fact that the guard didn't bother to check him out. After all, he was a civilian.

They dashed up the stairs and were ushered into Olbricht's office. There, talking to Olbricht, were Stauffenberg and his aide, Lieutenant von Haeften.

Stauffenberg was bathed in sweat. A little smile played around his lips. He actually radiated triumph. Gisevius was more baffled than ever.

Beck, also present, shook hands gravely with Gisevius and Helldorf. Olbricht, his voice quivering with excitement, informed Helldorf in dramatic tones that Stauffenberg had reported that the Führer had been the victim of an assassination. The army had taken over direction of the government. A state of siege was being proclaimed. The Berlin police were hereby subordinated directly to German Army headquarters. Helldorf was to take all necessary measures at once.

Helldorf saluted and started to leave the room, but Beck motioned him to wait. "In all fairness, Olbricht," Beck said, "I think we should tell the chief of police that according to certain reports from headquarters, Hitler may not be dead. . . ."

Olbricht interrupted excitedly. "Keitel is lying! Keitel is lying!"

Stauffenberg smiled, but Gisevius noticed that Von Haeften did not.

Beck said that it didn't matter whether Keitel, Hitler's chief of staff, was lying or not. "What is important is that Helldorf knows what the other side is claiming," he added.

Helldorf left to return to his office, just as General Hoepner entered the room to fetch a suitcase he had left with Olbricht. Having been deprived of the right to wear a uniform ever since Hitler had fired him, Hoepner was determined to don the uniform again so as to be properly dressed for the demise of the man who had so humiliated him. Gisevius claimed this gesture of Hoepner's was typical of the vanity and rigidity of the highest echelons of the military which, he believed in retrospect, had made the failure of the putsch inevitable.

Olbricht announced that they must give General Fromm an ultimatum before he became alarmed by phone calls asking what was happening. Fromm had been one of the generals whose vacillations had caused the conspirators endless disappointments. Yet, after one of his withdrawals from the conspiracy, he had said to one of the conspirators, "But when and if you *do* make your putsch, don't forget to get Keitel for me!"

It was particularly important to get Fromm to commit himself now since, without his knowledge, orders for the imposition of a state of siege signed with his name were already going out over the Teletype.

Gisevius asked Beck what had happened. Beck shook his head. "Don't ask me! You can see how excited they all are. But we can't change anything now, only hope for the best."

Something had obviously gone wrong at headquarters. Confirmation of the assassination had not been received until Stauffenberg's return some hours later. The code word had come through all right, but then . . . Beck shrugged. Apparently the communications center had *not* been destroyed. Fromm had been able to get through and talk to Keitel, who had said that there had been an attempt on the Führer's life, but that the Führer was alive and only slightly wounded.

Hitler's conferences were often held in an underground bunker. The explosive force of the bomb had been calculated with that in mind. But on July 20 Hitler, with his deadly intuition probably at work, had ordered the conference held in a wooden-reinforced conference barracks. When Stauffenberg had arrived at headquarters, he had placed the briefcase containing the bomb under the table over which Hitler was leaning. At an auspicious moment, through a prearranged signal with Von Haeften,

Stauffenberg had had himself called to the phone. With a quick movement of his foot, he had set the bomb mechanism and left the room. He and Von Haeften were not more than a hundred yards away when there was a thunderous explosion. They saw flames and several bodies, as well as part of the barracks, shoot into the air. They raced for their car and, in the general confusion, were able to reach the airport and take off for Berlin. In the meantime, Olbricht had been given the code word over the telephone. In the few seconds between the time Stauffenberg had left the room and the bomb had exploded, someone had moved the briefcase containing the bomb far enough away from where Hitler was standing so that he was protected from the full force of the explosion by the massive structure of the oak table over which he had been leaning.

When Olbricht had received the code word, Valkyrie, he had stormed into Fromm's office and told him he had just received word that the Führer had been the victim of an assassination. Fromm's duty was to immediately issue the code word for internal disorder to the various deputy headquarters indicating that the power of the state had passed into the hands of the army.

Although he had naturally been startled, for some reason Fromm was not quite convinced. He insisted on trying to reach the Führer's headquarters to check for himself. Olbricht told him to go ahead; he would listen in on another line.

Fromm made the call and Olbricht was aghast when it not only went through but Keitel answered and denied that anything had happened to Hitler.

Beck told Gisevius that when Fromm hung up after talking to Keitel, he said to Olbricht, now greatly shaken, that under the circumstances he saw no reason to issue the code word for internal disorder. Olbricht didn't know what to do since orders containing the code word were already going out over Fromm's name without his knowledge. When Olbricht returned to his own office, where various members of the Stauffenberg group were gathered, and told them what Keitel had said, they were as confused and upset as he was.

Beck confided to Gisevius that when Stauffenberg had arrived at the Rangsdorf airport on his flight back from headquarters and learned that nothing had been undertaken, he was furious. As soon as he had reached the Bendlerstrasse, he insisted that the putsch be set in motion at once. He had still been arguing with Olbricht when Gisevius and Helldorf had arrived.

While Gisevius was still being filled in by Beck, Stauffenberg, accompanied by Olbricht, had gone to Fromm's office and told him that Hitler was dead and that he, Stauffenberg, was able to confirm this. Nevertheless, Fromm chose to believe Keitel's report and tried to place Stauffenberg and Olbricht under arrest. Olbricht protested, "You can't arrest us. You don't seem to realize who has the power now. We arrest you!"

This exchange was followed by an angry but fairly harmless scuffle, the net result of which was that Fromm finally agreed to let himself be locked up in an adjacent room.

Gisevius told Beck that he thought Beck should now take over the direction of the putsch. But again Beck demurred. He didn't want to confuse the situation by intervening at this point. His role was to take over only after the putsch had succeeded, not before.

Gisevius said he admired Beck's self-control, but he personally felt that the situation required action. He told Beck about the experience he and Helldorf had had with the young major who had brought the outdated maps to Helldorf's office, hoping this might convince Beck that plenty was going wrong in the lower echelons, too. Beck's only reaction was to comment dryly, "A number of things seem to have gone wrong today!"

At this point Olbricht, accompanied by Hoepner, returned to the room where Gisevius and Beck were sitting to say that Fromm had asked permission to return home. He would give his word of honor not to undertake any action against the conspirators but would remain there quietly. Olbricht and Hoepner thought he should be allowed to go, pointing out that Fromm had always been "fair." He had known about their plans all along and had never betrayed them. Beck was inclined to grant Fromm's request—if Olbricht and Hoepner were willing to take the responsibility.

This was too much for Gisevius. "Fromm deserves to be shot!" he exclaimed as Stauffenberg entered the room.

Everyone was becoming increasingly excited. Gisevius suggested that at least they ought to discuss what police measures should be taken. More than an hour had passed since Helldorf had returned to his office. It was high time he and Nebe received further instructions.

For some reason, this suggestion seemed to infuriate Stauffenberg. Beck laid a restraining hand on his arm, suggesting that the others leave him alone with Stauffenberg for a few minutes.

Adjutants rushed in and out. Phones rang incessantly. Suddenly heavy footsteps were heard on the stairs and SS Oberführer Colonel Piffraeder entered the room. He was one of the worst of the Gestapo crowd that had been placed in charge of the Abwehr after Admiral Canaris had been removed from office. Gisevius's first reaction had been, "This is it!" But the Oberführer only inquired very politely if he might speak to Colonel von Stauffenberg—"On orders of the chief of the Reich's Security Office," he added somewhat pompously. At this Gisevius realized that the Gestapo was still in the dark. Apparently Piffraeder only wanted to inquire why Colonel von Stauffenberg had returned in such a hurry from the Führer's headquarters. If the Gestapo had known what had actually happened, Gisevius reflected, they never would have sent just one man, and such a highly placed one at that, to the Bendlerstrasse.

When Stauffenberg's only reaction, when told of Piffraeder's appearance, was to order him locked up, Gisevius was incensed. "You should have shot that murderer on the spot, Stauffenberg!" he said angrily.

"His turn will come," Stauffenberg replied calmly.

"We can't just sit here passively for three full hours," Gisevius continued. "If you don't want to shoot this man, at least send an officer with some shock troops to Gestapo headquarters on the Prinz Albrechtstrasse. You should at least get Goebbels and Mueller!"

Stauffenberg replied that he himself had thought of that. He'd speak to Colonel Jaeger, a well-known daredevil whom the conspirators had long considered using in just such an emergency and who was already in the building.

Then Gisevius was called to the phone and informed that Helldorf's adjutant was downstairs. The adjutant told him that Helldorf was becoming extremely impatient and wanted to know what was going on. Couldn't Gisevius accompany him back to Helldorf's office?

This struck Gisevius as a sensible suggestion, so he left word with Olbricht's aide that he would be back within an hour. When Gisevius reached Helldorf's office around six o'clock, he found Helldorf and Nebe drinking coffee.

Gisevius tried to be as optimistic as possible, but Helldorf refused to be encouraged. In the previous two hours nothing, absolutely nothing, had happened. He had frozen his entire police force as ordered by Olbricht, but no representative of the military had been to see him.

Gisevius turned to Nebe. What was the situation at Gestapo headquarters? Nebe said that at five-thirty when he had left there, nothing had been known about the details of the putsch. They weren't even sure that it was Stauffenberg who had set off the bomb.

Gisevius returned to the Bendlerstrasse, where he met Olbricht on the stairs. "Beck wants to see you," said Olbricht. "But come into my office for a minute first. I want to discuss something with you privately."

A radio statement about the failure of the assassination had been made, Olbricht said. No details, not a word about who the assassin had been, were given. Olbricht now had no doubts that Hitler was still alive. Furthermore, he had learned that Hitler was having tea with Mussolini, who, in another one of those incredible coincidences of that fantastic day, had chosen that particular moment to pay a call on the Führer.

Gisevius waited impatiently for Olbricht to come to the point. Surely Olbricht hadn't invited him into his office simply to convey this discouraging bit of news. Finally, Olbricht said, "My dear Gisevius, just for the sake of discussion, I'd like your opinion . . ." Pause. "Of course, we can't call it off now, can we?" Pause. "Deny it at this point, I mean . . ."

Gisevius, dumbfounded, said, "No! We can't!"

Something about the timid, crestfallen way Olbricht asked the question, Gisevius said, had drained all the anger out of him. He excused himself and headed toward Fromm's office. Beck rushed forward to greet him. Hitler himself was about to speak on the radio. Was Gisevius prepared to make a radio statement for their side? Again Gisevius was dumbfounded. The arrangement had been that General Fritz Lindemann, head of the Ordnance Office, was to read such a statement. If having a general make it now seemed inadvisable, surely either Beck or Goerdeler would be a more appropriate choice. Beck pointed out that Goerdeler was not there and he himself felt obliged to remain at the Bendlerstrasse.

The thought flashed through Gisevius's mind that such a statement might well be all the general public would ever learn about the conspiracy. Consequently, appropriate or not, perhaps he should make it. He asked where the proclamation General Lindemann had intended to make was. Beck admitted that Lindemann had the only copy—and he had left the building. Gisevius drew his own conclusions about the reasons behind this sudden disappearance, but not wanting to upset Beck further, he sat down to outline a radio statement.

Fromm's office, where Gisevius was now sitting, was separated from Stauffenberg's by a half-opened sliding door. Gisevius listened, fascinated, as Stauffenberg went through the same routine with each phone caller:

"Keitel is lying! Don't believe Keitel. Hitler is dead. Yes, he is definitely dead . . . Yes, here the action is in full swing . . ."

At first Stauffenberg's voice would be firm and commanding, then friendly and persuasive, finally imploring, "You must hold firm! See that your chief doesn't weaken. I'm depending on you. Please—don't disappoint me. We've got to hold firm! . . ."

Stauffenberg seemed to be the only man who knew what he wanted. Beck, although impressed by Stauffenberg's firmness, regarded all the phone calls as proof that the officers in the provinces were vacillating.

Occasionally, Stauffenberg would pause to assure Beck that everything was proceeding according to plan. The Panzer troops were on their way and should reach the center of the city by seven-thirty at the latest. Then the main action could begin. As yet there had been no reports of Gestapo or Waffen-SS activity. Gisevius reflected that maybe the conspirators did have a chance after all. Yet he couldn't shake off a feeling that valuable time was being wasted and again he urged Stauffenberg to send troops to arrest Goebbels and Mueller, the Gestapo chief, in order to paralyze the other side, at least temporarily.

Stauffenberg replied that the tank troops would arrive shortly. The important buildings could then be surrounded and nobody would be able to escape. Gisevius replied that it was not a question of nobody being able to escape but rather of the psychological effect of at least getting Goebbels and Mueller. This seemed to impress Stauffenberg and he dashed off, saying he would get Colonel Jaeger to lead one shock troop. This did little to reassure Gisevius. Stauffenberg had been looking for Jaeger an hour before. Why hadn't he found him then?

Beck suggested that he and Gisevius go over point by point what should be said on the radio. Suddenly, there was great excitement. Paris was on the line. This was the first call from any of the occupied territories.

Beck hurried to the phone to talk personally to the Paris Commandant, General Karl Heinrich von Stuelpnagel, who reported that he had already taken all appropriate measures. When Beck asked about Field Marshal von Kluge's reaction, Stuelpnagel suggested Beck talk to him personally and had the call switched to Von Kluge's headquarters on the front near Paris.

Beck spoke to Von Kluge in friendly, persuasive tones, described the measures that had been taken in Berlin, and urged the field marshal not to vacillate at this psychologically critical moment.

Listening on a second phone, Gisevius found it impossible to gather Von Kluge's true intentions from a few ambiguous remarks that he made. But the gist was that the failure of the assassination attempt had created a quite different situation. He would have to confer with his staff, then he'd call back in half an hour.

Beck hung up and turned to Gisevius. "Well, there you have it. That's Von Kluge for you."

At that point, Fromm sent word that he was hungry. Wouldn't they please reconsider and let him go home? This time everyone agreed that Fromm should not be released, but so that he would not be able to complain about his treatment at their hands, they decided to have some sandwiches and a bottle of wine sent in to him from the officers' canteen.

Then, the guard at the entrance phoned that Field Marshal von Witzleben was on his way upstairs. Everyone snapped to attention as Witzleben, his face beet red, entered the room. Obviously he was very angry.

Stauffenberg stepped forward and saluted. Witzleben glared at him. "This is a fine mess!" he growled.

Witzleben had always shown great respect and admiration for Beck. Despite his anger, he took Beck by the arm and led him to the far side of the room. They stood there talking in low tones for some minutes, then were joined by Stauffenberg, who, according to Gisevius, "had been standing aside like a drenched poodle."

The discussion between Beck, Witzleben, and Stauffenberg went on for at least thirty minutes. Meanwhile, Gisevius could hear Hoepner and Olbricht quarreling loudly in the next room. Olbricht's voice was angry, Hoepner's almost tearful. At one point, Olbricht caught Gisevius's eye and beckoned to him to join them.

"Now ask Gisevius, Hoepner," Olbricht said.

"No! No!" Hoepner replied. "If it's such a risk, one shouldn't take the gamble."

"There's a risk in every coup d'etat!" Olbricht countered.

"Yes," Hoepner replied. "But there must be a ninety percent probability that the putsch will succeed . . ."

"Nonsense," snapped Olbricht. "You'll never have a ninety percent probability. Fifty-one percent is enough."

"No," said Hoepner. "Fifty-one percent is *not* enough! Let's say at least eighty percent . . ."

"Eighty percent? How do you expect to get eighty percent?" Olbricht retorted.

"There you are!" said Hoepner. "Not even eighty percent! You can't go ahead and try to make a putsch—"

Olbricht interrupted him. "Ask Gisevius. What about it, Gisevius?"

Gisevius said he was actually speechless. Here were two generals at this moment of crisis arguing about percentages like a couple of economics professors. Fortunately, Gisevius didn't have to reply, because at that precise moment an officer appeared to say Helldorf was on the phone asking that "the gentleman who had been with him before" come to his office at once. He had something of great importance to communicate.

Gisevius had no desire to listen to Helldorf's complaints. Besides, he felt it was important for him to await the result of the Beck-Witzleben discussion with Stauffenberg. But Olbricht and Hoepner insisted he answer Helldorf's summons. Helldorf might have some vital new information to convey. Certainly nothing would be happening within the next half hour at the Bendlerstrasse. By then Gisevius could be back.

Stauffenberg then was told that Helldorf had sent for Gisevius. Stauffenberg said his discussion with Beck and Witzleben would not be through for at least another thirty minutes. He, too, thought it important that Gisevius find out what Helldorf wanted. Gisevius objected that he'd had trouble enough getting into the building before. By now getting through the blockaded street probably would be impossible. Stauffenberg went back to his desk, picked up a pass on heavy brown paper he had signed himself, and handed it to Gisevius.

XXIX

When Gisevius's car reached the first intersection, it met a heavily armed detachment marching in the opposite direction. Gisevius was so delighted at the thought of how happy his friends would be to see these men, who, he naturally assumed, were marching to protect them, he couldn't resist waving cheerfully at them! Little did he imagine that, far from going to protect the conspirators, the troops were going to arrest them.

Gisevius experienced his first qualms when a heavily armed double guard refused to let them through the Brandenburg Gate. However, still under the illusion that the putsch was under way, he was gratified to see that certain buildings were at last being surrounded. Then, glancing down a side street, he was disturbed to see a company of soldiers marching in a direction opposite to that he would have expected.

At the Alexanderplatz, he stopped the car, got out, and, as a precautionary measure, made his way on foot, entering the building by a rear entrance. Helldorf was not in his office but in his air-raid shelter. Gisevius didn't want to give his name, but the man in charge of the phones refused to connect him to Helldorf unless he did. Finally, Gisevius persuaded him to let him talk to Helldorf's adjutant, who recognized his voice and said he would fetch him in a car.

Gisevius went back to dismiss his own car and, deciding he had better get rid of any incriminating papers, gave the driver his notes for a radio statement to keep for him until he returned to the Bendlerstrasse.

As Gisevius entered the room where Helldorf and Nebe were sitting, he was still convinced that the putsch was proceeding. One glance at the faces of the two men, however, and he knew the game was up. Helldorf was very calm but, as Gisevius said, "not with the calm of an idealist who feels his fate depends on a higher power, but rather with the calm of a man who had been a gambler all his life." Nebe looked as gloomy as ever, but Gisevius sensed a touch of satisfaction in his melancholy glance, as if to say, "You see? I was right all along."

Helldorf began at once to outline the fragmentary information that he and Nebe had been able to piece together: The Grossdeutschland Guards Battalion and its Commander, Major Otto Remer, had been alerted and ordered to arrest Goebbels. At that very moment, however, Remer was marching instead on the Bendlerstrasse to arrest the conspirators. Neither Helldorf nor Nebe knew what had actually occurred. Later, it turned out that earlier in the day a Nazi "morale officer" had delivered a lecture to the Guards Battalion. After that, Remer had invited the man to have a drink with him, and it was then that word of the imposition of a state of siege had arrived. The morale officer, in civilian life an official of the Propaganda Ministry, pleaded with Remer to let him check with Goebbels as to whether Hitler was actually dead or not. Goebbels had a direct line to the Führer's headquarters and could easily find out the truth. At first Remer hesitated; Goebbels was not his superior officer. Then he thought better of it and yielded. The call was put through and Goebbels asked Remer to come to his office at once.

Actually, at this moment, Gisevius pointed out, the thirty-year-old Major Remer was probably the single most important army officer in Germany. The minute Remer arrived in Goebbels's office, Goebbels put through a call to the Führer's headquarters and handed the phone to Remer. Hitler himself was on the other end. Countless young majors had never spoken to Hitler. But just a few weeks before Remer had talked with Hitler personally when the latter had conferred on him an oak-leaf cluster to the Iron Cross. There was no doubt in Remer's mind that he was talking to Hitler. When the Führer charged him with the responsibility for crushing the putsch, that was all that Remer needed.

"Well," said Helldorf jauntily, "only sheer gall can save us now. We'll just pretend that nothing's happened. We'll deny everything!"

Helldorf could invent a thousand alibis and Nebe spin some fancy tale for the Gestapo, but how was Gisevius, who at the moment was supposedly performing his duties at the consulate in Zurich, to explain his presence in the Bendlerstrasse or even at Berlin police headquarters?

"That's quite simple," said Helldorf. "Obviously you must disappear."

Nebe excused himself. Gisevius, left alone with Helldorf, said that before "disappearing" he intended to return to the Bendlerstrasse. "Tell me the truth, Helldorf. Wouldn't you be thoroughly disgusted with me if I didn't?"

"Certainly not," said Helldorf. "Don't kid yourself, Gisevius. For years these generals have promised us everything. They've kept none of their promises. What happened today was right in line with the rest of it—just more of their shit."

Downstairs, Gisevius found a small police car, climbed in and told the driver to take him to the Bendlerstrasse.

Everywhere troops were still marching away. At the Brandenburg Gate guards blocked their passage. Gisevius suggested another route, but again they were stopped. It occurred to Gisevius that he still might be able to give some kind of a statement over the radio, so he told the driver to forget about getting to the Bendlerstrasse and proceed to the radio station, a considerable distance away.

Suddenly, the ludicrousness of his situation struck him. Did every putsch have an element of the absurd? Or just those that failed?

Suddenly the chauffeur announced he could go no further. He must get back to police headquarters. Fortunately, they were not far from the Struencks', so Gisevius got out and made his way there on foot.

The Struencks were relieved to see him alive. They had some idea of what had happened but few details. Apparently, shortly after eight o'clock, the Guards Battalion had surrounded the Bendlerstrasse and Major Remer had announced that he was taking the conspirators under his "protection." Neither Olbricht, Stauffenberg, nor anyone else had thought to question him. For nearly two hours they didn't even realize what was actually happening but continued on with their phantom putsch.

At ten o'clock sharp the Guards Battalion was withdrawn. A number of officers who had gone along with the revolt in the afternoon were now getting cold feet and looking for a way out. One of these officers rushed into Stauffenberg's room and shot at him, only wounding him. Trailing a stream of blood, Stauffenberg dashed upstairs to Beck.

He reached Olbricht's office just as Fromm, now "liberated," entered the room. "Well, gentlemen," he announced, "now I am going to do to you what you wanted to do to me this afternoon!"

Flourishing his revolver threateningly, he barked, "Lay down your weapons!"

Beck was allowed to keep a pistol in case he chose to commit suicide.

After an abortive first attempt, he succeeded. Fromm sentenced Stauffenberg, Olbricht, and two others to be shot immediately.

That evening the Struencks and Gisevius sat around the radio. For an
hour there were announcements that Hitler would speak to the people,
but the broadcast was repeatedly postponed. Then, in the early-morning
hours, the music stopped abruptly and the announcer declared, "The
Führer will speak!"

With the first words it was obvious that the voice was Hitler's.

The putsch was over. The problem for Gisevius and the Struencks was
what to do next.

G isevius spent a sleepless night. Before seven the next morning, he left the Struencks' and headed for West Berlin, where he had a friend who had promised to give him refuge in an emergency. But when this friend saw Gisevius standing there on his doorstep, he blanched. He had, of course, been listening to the radio. He said apologetically that he was terribly sorry but his house was full of people bombed out of their homes. He offered Gisevius a cup of coffee and, while Gisevius was drinking it, suggested that he seek refuge with a neutral diplomat for whom Gisevius had done a great favor at a moment which but for Gisevius's intervention could have proved extremely embarrassing both to the diplomat and to his country. Again it was the same story: the diplomat was terribly sorry, but . . .

So Gisevius headed for the home of a lawyer friend, Hans Koch, a rather timid and extremely circumspect individual, who welcomed him with open arms. Gisevius said that he had a very special admiration for those with timid and cautious natures who at moments of great crisis performed acts of extraordinary courage. This was something that recurred again and again during the war. In Koch's case, the end of the story was particularly tragic. He was executed for having sheltered Gisevius only briefly.

On the morning of July 22, Mrs. Koch phoned the Struencks from a public phone and arranged for Gisevius to meet them later at a busy suburban railroad station where they figured they would be lost in the crowd. Mrs. Struenck had been in touch with Nebe, who had picked her up in his car and had told her that the Gestapo still had no idea that either he or Helldorf had been involved in the plot. Actually, the Gestapo was still confused as to how to proceed. Himmler and Goebbels wanted to cover up the plot, while others were pushing for revenge. Hitler had not as yet made up his mind which course to follow. Nebe warned that under no circumstances should Gisevius try to travel by train. All trains were being searched—by the military police looking for deserters, by the criminal police looking for escaped foreign workers and prisoners of war, and by the Gestapo seeking the traitors.

By Sunday, July 23, Gisevius's curiosity was such that he decided to risk making his way to Helldorf's office. Helldorf pretended to be perfectly at ease, but Gisevius could tell he was extremely nervous. He asked Gisevius what he knew about arrests or executions, which was precisely what Gisevius had hoped to learn from him.

After leaving Helldorf, Gisevius met the Struencks at the station as prearranged. They felt they really ought to get away, but not yet having heard from Hansen, they feared their flight might incriminate him.

Those urging revenge finally won out. Hitler ordered a clean sweep of the opposition. Helldorf and Hansen were eventually picked up and hanged in September. Although both had been mercilessly tortured, they had revealed nothing.

When Kaltenbrunner confessed to Nebe that he had heard that Nebe had often been seen in Helldorf's company, he added, "If that's the case, I guess I'll have to arrest you, too!" With that, Nebe had returned to his office, tossed a few things into his briefcase, and left the building. Unable to get any extra gas for his car, he started off with the small amount he had. He picked up Gisevius and the Struencks and headed for the country, where they had the address of a village pastor with whom they thought they might find shelter. But both this man and another clergyman to whom he sent them already had more people than they could accommodate, including some Jews whom they didn't want to endanger by taking in such dangerous new guests.

Their car was stopped frequently by military controls. Only the fact that Nebe was still wearing his SS general's uniform enabled them to get through. But they realized that at any moment Nebe's absence would be discovered and the order for his arrest would be issued. So, on the theory that the last place anyone would look for them would be in the lion's den, they returned to Berlin. There they separated, the Struencks going one way, Gisevius and Nebe another.

As Gisevius and Nebe were walking through West Berlin, they saw two men in a car watching them, so they quickly ducked into the nearest building. As it turned out, the men were watching for Dr. Carl Sack, the Chief Provost Marshal of the Army, who soon entered the building. Catching sight of Nebe and Gisevius, Dr. Sack muttered, "Clear out! I'm under observation! The Gestapo is following me!"

Ironically, Dr. Sack was the very official entrusted with the judicial investigation of the events of July 20. Eventually he was arrested and executed in April 1945, as the Americans were approaching.

Shortly, Nebe and Gisevius separated. Gisevius went into hiding, not far from Gestapo headquarters in the home of a woman friend. There he stayed until Allen Dulles managed to smuggle in false papers to him; with these he was eventually able to make his way to Switzerland.

Waiting for his false papers to arrive, combined with the devastating news about his friends, had pushed Gisevius's nerves nearly to the breaking point. Almost daily he learned of some friend who had either been picked up or executed. Then, in mid-January 1945, he had come down with a bad case of the grippe, which had done nothing for his morale.

Finally, on the evening of January 20, there was a ring at the front door. A woman Gisevius had never seen before asked if everything was "all right." When Gisevius said it was, she turned and vanished into the night. Shortly, the doorbell rang again. Gisevius opened the door in time to see a car driving away and a large manila envelope sticking out of the mailbox. When he opened the envelope, the first thing to fall out was a badge like that worn by all high Gestapo officials. Glancing through the papers in the envelope, Gisevius found they had been issued to a high-ranking Gestapo functionary called Hoffmann, obviously his new identity. The papers included a special pass and a letter from Gestapo headquarters signed by Himmler (a perfect forgery), instructing all governmental officials to assist said Hoffmann on an important secret mission to Switzerland. But there was no railroad ticket in the envelope and, to his dismay, Gisevius realized he would have to procure that himself.

Early the next morning, he went to the station, only to find it swarming with SS officers. SS General Kaltenbrunner was leaving on a trip to Austria. This was scarcely an ideal situation in which to find himself. But, as Gisevius put it, "After all, I have always been an expert in the haughty glare, the arrogant manner." He managed to push his way into an overcrowded train bound for Switzerland, on a track adjacent to the one on which Kaltenbrunner's train was standing. However, because of the tremendous number of people trying to clamber aboard, he did not succeed in getting on until he had flashed his Gestapo badge and cried, "Gestapo! Gestapo!" Even then he found himself in the baggage car, the other cars of the train having already been filled and their doors locked.

Once safely aboard, he made his way into one of the adjacent passenger cars and sat down, lifting a child up on his lap for protection. The conductor, who had apparently heard his cry of "Gestapo! Gestapo!" and had seen him flash his badge, pushed his way through the crowded train to where Gisevius was sitting and offered him the opportunity of going forward into a special compartment reserved for high officials. Gisevius said the poor man seemed quite baffled by Gisevius's insistence that he was quite happy where he was.

During the journey, the train stopped frequently, actually reaching the Swiss frontier twelve hours late. Hungry, thirsty, exhausted from the effects of his illness and the strains of the journey, Gisevius entered the waiting room at the frontier post at 6 A.M. on January 23. The regular customs official and his Gestapo colleague, unused to travelers arriving at such an hour, rubbed their eyes sleepily. Gisevius was wearing a summer suit, a dirty, light spring overcoat, a borrowed hat several sizes too large, and an oversized pair of fleece-lined boots. His appearance was scarcely reassuring. His heart sank as the Gestapo man studied his official papers suspiciously. But after careful scrutiny, he apparently decided his was not to question why, so he stamped the papers—and let Gisevius pass through into the safety of Switzerland.

He rushed to the nearest phone and some hours later reached the Zurich station, where Eddie Waetjen was waiting, overjoyed to see him again. Although everyone had hoped against hope that he would eventually make it to safety, nobody, including Gisevius himself, had actually believed he would. At one point when he was telling me about his adventures in Berlin, I said, "Actually I'm surprised, you know, by what you did. I never thought of you as a man of action."

He gave me a withering glance. "What was all that story in my book anyhow?" he demanded. "Morbid imagination?" And for a moment he was the Gisevius of old. But otherwise . . . At several points he nearly broke down, apologizing and saying that I should treat him like "a sick patient" for another month or so.

I asked him about his friends, the Struencks, of whom I knew he was particularly fond. He said that he didn't know whether they had been executed or not, but on the day he left Berlin, he had learned that they had been arrested. "That was one of the darkest moments of my life." He went on to say that during his flight with the Struencks and Nebe he had realized the true meaning of fear as well as what cowards some people could be.

After he had finished telling me about the attempted putsch and his flight with Nebe and the Struencks, Gisevius settled down to give me some of his personal reactions. He had begun almost at once writing on his book again to bring it up to date and had worked on it steadily for three months. This had required a tremendous amount of self-discipline as all the men he was writing about were being shot, hanged, or tortured while he was writing. He had been forced to come to terms with the meaning of his own life for the past ten years, and why he, in particular, was apparently being spared. With the news of each fresh arrest or execution, he had had to go through the whole process again, asking himself whether this new arrest or execution was in any way his fault. The results of this self-questioning were to make him realize what suffering for others actually meant and to give him a feeling of tremendous responsibility to his friends. Moreover, there was a conviction that far more depended on the story he had to tell than he had ever before imagined.

I had always thought it odd that Gisevius had never let his mother read his book, because I knew that he adored her. They shared a suite in a Zurich hotel and he often talked about her in a most affectionate way. I had told Jung that I had the impression that her own unfulfilled ambitions focused on Gisevius like a searchlight on a bug, very much the way Mme. de Charrière's unrealized longings had focused on Benjamin Constant. I thought that somehow, quite unconsciously, everything Gisevius did was living out his mother's ambitions for him in very much the same way that Benjamin Constant, as he admitted in *Le Cahier Rouge,* engaged in adventures simply in order to be able to tell Mme. de Charrière about them. I thought, to be so completely accepting of everything a son said and did, as Gisevius's mother seemed to be, was the very best way for a mother to hang on to a son and bind him to her. Jung said that this might quite likely be true.

One day in late March Gisevius's mother came to visit me, to see where Gisevius and I had worked. "Goethe's workroom," she called it. When I told Jung that she was a tiny, plump woman with a bright, merry face and a rather kittenish manner, he exclaimed, "That's just what I thought she would be like!"

While we were talking in "Goethe's workroom," I suddenly saw in that merry, kindly face the beady eyes of a crab peering at me from under a rock by the seashore, its claws quivering slightly as if waiting to grab its prey. Then the crab began to talk.

She told me Gisevius had never been able to do things he didn't want to do; he was "too superior as a personality to be able to take orders from anyone." That is why, in her opinion, he would never be able to take orders from "the occupying authorities." He had to give orders. He had to rule. She told me how wonderful all the people described in his book had been, how she had known nothing of what was going on. She had sometimes made coffee for them late at night and had been thrilled to be in the presence of such splendid men, all of whom so obviously admired and appreciated her wonderful son.

I had to show her where I had kept the manuscript, the machine on which I had typed my translation, and other such holy of holies. She told me how extraordinary Gisevius had been since a child. "He never had friends of his own age, never had time for women or girls." By the time he was twenty-two, he had a whole set of distinguished acquaintances, men in their fifties who lived on huge estates, who were interested only in culture—and in her son. Men who read to him, played the violin to him, walked through the woods, talking to him—her boy—while their huge homes were filled with distinguished guests whom they found boring by comparison.

To think that this *Wunderkind*, with a beautiful and extraordinary social life in a peaceful Germany of huge estates, was at the same time fighting and quarreling daily with *Bestien* ("beasts") like Reinhard Heydrich. She told me that the Reich's forester, "an unusually distinguished man with an unusually large estate," who played Beethoven "unusually well," had been particularly fond of her son. Arthur Nebe, who was at the house almost daily, "looked like Dante with his black hair, hooked nose, and beautiful, intelligent, sad, gray eyes." She felt Gisevius had not done justice to Nebe in his book—to this beautiful, strange, silent, gray-eyed Dante, who sat all during the war years in the heart of the Gestapo. Helldorf she had never met, although she had talked to him at least five hundred times on the phone.

In retrospect, she felt she had done a lot of dangerous things. She didn't think Helldorf was as careful as he should have been. He had a very bad reputation, had been a violent anti-Semite in the thirties, and she wasn't sure it was "nice" of him, with his reputation, to have seen so much of her son.

At that point, I couldn't resist pointing out that it had been a call from Helldorf, summoning Gisevius from the Bendlerstrasse to his office that had saved Gisevius's life. She said yes, that was true, but that had been "fate," not Helldorf. Whenever Helldorf had come to the house, she had been "whisked out of the way." There had always been a great mystery attached to his endless visits.

Suddenly, the crab glared at me and asked if I thought, because of how Helldorf was hated for his evil deeds in the early years of the Nazi regime, some of this hatred would now be directed at her beloved son simply because he had known Helldorf. I told her I didn't think so. In my opinion, it would be less compromising for her son to have known Helldorf than to have known Dr. Schacht, the great financial wizard. This gave her pause—and the crab blinked as the tide rolled in.

After the war, Schacht called Gisevius as a witness for him at Nuremberg. When I asked Gisevius if he wanted to go, his reply was, "Of course I don't want to go! Who likes to jump into ice water? But I owe Schacht a great deal. Now that he, an old man, is in trouble and I, a comparatively young one, whom he helped greatly in the early years of my career, am sitting here in Switzerland, in touch with the Americans, I can't say, 'Too bad! Your putsch is *kaput*! You are *kaput*! Germany is *kaput*! I wash my hands of the whole thing!'"

Wilhelm Frick, the Minister of the Interior, also called Gisevius as a witness, and apparently never noticed that Gisevius's testimony only helped to hang him. However, Gisevius's testimony against Goering was the most devastating he gave. Goering realized this almost at once, but his lawyer didn't, and he continued to question Gisevius until Goering passed him a note. Later, Gisevius was able to get that piece of paper. On it was written SCHLUSS MACHEN! ("Knock it off!").

After Jung had seen Gisevius, he told me that he found it enormously interesting how Gisevius had projected his own psychology on to Stauffenberg. It was probably just as well that the putsch had failed. Jung wanted me to be sure to tell Allen that in his opinion Gisevius and Stauffenberg actually had been fighting for the very same thing that Hitler had possessed, namely pure power. And he added, "They were like a pair of lions fighting over a hunk of raw meat."

When I asked Jung what he thought Gisevius's future would be, he said it was difficult to tell. Usually when disaster struck, any European who had shot up as Gisevius had into a very different class from the one into which he had been born would flounder at first, then gradually fall back into the class from which he had emerged. Gisevius's father had been a government official in Berlin. His mother came from Posen, where her family had owned properties that had been confiscated by Poland after World War I. Gisevius's early family life had been the solid, modest, genteel life led by middle-class civil servants in Germany for years before the Nazi seizure of power. Jung rather expected that Gisevius would fall back into this milieu. "Of course, he still has rather grandiose ideas, and if he goes to the United States, he might attach himself to some current of power there that would permit him to realize at least some of them." Then Jung paused, puffing on his pipe, and gazed reflectively out his study window at the Lake of Zurich.

"And if that doesn't happen?" I asked. "If he doesn't go to the United States and clamp on to some current of power, what then?"

Jung shrugged. "Well," he said, "then frankly I don't think he will ever amount to much. He may write a book or two. But that's all. It's too bad in a way. He's really a very nice boy!"

XXXI

Allen had been expecting his wife, Clover, to join him ever since the French-Swiss frontier had opened again. She had had to postpone her departure several times because of the illness of her mother. Unfortunately, just after she finally had sailed, her mother had taken a sudden turn for the worse. When news of her death had reached Allen, he phoned me to say he was leaving the following day to meet Clover, so as to break the sad news to her as gently as possible. He wasn't sure when they would be back in Bern, but the minute they arrived, he would call me so that I might meet Clover at last.

Ever since that first evening when Allen had said, "My wife is an angel!" he had told me little things she had said and done that had convinced me I would like her. I was not disappointed. Tall, slender, with high cheekbones and a profile like that of the Indian on a buffalo nickel, Clover had short, naturally wavy, light brown hair. Her voice was soft, cultivated, and she laughed easily. Yet at the same time there was something shy, almost other-worldly about her, that gave an impression of vagueness, particularly when she didn't like someone. She could be wondrously witty, but saved these displays of *esprit* for intimates. When describing the agonies of having to be gracious to people she didn't like at a party she had not enjoyed, she'd say, "Oh, Mary, it was all quite beyond the limits of human endurance!" and I'd know exactly what she meant. If she dismissed a book as "no good" after just leafing through it, I'd tease her about "snap judgments," but she'd defend herself with a laugh, exclaiming, "But, Mary, I *can* tell at a glance!" Actually, she could.

She had an unerring instinct for what was first class, but was relentless in her disdain of pretense and pomposity. Kind and compassionate, she was at the same time capable of awesome outbursts of rage—at God, at humanity, and at Allen. She and Allen had terrible fights, which Allen invariably won by the simple device of clamping an iron curtain down between them.

She had always been eager to share in his work, but he had never permitted it. In Bern, of course, he was able to profit from all the myths about the secret nature of intelligence work. I personally think the reason Allen went to such lengths to exclude her was that he had such a high regard for her moral and ethical values that he did not dare risk the unsettling effect of her possible disapproval.

Clover could be the soul of discretion if she wished and might well have been able to work with him. But since even I, far less idealistic than she was, sometimes had difficulty in overcoming a certain moral queasiness at various activities in which we were forced to engage, I think Allen was probably wise to exclude her.

When she and Allen became engaged, her professor father, who set great store on scholarly pursuits, had looked in a reference book to see if Allen had perchance ever written anything. To his delight, he discovered he had: "The Boer War." This was a booklet Allen had written at the age of eight, which ran into several editions and was most respectfully reviewed by *The New York Times.* The proceeds from its publication had gone to the Boer Relief Committee for aid to the destitute widows and orphans of those burghers killed during the war in South Africa. The eight-year-old had developed pro-Boer sympathies while listening to conversations between his largely pro-English elders and had been particularly incensed by the English.

Clover loved the little boy who had the temerity to stand up for those he considered mistreated, the same little boy who, when a neighborhood bully had him down and was beating him up, had yelled, "You may get me down, but you can't make me give up!" She also admitted frankly that a certain side of her personality that she had christened "Madame L'Elue" ("Madame, the Elected One") thoroughly enjoyed being the wife of a prominent and successful man. She was very proud of the citation that accompanied Allen's award of the Medal for Merit presented to him by President Truman after the war:

> . . . *For exceptionally meritorious conduct in the performance of outstanding services as chief of the foremost undercover operations con-*

ducted by the Office of Strategic Services on behalf of the United States government from November 1942 to October 1945. Mr. Dulles, within a year, effectively built up an intelligence network employing hundreds of informants and operatives, reaching into Germany, Yugoslavia, Czechoslovakia, Bulgaria, Hungary, Spain, Portugal, and North Africa, and completely covering France, Italy, and Austria. He assisted in the formation of various Maquis groups in France and supported the Italian partisan groups both financially and by pinpointing airdrops for supplies. The exceptional worth of his reports on bombing targets and troop movements both by land and sea was recognized by diplomatic military and naval agencies of the United States government. Particularly notable achievements by Mr. Dulles were first reports as early as August 1943, of the existence of a German experimental laboratory at Peenemunde for the testing of a rocket bomb, his report on the flooding of the Belgian and Dutch coastal areas long before similar information came in from other sources, his report on rocket-bomb installations in the Pas de Calais, and his reports on damage inflicted by the Allied Air Forces as a result of raids on Berlin and other German, Italian, and Balkan cities, which were forwarded within two or three days of the operations. Mr. Dulles, by his superior diplomacy and efficiency, built up for the United States enormous prestige among leading figures of occupied nations taking refuge in Switzerland. He carried out his assignments in extremely hazardous conditions, and, despite the constant observation of enemy agents, was able to fulfill his duties in a manner reflecting the utmost credit on himself and his country. After the German collapse, Mr. Dulles headed the Office of Strategic Services mission in Germany, which supplied highly important and essential intelligence to American Military Government, occupation, and diplomatic offices in the difficult post-hostilities period. His courage, rare initiative, exceptional ability, and wisdom provided an inspiration for those who worked with him and materially furthered the war effort of the United Nations . . .

However, between the eight-year-old boy defending the Boers and the grown man who had received one of his country's highest awards, was another Allen Dulles who held Clover at arm's length. It was constant anguish to her that she could never seem to break through the impenetrable barrier that he erected against her. She would often beg me to ask him something for her, and once when I asked her why she didn't ask him herself, she said, "Because he always gets angry at me. But he never gets angry at you. I think that's because you are the only person who is not afraid of him." I certainly wasn't afraid of him. However, I think the real reason why I could reach him when others couldn't was that in our work together, I had "got his number." He knew that there was nothing he could say or do that would affect in the slightest my deep affection for him. He was also aware that I knew his dark side—and that it didn't bother me in the least.

It did not take Clover long to sense the tie between me and Allen. In fact, the second or third time we were alone together, she said, "I want you to know I can see how much you and Allen care for each other—and I approve!" That was all that was said. I made no comment and the subject was never mentioned again, even though I remained close to them both until their deaths many years later, Allen in 1969 and Clover in 1974.

One day Clover said to me, "If I could only make out what Allen's *goal* is, what he wants from life, I might find it easier to understand all this sound and fury. Someone once said, 'The Dulles brothers are like sharks.' And I do think they are. I guess there's no solution but for you and me to be killer whales!" So from then on we referred to Allen as "the Shark" and to ourselves as the "Killer Whales." This little game once caused the Swiss a certain amount of alarm when Clover wired me from the Tessin what time she would arrive in Zurich and signed her telegram KILLER. An official from the telegraph office came to see me, clutching the telegram in his hand, to ask for an explanation of its signature. He listened with an expression of mistrust while I explained that "Killer" was a nickname for Mrs. Allen Dulles, wife of the special assistant to the American minister. Finally, shaking his head over the peculiar habits of Americans, he departed. But when I went to the station to meet Clover, I spotted him lurking behind a stanchion in the station, undoubtedly to check to his own satisfaction that I was not meeting some international terrorist.

Clover and I had one absorbing interest in common: analytical psychology. Over the years Clover had read a great deal of Jung and was eager to work, if not with Jung personally, then at least with one of his colleagues. The problem was that she had to participate in a certain amount of social and diplomatic activity in Bern as the wife of the special assistant to the American minister, a cover that Allen continued to maintain. So she was not sure just how often she would be able to get to Zurich. Wasn't there perhaps an analyst among Jung's colleagues who might be willing to go to Bern occasionally to work with her?

I thought Jolande Jacobi might be an ideal choice. Jolande had spent many years running an organization in Vienna known as the Kultur-bund, attached to the Austrian Ministry of Propaganda. It had been formed to attract writers, painters, scholars, musicians, and statesmen from other European countries, thus casting a kind of reflected glory on Vienna, as well as providing a cultural cover for all manner of high-level intrigues. This experience meant, I felt, that Jolande would understand and sympathize with Clover's many social obligations.

I had first met Jolande in 1938 when she had been planning a trip to the United States to lecture on Jungian psychology. I had advised her strongly against it, as I had felt her English at the time was inadequate. Usually, when you discourage anyone from doing something, you make an enemy. In Jolande's case, I made a friend.

In the early thirties when Jolande had realized that the Nazis were planning to occupy Austria, she had written to Jung, whom she had met through her work with the Kulturbund, to ask if she might come to Zurich and work with him. He had replied that he would be delighted, but first she should get her doctorate.

On the day of Hitler's arrival in Vienna, she had still to get twelve more credits and take her final exam for her doctorate. She went into hiding at a friend's house and attended the university with a heavy widow's veil over her face. In the meantime, an order had been issued for her arrest and the Gestapo had visited her home several times looking for her. When I asked her if the danger she had been in had not made it difficult to concentrate on her studies, she said no. Having been a wealthy woman all her life, the idea of having to start all over again with nothing was such a terrifying prospect that her terror at this possibility had re-placed any fear of the Nazis she might otherwise have had. She was convinced that her entire future depended on her getting her doctorate.

Jolande was inclined to overdress and had a passion for ultrafashiona-ble, often quite ridiculous hats. But I was sure that Clover would not mind these characteristics or a certain flamboyance in Jolande's personal-ity that did not sit too well with her introverted Swiss colleagues. Even Jung would sometimes make slightly acid comments about Jolande's ex-tremely un-Swiss personality. But he had the greatest respect for her brilliant mind and thorough understanding of his theories. He always counted on her help if his remarks were misunderstood by the press or if some angry Freudian attacked him.

She and I often joked about the problems of two extroverts like our-selves afloat in a sea of introverts like the Swiss. She had been of enor-

mous help to me in gaining an understanding of the difference between
the introvert's and the extrovert's psychologies—by using the analogy of
an electric light bulb. She said that when extroverts were with people,
they were like an electric light bulb with the current on. The introverts
functioned in exactly the opposite way: Extinguished when with people,
blazing brightly when alone. The difficulty the two types had in understanding each other was that the extroverts never saw the introverts
alone, and the introverts never saw the extroverts under similar circumstances. In short, the extroverts never saw the introverts at their best and
the introverts never saw the extroverts at their worst. An added difficulty
was that the introverts assumed that the extroverts were always as vi-
vacious and at ease as they seemed in a group. So the introverts were apt
to project a very subtle kind of power complex on the extroverts that the
latter saw quite clearly, but that the introverts themselves were not always aware of.

When I told Clover, who was extremely introverted, Jolande's analogy, she was delighted with it and sure she could work well with Jolande.
The result was a long and fruitful association. After Allen left Bern for
Germany, Clover moved to Zurich. On several occasions after the war,
she returned for prolonged visits until I myself returned permanently to
the States in the early fifties.

Eventually, Jolande put together a fascinating book, which unfortunately has never been translated into English, in which there are many
paintings and drawings by the people who worked with her. Some of
Clover's drawings are among the cleverest and wittiest in the book. In
two drawings Clover made for me, she has captured the way she felt
under certain circumstances. One of these drawings shows a large, fuzzy
donkey seated at a round table on which his forelegs are extended. His
head is down on the table and two huge tears are running out of his eyes.
The caption under this drawing reads, AND THE ASS PUT HIS HEAD DOWN
ON THE TABLE AND WEPT AS IF HIS HEART WOULD BREAK! Clover maintained that was the way she felt when Allen was rushing around, engaged
in activities she didn't understand but suspected were not as important as
his behavior implied.

The other drawing portrayed one of her sessions with Jolande. It
showed Jolande's study, with its rather baroque furnishings and a dainty
little lamb (Jolande), in an elaborate, frilly dress with a lace handkerchief
held in one tiny forefoot, seated opposite a huge, bulbous creature rather
like a lion (Clover) slumped in an armchair with an expression of stupid

incomprehension on its face. Clover said this was how Jolande often made her feel. Another picture—this one a lovely watercolor that is included in Jolande's book—showed a little blond girl in a Kate Greenaway dress, frantically clutching the blade of a huge wooden wheel that has already lifted the little girl high off the ground and is carrying her forward to a horrible fate. Clover entitled this picture "The Wheel of Life" and said it showed how she usually felt.

Allen was delighted with the satisfaction that Clover got out of her work with Jolande. He didn't heap as much work on me as he had done before Clover's arrival, but he still would ask me to do things for him. Whenever possible, I would take Clover with me.

In April 1945, as the Allied armies were pushing forward along the northern frontier of Switzerland, Clover and I went up to Kreuzlingen on the German-Swiss border to watch firsthand the approaching collapse of Germany. We strolled along the frontier, which ran through the middle of the town and separated Kreuzlingen in Switzerland from Constance in Germany. On the other side of a wire fence, marking the frontier, an elderly German, digging in his garden, was joined shortly by two other elderly men and a boy in an army uniform. One of the men went into an adjacent chicken yard and fed some very spritely looking hens. The other fetched a plate of food and set it down in front of a handsome, healthy-looking police dog, tethered to an apple tree in a corner of the chicken yard. Both men looked exhausted. Even the boy seemed weary and disoriented. After chatting briefly with the gardener, all three trudged off, a peculiar aimlessness in their gait, as if they had no idea where they were going and cared even less.

Along with wire fence on the Swiss side of the frontier were clusters of the curious. At practically every window in every house someone was staring out across the frontier into Constance, where white sheets or Red Cross flags were spread on the roofs or hung from the windows. There was a deathly stillness in the air and we were told, *"Konstanz hat schon kapituliert"* ("Constance has already capitulated"). An old woman kept emerging from her house to demand, *"Ischt der Ribbentrop noch nicht cho?"* ("Has Ribbentrop arrived yet?"), only to disappear inside again when she got a negative response.

Two tugs were drawn up alongside the wharf in Constance, guarded by a Swiss soldier, who told us that Mrs. Himmler had supposedly "sailed off down the lake on Saturday night." The whole town was obviously abuzz with rumors, mostly unfounded.

We watched the frontier formalities at a distance, German officers lifting and lowering the barriers and, with the greatest courtesy, ushering a steady stream of refugees through into Switzerland. I had previously watched refugees streaming across all the different Swiss frontiers, but these people were in far better condition than any I had yet seen. The women with children and the older people looked tired, but they were in comparatively good condition, their baggage amazingly neat and substantial. Most of the foreign workers crossing had been working on farms in southern Germany. They were sunburned and extremely healthy looking, many of them carrying sacks of potatoes.

When a young Frenchman caught sight of Clover, he nudged his companion; "*Pas mal—celle-là*" ("Not bad—that one"), he said.

"*En effet*" ("Right"), replied his companion, as they marched off to the delousing barracks.

The fields were just turning green, the fruit trees and many spring flowers already in bloom. As the sun began to set behind a pile of fluffy white clouds, it cast an eerie pink light over the landscape. The unearthly stillness in Constance, combined with the curious pink light, shading in places to lavender, created the impression of a muted *Götterdämmerung*. This gentle, pink, flowery scene, with the steady trickle of foreign workers and civilians trudging through the courteously raised and lowered barriers, as the Germans marshaled their Trojan horses—the foreign workers—up to the frontier and shoved them across into Switzerland, was certainly not as one had imagined the collapse of Germany. Maybe T. S. Eliot had been right when he had said the world would end "not with a bang but a whimper. . . ."

The next day when Clover and I reached Kreuzlingen, the fog was just lifting from the lake but there was little activity in either Kreuzlingen or Constance. However, down near the freight yards a group of Swiss housewives was peering through the fence, while up on a bridge over the railroad tracks Swiss officers were staring through binoculars at a corpse lying on the ground between two freight cars in Constance. We were told the dead man was a customs official, known in both Constance and Kreuzlingen as a brutal and corrupt man. On the previous afternoon, shortly before the French occupied Constance, he had tried to get into Switzerland by climbing over the fence. But the Swiss guards, "who knew him well," had trained their guns on him and said they would shoot if he tried to come across. At this he had dropped back and scurried off among the freight cars. A German soldier—"an Austrian"—yelled at him, demanding his name. When he replied "Rombacher," the Austrian shot him dead. This delighted the Swiss who kept emphasizing the fact that "they got the right one first." They seemed particularly pleased that it had been an Austrian who had "got" him.

As we were watching, a railway official went over to the body and began emptying the dead man's pockets. He tied up a few small objects in a handkerchief, covered the body with a blanket, and departed. Several people sunning themselves on a nearby wall appeared quite indifferent to the corpse, never even glancing in its direction.

At the delousing barracks, Clover approached one of the Swiss guards and said, in French, that we were Americans and would like to talk to some of the refugees. He looked skeptical, but said he would ask the commandant.

He returned shortly with the commandant, to whom Clover explained that she had heard about the wonderful way the Swiss were managing the refugee problem, and she would *so* like to see with her own eyes what they were doing, especially since in 1914–1918 she had worked in the White Russian camps in Constantinople. At the word *Russian,* the commandant looked slightly alarmed, but after disappearing briefly, he returned and with a flourish swung open the gate. "Forgive me, Mrs. Dulles," he said apologetically. "I didn't recognize you." We were conducted through the entire establishment, which was spotless and very efficiently organized. Then we were given permission to talk to the refugees in the "disinfected" building.

The first woman we talked to, wearing ski pants, heavy boots, and an expensive velvet turban, was a German married to a Swiss and had her four children with her. The children were so inordinately fat that we commented on it. She said this was because in Mannheim, where they lived, the bombings had been so severe that they had been given extra rations. Her husband had been "forced" into the German Army three months before and she had no idea where he was. When we began to ask further questions, she shrugged and moved off. We had this same experience with most of those with whom we tried to talk. At first they seemed only too glad to talk to us, but the minute we began to ask questions, they got that "Gestapo look" in their eyes and clammed up.

Talking with French collaborationists who in large numbers had come across the previous day, I realized for the first time how very tricky this problem of "collaboration" was going to be. If any kind of justice were to prevail, it was clear each case would have to be considered on its own merits. The news from France was that collaborationists were being shot. But in the differences in motive for collaboration of at least two of the people we talked to, it was possible to see how collaboration varied from individual to individual.

A woman who had her five children with her said her husband had been a druggist in Le Havre, where his shop had been patronized by the Germans. When the Germans retreated, they had forced the whole family to go with them. Her husband had been inducted into the German Army and she didn't know what had become of him. She knew her home in Le Havre had been destroyed, her whole family killed in the bombings. She had heard that all collaborationists were being shot. At the Swiss frontier, she had been given five minutes to decide if she would stay in Germany or return to France; under no circumstances would she be allowed to remain in Switzerland. She had chosen France and kept repeating *"J'ai trop souffert en Allemagne"* ("I suffered too much in Germany").

She had grown up in a home with Marshal Pétain's picture on the wall. Never at any point had she thought of herself as anything but a loyal citizen of France. Having no other way to feed their children, she and her husband had kept their pharmacy open. She had never dreamed the Germans would take her family with them when they withdrew; she certainly had never imagined they would force her husband to join the German Army. The Germans had always behaved correctly and had often played with the children, but they claimed she and her husband knew too much to be left behind. When they had protested, the Gestapo had appeared and threatened to shoot them all unless they went quietly. No longer caring what happened to her or her children, she was returning to Le Havre, on foot if need be, even if they shot her and the children. Death would be welcome after what she had been through. Neither Clover nor I had the slightest doubt of her sincerity. One look at the tragic expression in her eyes and the woebegone air of the children was enough. She had reached the end of her rope. The only thing she still had the strength to want was to reach France and die there if need be.

The other collaborationist, a weasel-faced, shifty-eyed man, was an electrical engineer who before the war had worked for German firms. His health was such that the French Army had not taken him, but when he realized after the fall of France that he was going to be sent to do forced labor in Germany, he had arranged to work for one of the German firms with which he had had previous connections. He had stayed with that firm throughout the war and boasted of what very good care he had taken of himself by various sly and shoddy means. He had told the officials at the frontier that he wanted to return to France, but he had no intention of doing so. He was planning to escape from the convoy and hide out in Switzerland until things either quieted down in France or maybe—just maybe—the Germans would win the war after all—something he considered not too remote a possibility. He was thrilled that Pétain had crossed the Swiss frontier the previous day on his way back to France and was only sorry he had not been at the frontier "to cheer the marshal in person." Probably it was just as well. He'd heard that De Gaulle had quite a following. Did we know anything about him? Would it perhaps be better for him to return to France eventually as a Gaullist rather than as a Pétainist as he had planned?

The difference in motive and character between this man and the woman from Le Havre was the difference between day and night, yet they had been lumped together in the same group—collaborationists.

O──

n July 26, 1945, Professor Jung celebrated his seventy-fifth birthday. I had been asked by the Associated Press, for whom I had occasionally worked as a stringer, if I could get an exclusive interview with him.

When I arrived at Jung's home in Küsnacht, I found him seated on his knees by the window in his study with a dachshund puppy that his wife had given him as a birthday present. I really knew very little about Jung's early years, for this was long before all the biographies, to say nothing of his own autobiography, *Memories, Dreams, Reflections,* had appeared.

He told me that he had been born in a small village on the Lake of Constance, where his father, from an old Basel family, was a parish preacher. When he was a year old, the family had moved to Schaffhausen. There, his father preached in the chapel of an old castle that overlooked the Rheinfall and served as the place of worship for the people of several surrounding villages. When he was four, the family moved to Basel, a city with which he had always felt closely identified. He was a great believer in "the spirit of place" and said that he felt that the humanistic tradition of Basel—where Erasmus and Jacob Burckhardt, among others, had lived and worked and where Friedrich Nietzsche had been a professor at the university—had had a great influence on him. Of Nietzsche, he said, "I thought him a poet, but a morbid poet! And I thought him a marvelous psychologist!"

Jung said he had intended to study ancient languages—"You know how fascinated Swiss students have always been by languages." But then he turned to natural science, adding with a smile, "I don't like to say that

I did this because I felt that in this way perhaps I could help humanity, but that was the real reason."

He had had an excellent humanistic education and was particularly well versed in Latin, which, with his father's help, he was able to read quite easily by the time he was six. "Of course," he said, "the real basis of my philosophical education was Kant. Anyone who doesn't understand Kant and Kant's theory of cognition cannot understand my psychology. Such people mix up psychology and metaphysics. They think that when I say 'God,' I mean God, rather than the *idea* of God."

He told me that he had said all he intended to say about Germany, at least for the moment, in a recent article—"After the Catastrophe"—published in the *Neue Schweizerische Rundschaut* the previous June. In that article, which he claimed was the most difficult for him to write of any he ever had written, he had dealt with the problem of collective guilt and the psychosis that had seized the German people. It was his first statement on the Germans since his "Wotan" article in the March 1936 issue of the same magazine. And he added, "Now the mythos has become reality and a large part of Europe lies in ruins."

One reason the article had been so hard for him to write was that, in touching on the problem of Germany, one was forced to look deep into oneself and face up to one's own share of responsibility for all that had happened. For what had happened in Germany was not Germany's fault alone. The guilt spread far beyond Germany's frontiers and touched not only all Europeans but all Christians as well. How would we react if a Hindu rejected the reproaches we made to him about conditions in India by replying that those particular crimes we were referring to had not taken place in Travancore, where he came from, but in Hyderabad? Wouldn't we say, "Oh, but India is India?"

When a European looked at what had happened in Germany from the standpoint of the East, he perceived his own participation in the German guilt. The crimes in question took place in Germany, but they also took place in Christian Europe. This had to be faced before the work of moral reconstruction could begin.

When I asked him what he was working on at the moment, he said, "I am writing an introduction for the American edition of the *I Ching* ["classic of changes"]. But I can assure you that trying to interpret a Chinese oracle that contains the wisdom of the ages for the American public is not an easy task! However, the publisher made it a condition for bringing out the book that I write an introduction. So I consulted the oracle myself when I was halfway through the introduction."

"And what was the result?"

"The *I Ching* is rather skeptical about the reception he will be accorded in the United States," Jung replied with a chuckle.

In my article, I also described Jung's house in Küsnacht, the simple way he lived, mentioned his wife, five children, and eighteen grandchildren, and closed by saying that engraved in stone over the entrance to his home were the words, *Vocatus atque non vocatus Deus aderit* ("Called or not called, God will be there").

I was rather pleased with my article and so apparently was the Associated Press; at least I received a check in payment promptly and looked forward to the article's publication so I could show it to Jung. But this was not to be. At some point along the chain of command within the Associated Press, an editor or rewrite person decided that my interview with Jung wasn't what Jung *should* have said on his seventy-fifth birthday. So this unknown individual got hold of one of Jung's more recent books and proceeded to compose a quite incredible dialogue in question-and-answer form, attached my name to it, added the words *exclusive interview,* and published the result. I could only creep out to Küsnacht and tell Jung what had happened. Fortunately, he thought it hilarious, although he agreed that it was certainly a prime example of journalistic irresponsibility.

At one point when I had been discussing Gisevius with Jung, I had mentioned that Gisevius was always talking about his friend Martin Niemoeller, the theologian, and how anxious he was to have me meet him. Jung said that it would be most interesting to talk to Niemoeller and added, "Niemoeller is someone with whom something might be done." He thought that Niemoeller might be useful in helping straighten out some of the religious and philosophical turmoil in which so many Germans found themselves, as well as helping them to face up to the problem of collective guilt that was so acute in Germany at the time.

Niemoeller and his wife finally did come to Switzerland and I was able to spend a weekend with them, Gisevius, and Gerda, his fiancée or "Fräulein Braut," as he called her. When Gisevius had talked to me previously about Niemoeller, I got the impression that he was actually fonder of him than of anyone, with the possible exception of General Hans Oster. Everything I had ever heard about Niemoeller, however, had made me think he would be a strong personality, but at the same time rather pompous and overbearing.

To my surprise, he was a simple, genuine person with an impressive ability to establish instant rapport with people of all classes, and an earthy, colloquial way of expressing himself. He also liked to drink. I found it difficult to believe that this was the world-famous clergyman about whom I had heard so much. To me he seemed far more like the submarine captain he had actually been during World War I.

He had just come from a meeting of the World Council of Churches in Geneva, where he had had the opportunity of talking with colleagues from other countries for the first time since his incarceration in Dachau in 1938. He was now fifty-four, but his hair was only slightly gray and, although in repose his face looked somewhat ravaged by all he had been through, the lively intelligence that shone from his eyes and his very winning smile made him look much younger than he was.

His wife, who was younger, looked very much older. They had had seven children, two of whom had been killed in the war. Mrs. Niemoeller said that she dreaded their projected trip to the United States, fearing she had a rather negative attitude toward Americans. The first news she had had of her husband's release from Dachau had been when a Jeep drove up to her country house and Klaus Mann, Thomas Mann's son, and Kurt Riess, a former German journalist, both in American uniforms, the latter with a pencil and notebook in hand, sprang out. "But," she said somewhat disdainfully, "neither of them was an American to me!" Klaus Mann had said, "The Americans have freed your husband from Dachau. You are to come with us." Riess, moistening his pencil, had demanded, "Were any of your children Nazis?" She had been appalled by the Germans who appeared in Germany in American uniforms, which was what had made her wonder what her own reception in the United States would be like.

Niemoeller said that eight years in Dachau, two of them in solitary confinement, had put him "above such things." He didn't really care what kind of a reception he received in the United States. His only concern was whether he would be able to cope with a world, which, under normal circumstances, would have been strange to him but which would be doubly so after having been isolated for so long. He felt no bitterness at being "assaulted" by the American press in Capri, where he had been flown after his release. He admitted, however, that it was certainly an odd experience to face the American press after so many years in a concentration camp. One reporter had shoved a slip of paper at him on which was scrawled: I WILL GIVE YOU FIVE THOUSAND DOLLARS RIGHT NOW IF YOU PROMISE TO LET ME HAVE THE FIRST BOOK YOU WRITE.

During his American trip, he hoped to plead for unity and understanding in the Christian community throughout the world and to ask for food and clothing for the needy in all countries, not just in Germany. What worried him most was whether he would be able to form such pleas effectively, granted the differences in the frame of reference between him and his audiences, differences that at the moment he was not sure he understood.

He seemed discouraged not only about Christianity but about human nature as well. He told us how very unsettling it had been for him to return and have Germans whistle, stamp, and even get up and leave the church when he had tried to tell them that they bore a heavy responsibility for all that had happened. He was pessimistic about the revival of the German church and personally thought "the spirit of the Nazis" had never been stronger in Germany, meaning not just the Nazis' political concepts but the whole evil, totalitarian, godless attitude that oversimplified everything and chose violence to achieve its ends.

One beautiful, sunny day we went up to Weissflujoch. The terrace and restaurant there were full of laughing, happy people. Niemoeller said it was impossible to imagine how good it was to see carefree people enjoying themselves. This was something he had longed for almost more than anything else during the long months of his incarceration. He dreaded returning to the ruins of Germany, being faced with "the isolated, sick mentality of my own people." He feared the Germans would continue to misinterpret their experiences of the past years, to their own detriment and that of the rest of the world.

When I commented on how fluently he spoke English, he said that during the two years he was in solitary confinement, his wife had been allowed to bring him books and had brought him exclusively English books. Counting them up, he had been astonished to find he had read more than four hundred English books during that period alone.

For the benefit of a reporter from the *Neue Zürcher Zeitung*, Niemoeller, at Gisevius's instigation, told the story of his one encounter with Hitler at a meeting of church leaders at the Reich's Chancellery. Goering had read the assembled clergy a transcript of a telephone conversation of Niemoeller's that had been bugged. Then Hitler had accused Niemoeller of receiving money from foreign countries, an accusation Niemoeller had vigorously denied. I asked him why he thought Hitler bothered to put him in Dachau rather than having him killed outright. He said he had often wondered about that, particularly after he had told Hitler at that meeting, so that everyone present could hear, that Hitler had no right to place himself above God. One explanation of why Hitler had not ordered him executed but only incarcerated might be that, unlike many of the other church leaders, he came from a background somewhat similar to Hitler's own. Consequently, he could also "see things primitively" and express himself accordingly. This may well have made Hitler think that he was up against "a leader of the masses like himself" and had better proceed cautiously.

Each evening around ten, Mrs. Niemoeller insisted on dragging a protesting Martin Niemoeller off to bed, claiming his health was poor and that he needed his rest. Within ten or fifteen minutes, however, he would reappear in the café, call for a bottle of wine, and spend another hour or so laughing and talking with the rest of us.

Wherever he went, he created a stir. In Klosters, the village pastor got so excited when he heard that Niemoeller was there that he arranged a special service at which he gave an incredibly long-winded and effusive speech in the course of which he compared Niemoeller to both Christ and Goethe. Niemoeller sat through this ordeal, looking extremely uncomfortable and embarrassed, but afterward he was very kind to the man, who simply couldn't contain his excitement at the great honor that had fallen upon him, his church, and the entire village.

There was another famous personality of those days in Klosters during that weekend, namely Fabian von Schlabrendorff, a survivor of the twentieth of July conspiracy. Schlabrendorff, working closely with Major General Henning von Tresckow, also a member of the conspiracy, had managed to smuggle a bomb aboard Hitler's plane when the Führer had visited the headquarters of Field Marshal von Kluge at Smolensk in March 1943. Schlabrendorff and Tresckow had repeatedly tested similar bombs, always with complete success. But this time Hitler's luck, or his Providence, as he called it, had protected him again. The bomb was an English type, compact yet powerful enough to blow up a plane in flight. In order to be on the safe side, they had wrapped two bombs in a package that resembled two bottles of cognac and had arranged with a member of the plane's crew to deliver the "cognac" to General Helmuth Stieff of the High Command, later a member of the conspiracy, when the plane returned to the Führer's headquarters at Rastenburg. They had to wrap the package very, very carefully so that it would be possible to press the fuse just before they handed it aboard the plane.

Schlabrendorff had accompanied Hitler, Von Kluge, and Tresckow to the airport, taken the package from the trunk of the car, and activated the fuse. After Hitler had entered the plane, Schlabrendorff had handed the package to the man who was to deliver it to General Stieff.

The plane took off. Schlabrendorff and Tresckow, waiting impatiently at Smolensk, were aghast when two hours later came the official announcement that the Führer had landed safely at his headquarters in Rastenburg. What could possibly have happened? It was bad enough that Hitler had escaped. What was worse was that if the bombs were discovered, it would not only lead to their own exposure but to that of a wide circle of collaborators as well. Finally, Tresckow decided to call the man to whom he had given the package—"the two bottles of cognac for General Stieff." He could tell by the man's manner that he still believed the story about the cognac, so he asked the man to hold the package for a day before delivering it. Early the next morning Schlabrendorff, on some military pretext, took a regular courier plane to Hitler's headquarters, picked up the package with the bombs in it, and replaced it with a similar package that really did contain two bottles of cognac. In the meantime he and Tresckow had been in touch by code with the leaders of the conspiracy in Berlin.

Terrified that the rough and careless way in which the man had handed back the package with the bombs in it might have set off the fuse, Schlabrendorff drove directly to where a special army train was to leave that evening for Berlin. Once inside one of the train's compartments, he locked the door and carefully opened the package, expecting that at any moment it might explode. Fortunately, it did not. What he discovered was that the bomb's mechanism had begun to work, then stopped. The fuse was supposed to break a small bottle of acid which would then eat through a wire holding back the firing pin. This had all happened, but for some inexplicable reason the percussion cap had not gone off.

Gero von Gaevernits, Allen's assistant, had been helping Schlabrendorff write up his version of this affair, and when Gisevius heard about it, he was greatly agitated. Would Schlabrendorff's book harm the sale of his own beloved manuscript? I personally thought not. I had seen Schlabrendorff's manuscript, in which he had said some nice things about Gisevius. I felt that Gisevius being mentioned favorably by Schlabrendorff would only help him and tend to kill those rumors that continued to circulate that Gisevius had been Gestapo.

Still, I had no desire to have Gisevius cross-examining me about either Schlabrendorff or his manuscript. So although I spent many hours that weekend talking to Schlabrendorff, I told Gisevius I had seen him only briefly. I found Schlabrendorff highly intelligent, with eyes that flickered like a snake's when talking about anything that interested him greatly. He was a lawyer by profession, born in 1907, which made him three years younger than Gisevius. At one point he told me half-jokingly that, in the next war, he would prefer to fight in a German Army under English political leadership, equipped by the Americans. When I repeated this to Gisevius, he turned to Niemoeller and said indignantly, "What did I tell you? You see, he is still a militarist!" Then he asked Niemoeller what he thought would become of *Der Schlager,* as they called him, a nickname that in this instance might be translated as "the hit man." Niemoeller replied that he thought *Der Schlager* might go far. He was very ambitious, very capable, with an intelligence in direct proportion to his ambition—but he would never do anything *unanständig* ("improper"). Actually Niemoeller thought· that within ten years Schlabrendorff might well hold any position he wished.

Niemoeller was right. The manuscript I had seen prepared and edited by Gaevernits was published in 1947 under the title, *They Almost Killed Hitler.* An expanded version of Schlabrendorff's story, *The Secret War Against Hitler,* was published in 1965.

That weekend Schlabrendorff's comment to me about Gisevius's book had been that although he had found it "fascinating," it was written "a little too broadly for my tastes." He felt Gisevius's criticism of the German generals was "too one-sided. The problems these men were up against were not as simple as Gisevius made them out to have been." That comment I did not repeat.

XXXIII

The Allied armies continued to push steadily forward. At the time they were approaching the frontiers of Liechtenstein, Allen suggested I go up there to see what information I could pick up.

A Soviet commission had been in Bern negotiating for the return of any Soviet prisoners of war who had escaped from Germany and sought refuge in Switzerland. Two members of the commission, uniformed officers of the NKVD, the Soviet secret police, would be going to Liechtenstein. A contingent of White Russians, who had been fighting in the German Army, had recently crossed the Liechtenstein frontier and had been given asylum. There was a rumor that among these troops was the man who had been in charge of the selection of partisan units that the Germans had left behind the Russian lines when they retreated. All the Allies were eager to lay their hands on this man, the Soviets most of all.

I left Zurich on a flawless spring day. The fruit trees were just beginning to burst into bloom and a cold wind was blowing down from the still snow-tipped mountains surrounding the tiny principality, whose capital, Vaduz, was actually little more than a small village with one main street.

Liechtenstein itself covers approximately sixty-two square miles, and during the war had a population of about eleven thousand people. It was a constitutional monarchy, but both the father and uncle of Franz Joseph II, the present ruling prince, or *Fürst*, had renounced the throne because the idea of being a ruling prince had bored them. But Franz Joseph had modernized the castle and taken up permanent residence there. I knew both Franz Joseph and his wife, Gina, the *Fürstin*, as well as their cousin,

Prince Constantine, who was a particularly good friend of mine. I had been to Liechtenstein on several previous occasions to visit them.

Prince Constantine met me at the station and, as soon as I had registered and left my bag at the hotel, we went up to the frontier, where a huge mass of refugees was gathered on the other side waiting to come through. The rumor was that the SS was planning to defend Feldkirch, a short distance away.

Pressed up against the barrier was a tall girl in a blue silk dress with a mink stole thrown around her shoulders. On her head she wore a tiny velvet hat with a veil and under one arm she clutched a Pekingese, a pink bow on its head. She was, I was told, an American. Would I please speak to her?

I was not particularly proud to have my country represented by such a specimen at that particular moment among those miserable and bedraggled refugees. But up I went to the frontier and asked her what she was doing there. "It's the war, you know," she lisped. "I want to get out of Germany because of the war. I want to telephone Daddy." I said I would call the legation in Bern and see what could be done. The official to whom I spoke said, "My God! Is she trying to get into Liechtenstein now? She's been trying to get across every frontier. She's the girl friend of an SS officer with whom she has been living for years. Let the SS take care of her!"

Gina, a bandana tied around her head, was ladling cups of soup out of a huge kettle and passing them across the frontier to the refugees. Suddenly, the crowd fell back, the frontier barriers were raised, and a cavalry company of White Russians in German uniforms passed through. They rode their horses over into a nearby orchard and dismounted. I have seldom seen more interesting faces on a group of men.

Then a murmur arose from the crowd at the frontier and, glancing in that direction, I saw a group of seven adolescent boys in the striped uniforms of the concentration camps limping across the frontier. They walked slowly over to the orchard where the White Russians' horses were now grazing and slumped down in the grass. The Americans had liberated Dachau that morning and these seven boys were the sole survivors of more than twelve hundred Dachau inmates who had been herded into a train that had just arrived at the other side of the frontier. The rumor was that all the others on that train had died en route either from exhaustion or from the excitement of their liberation.

The seven boys were all from Poland, where they had been picked up as children and shuttled from camp to camp throughout the war. They were unbelievably gaunt and filthy. The sweet smell of death that emanated from them made me reel. One of them produced an empty sardine tin from which he extracted a few grimy and torn family photographs to show me, but the others seemed too weak to speak. They just lay there in the grass until an ambulance arrived to take them to a hospital in Switzerland.

The emotions induced by the combination of the American girl, the White Russians, and those poor, wretched boys were such that I had difficulty pulling myself together to attend a dinner held that evening for the two Soviet officers in the uniform of the dreaded NKVD. Each had his own translator with him, but we had been warned that although the two officers pretended to speak only Russian, they actually spoke many languages and nothing should be said in their presence that we didn't want them to understand.

The dinner was held in one of the hotels in Vaduz; the dining room decorated with garlands of orange crepe paper. The food was delicious and a great deal of wine was consumed. Afterward there was dancing. One of the NKVD officers, a tiny man who came just up to my shoulder, clicking his heels and bowing before me, invited me, through his interpreter, to dance. He was a wonderful dancer. As we floated about to the strains of "The Blue Danube Waltz," it suddenly occurred to me that while I had met many people who claimed to know Communists or to be Communists themselves, I had never known anyone who had waltzed with a member of the NKVD. Furthermore, this little creature was the first member of the great Red Army I had seen. I found this all so absurd that I wanted to confide my thoughts to my partner. We were dancing in such perfect rhythm that I felt it symbolically encouraging for a future friendship between our two nations and I wanted to tell him so. I glanced about for his interpreter, but he was nowhere in sight.

"What's the matter?" asked my partner in flawless English.

"I'm looking for your interpreter," I said, only half-realizing that he had addressed me in my native tongue.

"Oh, don't worry about him," he said. "Tell me in English."

I recognized a familiar accent.

"Where did you learn English?" I demanded.

"In Brooklyn," he said, smiling.

At that moment, his interpreter appeared and my partner, assuming a ferocious expression, began to bawl the poor man out in Russian.

The following day, feeling extremely depressed, I left for Zurich. What I had seen in Liechtenstein had convinced me that not just a few nations were in trouble but humanity as a whole. An unhappy footnote to my experiences was that, under an agreement with the Soviets, the Allies eventually handed over those White Russians and they were all executed.

XXXIV

By the late spring of 1945, my colleagues had begun getting ready to leave for other posts. Allen was going to Germany to head the OSS mission there. He asked me if I wanted to go with him. Gisevius thought I should. I knew so much about Germany and Germans, he said, I would be extremely "valuable" there and could make "a very interesting career" for myself. However flattering that might be, I was exhausted emotionally, physically, psychically. I never wanted to hear the words *intelligence work* again. The strain had been enormous, so I told Allen no. He then asked me what kind of a "reward" I would like for my wartime services. "To go to Nuremberg when Gisevius appears as a witness for Schacht," I said. Allen said that could easily be arranged.

A few weeks later we started off by car, my OSS colleague Bob Shea at the wheel, with me beside him, and Gisevius and a Swiss, who had served the Allied cause above and beyond the call of duty, ensconced in the backseat. The Swiss kept exclaiming that for him this trip to Nuremberg was the high point of his life. Bob and Gisevius grew increasingly grim as the Swiss gentleman's ebullience increased by the minute.

Würzburg, on our somewhat circuitous route to Nuremberg, made a devastating impression on me. It had been razed to the ground in an air attack lasting eighteen minutes. A woman sitting in the sun on a wooden chair before the ruins of what had once been her home, a dirty white cat curled up at her feet, said she had lost her entire family in the bombardment and had herself been temporarily blinded. But she was all right now. She lived in the cellar of her former home. Everyone else was also living in a cellar. Yes, the Americans were all right. Yes, everyone got what was on the ration cards. No, she didn't know what she was going to do. For the moment, she just enjoyed sitting in the sun with her cat, who had miraculously escaped the bombs and now dozed contentedly at her feet. She waved her hand at the surrounding ruins: "We have our Führer to thank for this!" Adolf Hitler no longer held any place in her heart, but hers was one of the very few hearts in Germany of which I was personally persuaded that this was true.

There was a strange beauty in the ruins of Nuremberg. The reds and browns, mingled with the blacks and grays of the bombed-out buildings, contrasted strongly with the lime-green buds of the willow trees and the yellow flowers of forsythia bushes under the bright blue sky of a spring day. In front of a shattered statue, two little girls were quarreling over a wicker doll carriage piled high with dirty rag dolls, while a black GI, lolling behind the wheel of a Jeep, watched them with amusement.

We deposited our Swiss at the home of some friends. Gisevius was pale with exhaustion. Shea was still red-faced with annoyance at the ebullient Swiss, and I quite unable to believe that I was at last in Nuremberg.

It had been a warm day, but the air was growing cooler by the time we drew up in front of the hotel that served as American Army headquarters. An American woman stood in the doorway, a fur coat thrown carelessly over her shoulders. The light streaming out from the lobby of the hotel reflected off her high-heeled patent-leather pumps and her smart matching handbag.

Suddenly, an American officer materialized by her side. "Oh, Harry," she squealed. "This is going to be *such* fun! Have you got the whiskey? Only one bottle? Don't you think we'd better take *two*?"

The sun had set, but a sinister yellow light hung over the city. A shabbily dressed man limping past the hotel turned sharply as the woman's shrill voice floated out on the evening air. He gave her a harsh, penetrating look, spat contemptuously at his feet, and shuffled off down the avenue. Overhead hung that ubiquitous warning sign that the American occupying forces had placed over the highways in their zone: DEATH IS SO PERMANENT! DRIVE CAREFULLY!

In the lobby of the hotel, Shea quickly located the officer in charge of accommodations. After an exchange that I could not hear, the officer picked up a phone. "OK! OK!" he shouted into the receiver. "But they've got a *Kraut* with them!" Shea's accommodations were in order, but apparently no one had thought to specify that, of the two people accompanying him, one would be a *Kraut* and the other a woman.

Eventually, the problem was resolved and Gisevius and I were driven by a GI to a villa on the outskirts of the city, referred to as the Witness House. The door was opened by a maid who began wringing her hands at the sight of us. "Oh!" she exclaimed. "The Countess has just stepped out. She seldom goes out! I'm sure she will be right back!"

"Yes," echoed an older woman appearing by her side, "The Countess seldom goes out! She will be right back! Please, won't you wait in here for the Countess?"

She opened the door of a large, gloomy room furnished in nondescript fashion just as there was the sound of voices outside and the younger woman cried, "Here comes the Countess now!"

A slim young woman with blond hair falling to her shoulders entered, followed by a group of six or seven small men chattering and laughing. Snow White and the Seven Dwarfs flashed through my mind.

One of the men let out a shout of delight at the sight of Gisevius; it was followed by an equally delighted shout from Gisevius.

"What are *you* doing here?" asked the man.

"What are *you* doing here?" countered Gisevius.

"I'm here as a witness!"

"Me, too," said Gisevius. "For Schacht!"

"Schacht? You don't say! Have you heard about . . ."

I didn't catch the name, but Gisevius told me later that the reference was to a fanatical Nazi.

"No. What about him?" asked Gisevius.

"They've made him mayor of . . ." Again I didn't catch the name of the city. "It seems he never belonged to the party!" Shouts of delighted laughter.

The Countess was full of apologies. Nobody had told her we were coming. Did we plan to spend the night? Had we eaten? We must be hungry. We must be tired. Where had we come from? How dreadful that she had not been at home to receive us, but she and her guests had felt the need of some fresh air. She began introducing the men milling about in the hall. One of them, in a shabby Tyrolean jacket, scampered up the stairs. "Heinrich Hoffmann," the Countess murmured to me under her breath. "You've doubtless heard of him. He was Hitler's photographer. He thinks you are from the press. He refuses to talk to the press . . ."

Immediately after supper, Gisevius retired for the night. But I, curious about my fellow guests, joined them in the sitting room. I was particularly interested in a distinguished-looking elderly man in a shabby dark suit with a white silk scarf, yellowed with age, wrapped around his neck. He was, he told me, a naval officer who had been called as a witness for Admiral Raeder. He was anxious to have me understand, if I didn't already realize it, that the German Navy was the elite of the German armed forces.

A plump, dowdy woman with an air of great self-importance turned to me. "So," she said. "You come from Switzerland!" Pause. "How interesting!" Faint smiles from the other guests. "My husband and I always went to Davos. We haven't gone lately, but hope to next year. I am Mrs. Hoffmann! This is Mrs. Funk."

Mrs. Funk gave me a stiff little bow. "We met at dinner," she said. "I was explaining to this lady [meaning me] that my husband was among the twenty-one leading criminals of war. They haven't caught Bormann yet. Otherwise my husband would have been only the twenty-second!"

The air of pride with which she spoke seemed to imply that to be selected among the leading criminals of war was a great honor.

"Of course, you understand," said Mrs. Hoffmann, "that we are free. The others were under arrest."

"The others?" I asked.

"Yes. The witnesses for the prosecution. They all had guards."

These witnesses for the defense had simply assumed that the prosecution witnesses were under arrest, never dreaming that they were guarded to protect them from the wrath of those against whom they were about to testify.

A tall, scrawny woman, sitting on the edge of a straight-backed chair, glanced nervously from one guest to another like an inquisitive crow. She had been introduced to me by the Countess as Miss Take. I had assumed her family name was Take, but I learned later that the woman was there "by mistake." She had been picked up late one night at her home in the British zone by two GIs in a Jeep and carted off to Nuremberg, she knew not why. Neither did anyone else. Furthermore, nobody cared. So she had stayed on, far more worried about what would become of a Children's Aid project in which she, a retired schoolteacher, had been active than about her own fate.

She was not the first person to land in the Witness House by mistake. Some weeks before, a woman with the same name as an authentic witness and living in the same neighborhood had been brought to the house. She had been thrilled by the honor, feasted eagerly on the food provided by the Americans, and made a terrible fuss when the real witness had showed up, insisting the latter was an imposter. Eventually, she had had to be forcibly evicted by the military police.

After about an hour, the door of the sitting room opened and the Countess beckoned me to join her outside in the hall.

"You must forgive me," she said. "I don't know what I was thinking about. You know that lady beside Mrs. Hoffmann?" She paused. "Well . . . at first I intended to put you in the same room with her. But then . . ." She struck her forehead with the palm of her hand. "Then it occurred to me. No! I thought. *No!* I cannot allow you—an American—to sleep in the same room with the wife of a criminal of war!"

I assured her that it was a matter of indifference to me where I slept, but the Countess was adamant. She was moving one of her children in with her and giving me the child's room. She would never have been able to forgive herself if she had permitted me to sleep in the same room with the wife of a criminal of war. Little did she realize that actually I had been rather looking forward to the experience.

When I entered the Nuremberg courtroom the following day, Von Ribbentrop, his face the color of Camembert cheese, was on the stand. He seemed to have no idea why he found himself in his present humiliating position. In his opinion, he had never done anything wrong.

Goering, in a plain jacket, was in the place of honor at the far left of the front row of defendants, turned slightly catercorner and leaning back against the side of the dock, watching the proceedings with an expression of sardonic contempt. His dark blond hair was combed straight back from his receding hairline and he had lost a tremendous amount of weight. But there was something about the set of his jaw and the tilt of his head that suggested that there was still plenty of fight left in him.

Beside him sat Rudolf Hess, staring catatonically off into space. He looked utterly demented, like a character out of *The Cabinet of Dr. Caligari.*

Wilhelm Frick, in a plaid tweed sports jacket, was chewing gum and appeared quite unconcerned. I got the impression he fully expected to be acquitted. He was not. He was hanged.

Schacht's high, stiff collar and bullet-shaped head instantly identified him. His whole posture was arrogance incarnate. I have never seen such disdain displayed by any defendant in any courtroom. He obviously never doubted that he would be acquitted. Actually, he was, on all counts.

After Von Ribbentrop had finished his testimony, General Keitel was the next defendant called to the stand. It was difficult to believe that this subdued, almost groveling creature had been Hitler's Chief of Staff. In answer to the prosecutor's opening query, he replied in a low voice, *"Mein name ist Wilhelm Keitel."* It was strange to hear those words translated by a soft, female American voice: "My name is Wilhelm Keitel."

By turning a switch on the earphones provided to the spectators, it was possible to listen to the proceedings in French, English, German, or Russian. Occasionally, a ripple of laughter would break out among a particular group of spectators when a translator missed a point. The translators were tops in their field, but this trial was unique in that concepts were being dealt with here that had never before been dealt with in a court of law. This caused most of the slips. The translator would give the words correctly but misunderstand the concept, thus giving the words an oblique, if not actually incorrect, meaning.

On my last night in the Witness House I was chatting with the other guests when the door of the sitting room opened a crack and Heinrich Hoffmann beckoned to me. I glanced at Mrs. Hoffmann. She nodded benignly. "My husband wants to talk to you," she murmured.

I knew I would never have a chance to talk to anyone who had known Hitler as well, yet until that moment Heinrich Hoffmann had avoided me like the plague. Motioning me into the dining room, he closed the door and, with a sweeping gesture, indicated I should take one of the chairs drawn up to the dining-room table while he took the chair beside me. He was wearing the same shabby Tyrolean jacket he always wore. The collar and cuffs of his dingy white shirt were frayed around the edges. His fingernails were dirty and he smelled slightly rancid, rather like an old dishcloth, as many people did in those days when soap was at a premium. His eyes, however, were bright and shrewd, his whole expression that of an inquisitive weasel.

"So," he said, "you write for the press?"

"Sometimes," I answered cautiously.

"Is that why you are here? Are you going to write about your trip for the press?"

"Not necessarily. Maybe . . ."

"It doesn't matter!" He tilted back in his chair and studied me appraisingly. "I know you accompanied a witness to Nuremberg." He paused. "You realize, of course," he continued in a rather lordly tone, "that I was a *world-famous* photographer long before Adolf Hitler ever crossed my path."

I allowed as how I knew he was a very famous photographer but—

Hoffmann held up his hand.

"Yes," he said. "World famous! I photographed Stalin years before I even met Adolf Hitler. People seem to have forgotten that I was in the Kremlin. Stalin made my reputation . . . even in America my pictures of him were greatly admired!"

He paused to let this bit of information sink in. Then, with a casual gesture of dismissal, he observed disdainfully, "Adolf Hitler? Adolf Hitler was but an episode in my life. A rather long episode, I grant you. But still—only an episode."

For nearly an hour he rambled on, explaining in great detail his views on life, art, and the value of the human personality. He stopped periodically to extract a promise from me that I would not publish any of these pearls of wisdom in the foreign press. "The press today is a thoroughly unreliable channel for the dissemination of my ideas."

He said that the diaries of Eva Braun that had begun to appear in several countries, including Switzerland, were forgeries. He opened his wallet and showed me a picture of Eva Braun that bore no resemblance to any of the photographs of her that had so far been published. The diaries then appearing, written in a crude and simplistic style, were obviously forgeries, he said, because "Eva had a fine literary style." He had personally introduced Eva to the Führer. "I have, of course, been called as a witness for my son-in-law, von Schirach. When I've finished my testimony, the whole world will realize what a tremendous injustice is being done!"

Von Schirach's comment after the verdict condemning him to twenty years imprisonment on one count of a four-point indictment was, "The whole misfortune came from racial politics."

Shea and I left Gisevius in Nuremberg. On our way to Munich, our next stop, we spent the night with the American civilian administrator in one of the districts occupied by the Americans. There were two other guests at dinner: a young American vice-consul newly arrived from Chicago, a great admirer of the works of e.e. cummings, who evaluated every experience he was having on the basis of what it might do for him and his future career, and Dr. Wang, the Chinese observer at the Dachau trials that were taking place nearby. This charming and cultivated gentleman was greatly amused by the American vice-consul, particularly when the latter began explaining to him the difference between a *fille de joie* ("prostitute") in Italy and a *fille de joie* in China, although he had never been in either country. When he had finished his analysis, Dr. Wang observed gently in French, "Young man, I am sure that one day you will marry *une fille de joie!*" This delighted the vice-consul who, missing the irony, countered with, "Did you know, sir, that you can get married in South Carolina but you can't get divorced there?"

"Extraordinary!" murmured Dr. Wang.

Dr. Wang told me that he found it absurd to try the Dachau guards in a court of law, wrong to kill them outright. "They should be tortured as they have tortured others. I see no reason for opening the door that is death to such monsters so that they may depart this vale of tears so pleasantly." His forehead wrinkled slightly, his lips curled in a satisfied smile, and his exquisitely manicured hands fluttered, like dying butterflies, down on the arms of his chair.

Dr. Wang had lived for some time in Switzerland, having studied at the University of Freiburg. He admired the Swiss but described them as a people great "because of their pettiness." Then he added with a sad little smile, "The Swiss have so few pleasures!"

I had remembered Munich as a friendly city, with beautiful parks and wide boulevards, but now its atmosphere was tense and ugly. A black market flourished openly and there were a great many displaced persons—or DPs as they were called—skulking through the streets.

I had a package to deliver that had been given me by Count Lingen, a hearty, florid gentleman with a booming voice, who had come to tea with his sweet-faced wife and his tall, handsome daughter. Count Lingen loved bananas, a great luxury in those days, and had arrived with a bag full of them to share with me.

As he had strutted happily up and down our living room, waving a banana in one hand and telling one of his fascinating stories, I was overcome by a sense of unreality, of disbelief. For Count Lingen was a son of that bogeyman of my childhood, Emperor William II of Germany. As he pranced happily around the room under the affectionate gaze of his wife and daughter, it was certainly a very different scene from anything I had imagined when I had chanted with the neighborhood children:

> *We will hang the Kaiser*
> *To a rotten apple tree!*
> *Out goes Y-O-U!*

When the Count asked me if I would take a hot-water bottle and a pair of shoes to an old family retainer—"Such a devoted soul!"—in Munich, I naturally said I would be delighted. Why shouldn't I run errands for a Hohenzollern?

We found the lady in question living in a tiny, two-room flat with glazed paper covering the windows that had been shattered in a bombardment. She had not wanted to fix up the apartment too much for fear the Americans would requisition it.

On the street outside the building, DPs were doing a lively black-market trade in wearing apparel of all kinds. Each day, she said, they would show up at a different UNRA center that was distributing clothes, get themselves a new outfit, promptly sell it, and repeat the same routine the following day.

After I had delivered the hot-water bottle and all the messages the Lingens had asked me to convey, the little lady begged us to stay for a cup of tea with her. We were the first people she had met since the outbreak of the war that she felt could tell her what had actually happened. She herself had finally become convinced of the existence of the concentration camps. Although horrified, she had not been surprised. She was quite willing to attribute anything to the Nazis, whom she had always considered "vulgar and brutal men." She asked if it were true that Rotterdam and Coventry had been destroyed. She had never believed anything she had read in the Nazi-controlled press or heard over the radio. As for air raids on London, she had imagined, "Perhaps it was the work of some dashing squadron leader, exceeding orders, and Goebbels had simply taken one incident and exaggerated it, as was his custom."

Tears rolled down her cheeks as we assured her that it was true that Rotterdam and Coventry had indeed been flattened and London bombed repeatedly. She looked so frail that I asked her if she needed any food. She confessed that she had had very little to eat in recent months. Since the Occupation, she had been afraid to go out. She had had to count on the kindness of neighbors to bring her anything they had left over from their own meager food supplies. I asked her if she didn't have any friends or relatives with whom she could stay in the country; conditions were said to be so much better there than in the cities. No, she said, unfortunately she was alone in the world. But even if there had been someplace where she could have gone, she doubted if she could have brought herself to leave Munich, which held for her so many memories of happier times.

If there was anyone in Germany who belonged to a world that had gone forever, it was this genteel little lady, existing on tea and crusts of bread, surrounded by pictures of the Hohenzollern family. When we were leaving, she accompanied us to the head of the stone staircase out-side her apartment, still clutching the hot-water bottle I had brought her and thanking us over and over again for having come to see her.

As we pushed our way through the grimy, haggling DPs, the hysteri-cal shrieks of the German girls fraternizing with the GIs ringing in our ears, I felt that at last I had closed a book that had begun for me nearly thirty years before, when I'd followed with such passionate interest that "war to end all wars," had wept over Alan Seeger's "I Have a Ren-dezvous with Death," and had banged out all those World War I songs on my grandmother's piano.

Now another war had come and gone. More millions were dead. Was this just God's will, as Maria proclaimed? As we made our way through the crowd of wretched DPs to our car to begin our trip back to Switzer-land, I wondered if anything had been learned from any of it, and if anyone actually cared.

XXXV

When I went to France for the first time after the cessation of hostilities, the object of my trip was to supervise the publication of a book on Switzerland on which I had done some work. This publishing endeavor was one of those enterprises that cropped up frequently in those days when people who had blocked currency in some country engaged in activities they had never engaged in before in order to use their blocked money. This particular book was to be published by a group of Balkan businessmen with cultural aspirations, who had decided that book publishing would be a "safe" venture to engage in with capital acquired in black- or gray-market activities during the war. They disliked and mistrusted each other, which certainly didn't facilitate the project. They also wanted to publish the book in English, figuring this might help them get that American visa that was the dream of everyone in Europe in those days. They chose me both to polish the translation and to go to Paris to oversee the details of publication. In their eyes I had "connections," which figured so highly in European calculations. They had stared at me with a total lack of comprehension when I pointed out to them that any connections I might have, I retained only because I never used them. That was certainly not how business was done in the Balkans.

Jean had been responsible for introducing me to these gentlemen, who had been extremely helpful to him on his trips to Rumania. They had offered to pay well for the job—"And better that you get the money than anyone else!" said Jean. I was no longer as naive as I had been in earlier days, no longer had any of those attacks of moral indignation that had so troubled me during my first few years in Europe. However, I still had much to learn, as a recent experience in Liechtenstein had taught me: I had been summoned to Vaduz by a gentleman, a German who had built a house there and was wanted as a "minor" criminal of war. He was interested in engaging me to help him write his memoirs.

After he had shown me a general outline and certain documents he intended to include, I felt we should get down to business. One of my weaknesses is that if I'm interested in any writing job, I don't care how much I am paid. If I'm not interested, no sum is large enough to persuade me to take it on, because under such circumstances, my imagination completely evaporates. This attitude had always been a source of great irritation to Jean. He always insisted whenever I went for a job interview that I be sure that I was to be paid, and paid well, preferably ahead of time.

The one time I had defied Jean on this point had taught me a lesson: A Hindu gentleman had asked me to translate a manuscript from French into English for him. He had not written it himself; he neither wrote nor spoke French; but the manuscript was on a subject that interested him greatly and he wanted to be able to read it. Jean warned me that I should insist on being paid in advance. "You'll see that if you don't," he had said, "that once you've given your fine friend the translation, he'll be so sure that the whole experience has been of such enormous spiritual benefit to you that he won't dream of tarnishing it by giving you money!" I thought Jean was just being impossibly cynical and prejudiced. The translation was extremely difficult, but the Hindu gentleman was delighted with it, gave the attached bill a pained glance, folded it, and slipped it into his pocket with no comment. Shortly thereafter, he left Zurich to return to Bombay. I never got my money.

So, with that in mind, I brought up the subject of money that day in Liechtenstein. The gentleman in question made a gesture of protest. "Please, this is not a question of money! I will pay the sum you suggest." He summoned his secretary, asked for his checkbook, and, tearing out a check, signed it blank, and handed it to me.

"Fill in any sum you think fair," he said with an engaging smile.

I handed the check back, saying I couldn't possibly accept any such arrangement. He looked faintly annoyed, shrugged, and said, "As you like! But think it over. Let me know if you change your mind."

Later, I told Gisevius of this experience. "I'm afraid I offended him," I said. "I guess he'll now get someone else to do the job. . . ."

"Undoubtedly," said Gisevius scornfully. "But really . . . what is the matter with you?"

"What do you mean?"

"You didn't offend him. He just realized you couldn't be bribed."

"Is that what he was trying to do?"

"Of course," said Gisevius with a sigh. "Really! You Americans! Don't you understand anything? Of course that's what he was trying to do. You should have filled in the check for twenty-five thousand dollars, cashed it, then denounced him. Now he's got to find someone else, who is not as stupid as you are, to bribe!"

When I repeated Gisevius's remark to Allen, he asked with an air of innocence, "So twenty-five thousand dollars is the going rate?"—and burst out laughing. "Don't you realize," he said, "that one reason you've been so useful to me is that I know you can't be bribed?"

When I repeated this to Gisevius, he gave me another of his withering glances, observing with a sneer, "Naturally!" He then proceeded to lecture me on the problems of bribery and corruption "in our business" and the great advantage to a spy master of having agents who cannot be bribed.

My trip to France was actually in many ways a *recherche du temps perdu.* In one of those inexplicable coincidences that seem to occur periodically, I was assigned to the same room in the same hotel where I had stayed when I had been conducted, together with my schoolmates, through five European countries in six weeks and force-fed endless cathedrals, art galleries, and museums. I had learned in school about the Marquis de Lafayette, who had helped the United States win its freedom from the perfidious English in 1776. I could remember how proud I had felt during World War I when an editorial in the Boston *Evening Transcript* had pointed out that, by going to the aid of the Allies, we were paying our debt to the elegant Marquis de Lafayette. This feeling had reached its zenith when I had read the report of General Pershing's announcement as he landed in France: "Lafayette! We are here!" When on that earlier trip we had motored through the dusty battlefields of the war, I had been impressed and horrified by their stark and ugly desolation. Once back in our hotel rooms, I had recited to my companions, "In Flanders fields the poppies blow/Between the crosses, row on row . . ."

And as always, "I have a rendezvous with Death . . ."

We had all been deeply impressed that the soil of France was filled with dead Americans. This fact had had a particularly devastating effect on my imagination. Verdun, Somme, Marne—those names had haunted me—particularly Verdun, for which Marshal Pétain had become a symbol. But now the marshal was in disgrace and had been replaced by the towering figure of Charles de Gaulle.

In 1919 we had not known how to find our way into the life of France, to establish contact with the French people. We had been as puzzled, as lost, as miserable as the hordes of GIs now sitting at the sidewalk cafés, staring blankly at the passing crowds after another world war had been fought and still more dead Americans lay beneath the rich, fertile soil of France.

I talked with many of those GIs and found them an amazingly disconsolate lot. It was hard to believe they were the same GIs I had seen on leave in Switzerland, yet many of them told me they were. Their attitudes and reactions to France reminded me very much of my own and those of my classmates so many years before. The cleanliness and modernity of Switzerland had reassured them. The warmth and friendliness of the Swiss, who had been so grateful to them and eager to show their appreciation, had made them feel at home. But gratitude was not a characteristic of the French.

"Do you really believe the problem is partially something as trivial as a question of plumbing?" a French friend asked me when we were discussing how unfortunate it was that in both world wars so much friction had existed in France between the French and the Americans. I answered frankly that in many ways I thought it was. It was impossible to grow up in the United States with its high-pressure attitude toward hygiene and cleanliness, and not be appalled by certain aspects of French life. Actually, the average German was much more like the average American than the average Frenchman. It had been a very unsettling experience for many GIs to find themselves feeling closer to their former enemies than to their supposed friends.

There was also the French attitude toward work. We Americans shared a work ethic with the Germans, but even as early as the 1930's, the whole French nation seemed to expect life to be nothing but a protracted *vacance payée* ("paid vacation"). The French, it is true, were exhausted. On the other hand, the Germans were exhausted, too. Furthermore, they had been defeated rather than emerging victorious and finding themselves on the winning side as the French had managed to do. Yet all the Germans still seemed to care about was work. More than one American officer in Germany had told me that until he got to Germany and was able to have Germans working for him, he had been unable to get anything done properly.

Last but by no means least on the roster of difficulties between the French and Americans was the French ability to hate. Americans don't seem to be very good at hating, not only because it is generally regarded as not a very "nice" thing to do but because real hatred requires the kind of sustained emotional effort which, it seems to me, strikes most Americans as rather a waste of time. The French, however, hate with a positive splendor. A French friend told me that when she showed some GIs where five Resistance fighters had been killed, one of them had asked her, "Where are the bodies?" She had been baffled by this, but I told her I thought it simply the embarrassed reaction of a young, unsophisticated American to the intense hatred she herself felt, and to her concomitant desire for revenge, which she made no attempt to conceal.

I felt very sad in France. The city of Paris and the French countryside were as beautiful as ever; the French people I met seemed just as *spirituel*. I was aware that the world would indeed be a much poorer place without their taste, and their *esprit*. My own attitude toward the French themselves had changed, largely because of the incredible bravery of the men and women I had known in the French Resistance. But there was an enormous sense of fatigue and exhaustion in the air of Paris that depressed me immeasurably.

I lunched with a friend whose two sons had been in the Resistance. My friend's father, a distinguished banker, was off to the races. He observed courteously that he hoped he would see me again before I left Paris. Was I there for long? I said I was staying over a few days to attend the Peace Conference. "Oh," he observed with apparent surprise, "are we having a Peace Conference? Oh, yes, I believe I read something about it in the papers. You will excuse me, won't you? I have a horse running in the third race. I trust you will find the Peace Conference interesting!" And off he dashed.

There were still touches of elegance in Paris, floating, as it were, on a vast sea of misery. From Germany I had brought back, locked forever in my memory, a picture of that warning sign placed over the highways by the conquerors: DEATH IS SO PERMANENT! DRIVE CAREFULLY! The picture I carried back in my mind from France was the sight of the chalky-white, stockingless legs of the women of France. Sitting at the sidewalk cafés, watching the crowds, my eyes were inevitably drawn to those legs, hurrying along the boulevards. None of these women apparently ever had time to sit in the sun. Instead, there they were, hurrying down the boulevards, their legs whipping along in a nervous, frantic rhythm. Where were they going on those chalky legs? Women have always played an important role in every aspect of French life. What did these women, with their expressions of grim desperation, mean for the future of that proud and wounded country?

After just one day in Paris, I realized they were hurrying to find a way around, over, through, the difficulties of daily living that were still unresolved in France. When I phoned old friends, their first question was, "What can I do for you?" Did they think I had called only because I wanted something? I quickly realized this question was simply a habit that had developed during the war, and very little had changed since. People still had to help each other, trade favors, pull strings, share information about where and how various necessities might be obtained.

I stood in line at the station for nearly three hours to get my ticket back to Switzerland, for another hour with a friend waiting to purchase a loaf of bread. People in the lines kept up a steady chatter of advice, gossip, suggestions about where to go, what to do, and how to do it. Yes, the telephone was on strike. Yes, the post was on strike. Yes, everyone was off on a *vacance payée*. Yet it was a Frenchman, not a foreigner, who had said to me, "England today makes me sad. France, on the other hand, makes me mad!" He thought the French should feel more ashamed of themselves. He was one of those still suffering from the searing humiliation of 1940. But, under certain circumstances, shame can be a luxury. Life was still too difficult for the French people to indulge in such emotions. They needed all their energy to solve the problems of daily living.

I attended the Peace Conference on the day Jan Masaryk, son of the founder of Czechoslovakia, pleaded in fluent English his country's case. His address was short and very moving. He thanked the hostess nation— *la France éternelle*—and pointed out that France and Czechoslovakia shared a restless and predatory neighbor. Europe was now faced with making peace—"permanent peace"—or destroying itself. When he had finished, he sat down to a polite ripple of applause.

The Palais Luxembourg, where the conference was held, was beautifully decorated with the flags of the participating nations. Long lines of French police, in chic uniforms, added color to the scene. Within the hall, the eyes of all visitors were focused on Molotov, the Russian Foreign Minister, seated quite far back in the hall. Having been seated alphabetically, the United States, by calling itself America, had a front-row seat. The presiding officer for the sessions was Georges Bidault, the French statesman and Resistance leader. Certainly no statesman had been so elegantly attired since the days of Anthony Eden. But it was a member of the Ethiopian delegation who provided the journalists with the most copy by appearing each day in a different brilliantly colored robe that set off his luxurious henna beard to great advantage.

I knew some members of various Balkan delegations. They would periodically become greatly agitated at some speaker's suggestion that a boundary might be shifted hither or yon. However, after a brief, impassioned plea in which they referred disdainfully to the perfidious motives behind some neighbor's intent, they would subside wearily. When I later asked one of them why he had given in so easily, his comment was, "What does it matter? What can we do? Except be grateful that we can spend the last days of Europe here in Paris!" This atmosphere of the last days of Europe—*les derniers jours de l'Europe*—hung over the Palais Luxembourg like a faint, fading fragrance, mingled with a miasma of fatigue and despair.

As I glanced from the elegantly attired Mr. Bidault to the small, plump hands of Mr. Molotov, I thought of those chalky-white, stockingless legs of the women of France, nervously hurrying along the boulevards of Paris. Obviously, nothing was ever going to change until human nature itself changed. There was certainly nothing in France, or at that Peace Conference, to indicate that any such change was coming soon.

XXXVI

Both before and after my trip to Paris, I had several experiences that stand out with special vividness in my memory. They had about them the curious, dreamlike quality that sometimes made me feel like pinching myself to see if what was happening was actually real.

The first was my encounter with Lily Abegg, a Swiss journalist and Far Eastern expert who had served in Tokyo throughout the war as correspondent for the *Frankfurter Zeitung*. After her return from Japan, she had come to Zurich to visit a friend of mine who told me that Lily was anxious to get in touch with the Americans. She wanted to give them her version of the story of "Tokyo Rose," the young nisei girl, arrested by the Americans and accused of treason for broadcasting to the GIs in the South Pacific.

Lily had been arrested at the same time as this girl and accused of writing the material for her broadcasts, which she had not done. For three months, however, she had been confined in the same cell with Tokyo Rose, whose maiden name was Iva Toguri. Lily felt that a great injustice had been done to Iva. She was convinced that Iva, in reading the broadcasts given her by two Allied officers who were prisoners of war and then playing records, thought she was simply bringing comfort and entertainment to lonely, homesick GIs on isolated islands in the Pacific.

Lily gave me a long and carefully documented report that she had prepared, outlining from her knowledge of Far Eastern customs as well as of Japanese bureaucracy various incidents that she felt might have contributed to Iva's being accused of treason. It was her belief that Iva's situation was the result of American misunderstanding of Eastern customs and the mysterious intricacies of Japanese bureaucracy.

It was strange to have this episode of the war in the Pacific reaching out to me in Switzerland. To those of us confined within *Festung Europas* ("the fortress of Europe"), as it was called, the war in the Pacific seemed very remote indeed. Yet this was not the first time the war in the Pacific had been brought home to me suddenly and unexpectedly. In this modern age, a world war is precisely that.

The first time had been when an advertisement appearing in the Zurich papers had sought the rental of an unusually large villa. Jean had first alerted me to the ad and at the same time mentioned an enormous increase in the staff of the Japanese consulate. There had always been close commercial ties between Switzerland and Japan, largely because of the silk business. I, after all, had first met Jean when he had been returning from reorganizing a Swiss silk firm in Japan.

Because of conditions in Indochina, France had never officially declared war on Japan. Consequently, Japanese citizens could circulate freely throughout France. Nothing was easier for them than to note the number and movement of Allied troops, pass this information along to the Japanese in Zurich, and then have it cabled to Berlin via Tokyo or even directly to Berlin itself. Late each evening, several Japanese chattering happily in their own language, incomprehensible to most good Swiss burghers, made their way to the telegraph office in the Zurich station. Very shortly after the ad appeared, Allen had his own Japanese expert working on this situation.

Another incident that also stands out vividly in my memory was an interview I had with Wilhelm Furtwängler, the German composer who for many years was conductor of the Berlin Philharmonic Orchestra. Furtwängler had sought refuge in Switzerland at the end of the war and was eager to be "de-Nazified" so that he could return to Germany.

Clover and I had gone to Rolle, a small village on the Lake of Geneva between Lausanne and Geneva, where Mary Jane was at the girls' school La Combe and Clover's nephew, the son of Allen's sister, Eleanor, at the neighboring boys' school Le Rosey. Clover returned that evening to Zurich, but I stayed on to see Furtwängler, who was living near Lausanne.

I spent many interesting hours with him, including a long walk along the lakeside below Lausanne. There he told me that he was sure that if he signed a document guaranteeing that he would never leave Germany and travel to any country where any other famous conductor, particularly Bruno Walter, was conducting, his problems would rapidly be solved. He also was convinced that the fact that he had several illegitimate children by various former mistresses was causing him more difficulties than any possible Nazi connections he might have had. Nine was the number of these children that he told me he had. But I took this information with a grain of salt, having noticed over the years that nine was a number that popped up frequently when men were boasting of their sexual prowess. Even Napoleon claimed to have had nine mistresses—but to have loved only one: Josephine.

Furtwängler had made his career and achieved his position of prominence in the German musical world before the Nazis had come to power. His personal assistant had been a Jewish woman. Early in the Nazi regime, at a banquet arranged for him by Goebbels, he had discovered on his arrival that his personal assistant had not been invited. He had promptly left the hall and refused to attend the banquet, thus winning Goebbels's undying enmity. Although Furtwängler had refused to conduct concerts for the German occupying forces in France, Goebbels announced periodically that he had conducted such concerts.

In the beginning Furtwängler had imagined that, because of his position and reputation, the Nazis would not dare touch him and that in addition he would be able to protect the many Jewish musicians who played in his orchestra. He had a large dossier of letters from many of these men, thanking him for what he had done for them, written from the countries to which he had helped them flee. When I asked him why he himself had not left Germany, he said that although his reputation was based largely on his conducting, what lay closest to his heart was his composing. And he was quite unable to write music anywhere but in Germany itself, on German soil, as it were.

I had seen a report from Dr. Maria Dahlem, a doctor on the staff of one of the large hospitals in Berlin who had lived openly with Furtwängler for seven years and had been involved in the July 20 conspiracy. Her report completely cleared Furtwängler of any taint of Nazism. This was a particularly generous gesture of hers, in view of the fact that Furtwängler had, as their own affair had been drawing to a close, married her sister without even telling her he planned to do so. Obviously he had quite a way with the ladies!

His was a most complicated case, an amazing confirmation that "hell hath no fury like a woman scorned." Although he had actually stood up to the Nazis and could prove it, he was quite right, I discovered, in his contention that his former lady friends were busily intriguing against him. Only many months later, when Yehudi Menuhin finally arrived in Berlin and became interested in his case, was Furtwängler eventually de-Nazified.

I had intended to return to Zurich after seeing Furtwängler, but I longed for at least twenty-four hours of perfect peace, with no one even knowing where I was. So I called Maria and told her I would not be home until the following day, taking care not to tell her where I could be reached. Then I went to the Beau-Rivage Hotel at Ouchy and took a room looking out over the hotel's magnificent garden across the lake to the Alps of Haute-Savoie.

I ordered a delicious dinner in my room, secure in the thought that I was unreachable. As I sat there wondering if there was a more beautiful view anywhere than that from my hotel window, the phone suddenly rang. I picked up the receiver to hear an agitated Bob Jungk on the other end. "How in the world did you find me?" I demanded crossly.

Bob laughed. "I called Maria and she said you would not be home till tomorrow. She didn't even know where you were. Then I remembered that once you had said that if you ever wanted to go into hiding, you'd take a room at the Beau-Rivage because you so loved that garden and that view!"

"Well," I said, relenting slightly, "what do you want?"

"I want you to call Don Juan, the pretender to the Spanish throne, and ask him if he is planning a putsch. I've been asked by one of the English papers to do an article about this and I simply must find out about it. But I'm persona non grata with Don Juan. He will neither see me nor talk to me on the phone."

"Are you crazy?" I demanded. "Why should he talk to me? I don't know him. He's never even heard of me."

"Please, Mary," Bob pleaded. "It's terribly important to me. You promised to help me if I ever needed it badly—and I do now."

"Oh, all right," I said, weakening. "What's his number?"

Bob gave me the number and promised to call back in twenty minutes.

I dialed the number. A cultivated man's voice answered. "I would like to speak to Don Juan," I said in English.

"Who is this?" the man asked, also in English.

"My name is Mary Bancroft," I said. "Don Juan doesn't know me, but I believe he knows my friend, Mr. Allen Dulles, assistant to the American minister."

"This is Don Juan," said the voice. "How is Mr. Dulles?"

"He's fine," I said. "You must forgive me; I'm not calling for him, but for someone to whom I owe a great favor. He has asked me to call you and ask you if you are preparing a putsch against Franco. If you are, I can't imagine why you would tell me. But I promised to ask."

Don Juan laughed. "You're quite right. I would *not* tell you if I were preparing a putsch! But the fact is that I am not. You can assure your friend of that."

Then, after a few pleasantries and further apologies on my part, I hung up.

Within minutes, Bob was on the phone again. "Don Juan is not planning a putsch," I said. "He told me to assure you of that. He must be a very nice man . . ."

"He is," said Bob. "Thanks!" And he hung up.

Another incident that also had its amusing side took place on the day General Mark Clark, together with his wife, his son, and his daughter came to Zurich to do some shopping and I was asked to escort them around the city. The general was in full military regalia, as was his son, also an officer in the United States Army. They arrived in a US military car flying the flag of a five-star general.

When we met at the Baur au Lac, the general said he wanted to cash a check. So we proceeded to the Paradeplatz, where we entered one of the large Swiss banks. The Swiss are so accustomed to having famous people in their midst that they usually ignore them. But a five-star American general—and General Mark Clark at that, whose picture had appeared frequently in the Swiss press—was quite another matter. We were greeted with open mouths and popping eyes as we made our way across the lobby to the teller's window.

"I would like to cash this check," said General Clark, taking an official-looking check from his wallet and handing it to the teller.

"*Ihrer Pass, bitte,*" said the teller, without changing expression. "Your passport, please."

General Clark looked surprised. "I haven't got a passport," he said.

"*Ohne Pass, kein Geld!*" said the teller. "Without a passport, no money!"

The general turned to me. "What shall I do?" he asked. "I've *never* had a passport!"

I stepped forward to the window. "This is General Mark Clark who commanded the American Army in Italy," I said to the teller.

"*Ohne Pass, kein Geld!*" he repeated, still expressionless.

I was very much annoyed, but General Clark seemed amused. "I understand now how the Swiss were able to preserve their neutrality," he observed good-naturedly.

Fortunately, a bank official, realizing that something untoward was happening, had dashed off to get the bank's president, who now came rushing up, full of apologies to General Clark. Then, turning to the teller, he berated him furiously in Swiss-German. The teller, still muttering under his breath about how the regulations were that no one could get money without a passport, reluctantly handed over the money to General Clark.

This episode reminds me of another occasion when a Swiss bureaucrat participated in a special kind of contretemps during the early years of the war when the Swiss were negotiating the renewal of a trade treaty with the Germans. Such negotiations were always tricky.

On this particular occasion the negotiations were unusually delicate. But when the Swiss negotiator opened the dossier prepared for him to handle the negotiations, he was astonished to find lying on top of the other papers a letter from the German Foreign Office. The letter obviously contained directions to the German delegation, cautioning them to make every possible difficulty for the Swiss but under no circumstances to let the negotiations fall through.

After the negotiations were successfully completed and the Swiss negotiator, feeling very pleased with himself, was leaving the room, he encountered the head of the Swiss Federal Police waiting outside the door for him with a smile on his usually impassive countenance. "How did you like my little present?" the police chief asked.

"It was of enormous help to me," said the negotiator. "But how in the world did you ever get hold of it?"

The police chief chuckled and told the following story: A member of the German delegation had attended school in Switzerland and had a former girl friend, now married and living in Bern, where the negotiations were being held. Her husband, a Swiss bureaucrat, always left for his office extremely early in the morning. So the German delegate arranged a rendezvous with his girl friend between the hour her husband left for his office and the time, some three hours later, when the meeting to renegotiate the trade treaty was scheduled. On that particular day, as fate would have it, the girl friend's husband had forgotten his spectacles. Returning home to get them, he saw a man's hat and coat hanging in the hall and the door to the bedroom shut. He burst into the bedroom, catching sight of a man's clothing thrown across a chair and a man in bed with his wife. Grabbing the man's pants, and without a word to the culprits, he rushed from the house and headed for the nearest police station. There he demanded that the police proceed at once to his home and arrest the man in bed with his wife, handing over the man's pants as proof of his wife's delinquency.

By chance, the chief of the Federal Police happened to be in that particular police station at that precise moment. He reached for the pair of pants, searched the pockets, and found the letter of instructions to members of the German delegation. Realizing at once how invaluable this document would be to the Swiss negotiator, he left his colleagues to deal with the irate husband and hurried off to place the letter from the German Foreign Office in the dossier prepared for the Swiss negotiator.

XXXVII

I must now backtrack somewhat in my story—to the late winter and early spring of 1945—to describe some important events.

On May 2, 1945, Winston Churchill had made a surprise appearance in the House of Commons to announce that close to a million Germans had capitulated in northern Italy, thus bringing the war on the Italian front to a close. This mass surrender, the first great German surrender to the Allies in World War II, was the result of Operation Sunrise, conducted by Allen from Bern. Allen himself described Operation Sunrise in detail in his own book, *The Secret Surrender,* published in 1966.

I knew vaguely about Operation Sunrise, but as Germany, not Italy, absorbed most of my time and attention, I did not participate in Sunrise in any significant way. At one point I stayed with Clover for a few days in Ascona, where some of the negotiations were being conducted. Before that, I had warned Allen that if he wanted to keep the negotiations secret, something had to be done about the small dog that one of the Allied negotiators had brought with him to Switzerland and which the sharp-eyed Swiss had spotted waiting forlornly outside the most unlikely places, including Allen's own apartment on the Herrengasse. The dog's master, I said, had better take the little dog into the negotiations, otherwise some journalist could get wind of the fact that "something" was going on, tie it in with those mournful vigils on Herrengasse, and the secret would be secret no longer.

The story of Sunrise is a fascinating one. After it was over, an article appeared in the *Weltwoche,* pointing out that Allen deserved the Order of Maria Theresa, which during the reign of Empress Maria Theresa of

Austria had been given to those who had disobeyed orders, yet had brought their endeavors to a successful conclusion. At one point during Sunrise, the Russians, extremely suspicious of any negotiations in which they were not included, had got wind of it and protested to Washington. Allen had been ordered to break off all negotiations completely, but by then matters had reached a stage where success was in sight. So Allen withdrew personally from the negotiations, but indicated, without saying so in so many words, that it would be quite all right for others to proceed—as long as he didn't know anything about what they were doing. This was an old trick, similar to the one practiced by Admiral Canaris in connection with the July 20 conspiracy.

While Allen was still involved in the Sunrise negotiations, however, and before I realized how serious they were, one evening in Zurich I had been walking home just as a train from Italy pulled into the Bahnhof Enge, a station preceding the Zurich main station where trains coming over the Gotthard sometimes stopped to discharge passengers. To my surprise, Gero von Gaevernits, together with several other men, descended from the train and started walking in the direction of the Genferstrasse, where the apartment that served as Allen's Zurich headquarters was located. Gero did not see me, for I had quickly stepped into a small shop near the station so I could take a closer look at the men accompanying him. Unless I was very much mistaken, one of those men, all of whom were in civilian clothes, was General Karl Wolff, commander of the SS in Italy, whose picture I had often seen in newspapers. Later, I told Allen about seeing Gero, adding, "I may be crazy, but I could swear that one of the men with him was SS General Karl Wolff."

"You must be crazy," said Allen, laughing that hollow, mirthless laugh of his. "What would an SS general be doing in Zurich? And why were you hanging around the Bahnhof Enge instead of doing something useful?"

Allen eventually confessed that it *had* been General Wolff whom I had seen on his way to meet Allen for the first time. It was after that encounter that General Wolff kept lamenting to those accompanying him, "Why—why—didn't anyone ever tell me there were Americans like Dulles?" Why indeed!

The seven years until the autumn of 1953, when I returned permanently to the United States, have faded into a haze in my memory. I still have my diaries and journals of those years, but they haven't the focus of the war years. For me, at least, it was a time of recovery, a kind of emotional mop-up operation. I continued working on multilingual films, wrote commentary for documentaries, and did a great deal of translating.

In 1947 Mary Jane and I spent six months in the United States. We had a good visit with Sherwin, Jr., who was then at Dartmouth, and took a long motor trip through the West. We also spent several weeks with Clover and Allen. In the fall Mary Jane and I returned to Zurich, where she entered the School of Applied Arts.

In early 1950 I made another, much briefer trip to New York to sell my first novel about my early years in my grandparents' home in Cambridge. While I was away, I received a letter from Jean, whom I had divorced in 1947, saying that Mary Jane was seeing a good deal of a young American studying physics in Zurich. "I think I should warn you," Jean wrote, "that I view her interest in this Horace Taft as far more serious than her interest in either the Norwegian ski team or in members of the RAF!"

In the early summer of 1952, Mary Jane and I again returned to the States, and she and Horace Taft announced their engagement at the Republican Convention in Chicago, where Horace's father, Senator Robert A. Taft, was contending with General Dwight D. Eisenhower for the presidential nomination. Mary Jane and Horace were married that September in Washington, where we made our headquarters with Clover and Allen. Sherwin could not make the wedding because by then he was a lieutenant in the United States Navy serving off Korea. Clover and Allen's son was also in Korea serving as an officer in the US Marines.

Oddly, throughout the years our lives had continued to be intertwined. Clover had been staying with me in Zurich when she received word that her son had been badly wounded. She flew off immediately to Tokyo where, as fate would have it, she found Sherwin, whose ship had pulled into Tokyo for repairs, waiting for her. Later, after Sherwin's demobilization, when he was in a bad automobile accident in Washington, Clover telephoned from his bedside to tell me that she was with him.

After Mary Jane's wedding, I had returned to Zurich. There, in the summer of 1953, Sherwin came to spend several weeks with me, to see all the places and meet all the people he had heard so much about. That fall he helped me move back permanently to this country, where I settled in New York and where Sherwin started working for *Time* magazine.

Gisevius married his Fräulein Braut, spent some time in Texas, then returned to Germany where he published several more books; he finally settled on the Lake of Geneva near Vevey. We kept in touch until his death in 1974. In his very last letter to me, he enclosed, at my request, a copy of the official floor plan of the Ministry of War on the Bendler-strasse so that I could figure out to my own satisfaction who had been where during the horrendous events of the twentieth of July. In that letter he observed sarcastically that he could not see just what practical use this floor plan would be to me now.

Both Gisevius and Allen had always urged me to write the story of my wartime years from my own point of view. When Allen retired as head of the CIA in 1961, he took my wartime reports home with him. Periodically, he would suggest that I come to Washington and go over them with him so as to get started on my book. But somehow I couldn't face plunging back into what, for me, had been such a tumultuous and exhausting time, laced with so many poignant memories. Besides, my own life had moved on and I was deeply involved in the Byzantine plots and intrigues of local New York Democratic politics. So I procrastinated.

I was listening to the radio in January 1969 when Clover phoned to tell me of Allen's death. It seemed curiously appropriate that the lyrics floating out of my radio when the phone rang were:

> *Those were the days, my friend!*
> *We thought they'd never end . . .*

After Allen's death, I felt increasingly guilty that I had never attempted to write the book he had so often urged me to write. So I asked Clover if I could have my wartime reports. To her chagrin, she discovered that they had been with other papers in a filing cabinet carted off by the CIA. She said she would speak to Richard Helms, then CIA director, and urged me to write him, too, which I did. I received a nice letter from Helms, saying that everything in Allen's possession had to be evaluated to see what belonged to the CIA or to OSS archives, but he would see what could be done.

Two years passed in which I figured I had better forget about my book. Then one morning three huge, unmarked envelopes arrived in the mail: my wartime reports. When I called Clover to tell her the good news, I asked her what she imagined had happened. She replied, "Well, I guess Dick Helms must have had a vision in the night!" If this were true, I certainly owe a great deal to that vision in the night. For the foregoing pages are based largely on those reports, supplemented by my own journals and scrapbooks of those faroff days.

It would seem that every generation has to have its war. World War II was certainly mine. It changed me, my life, my whole outlook on the world. I have never been able to see anything in the same way since.

I still hear from Maria. After we left Zurich, she went to work for an elderly lady who, on her death some years ago, left Maria enough money to live out the rest of her days as a lady of leisure. Her letters to me are full of observations about human nature, the dangers of communism, and how, after all, one must be philosophical because everything that happens is only "God's will."

Clover and I remained close friends until her death in 1974. And I continue to keep in touch with her daughter, Joan, who shares my Jungian interests.

Elizabeth Montagu, now Mrs. Varley, lives on the estate of her brother, Lord Montagu of Beaulieu, in England. Elizabeth is not a very good correspondent, but she has made several trips to New York and we have always been able to pick up just where we last left off.

Mary Briner makes regular visits to New York, where we always have at least one good evening together, catching up on all we have done since we last met. Still in Zurich, she also was analyzed by Jung and works now as an analyst.

As I come to the end of this story about the first fifty years of my life, I can't help wondering what Nolan and CW, my first two trusted confidants, would have had to say about it all. I imagine Nolan, pushing back his dirty old cap and scratching his bald head with a puzzled expression in his bright blue eyes, would comment in his lovely brogue, "You don't say, Miss Mary! You don't say!" CW, beautifully manicured hands folded across his massive stomach, his equally blue eyes flashing with journalistic interest, would advise, "Write it up, Mary! Write it all up!" Then he would add his usual admonition, "But remember that facts are not the truth. They only indicate where the truth may lie!"

INDEX

H